THE PROMISE
of
HEAVEN

31 REASONS TO GET EXCITED
ABOUT YOUR ETERNAL HOME

DR. DAVID JEREMIAH

W PUBLISHING GROUP

AN IMPRINT OF THOMAS NELSON

To Dr. Charles "Chuck" Emert
1934–2025
Wonderful friend,
World-class encourager,
With Jesus in the Father's House

CONTENTS

CONTENTS

THE APPOINTMENTS OF HEAVEN

THE ANSWERS ABOUT HEAVEN

THE APPLICATION OF HEAVEN

INTRODUCTION

Just as I started working on this book, I read in the news that entertainer Dolly Parton's husband had died. She and Carl Dean were married for six decades. The headline said, "Dolly Parton Holds to the Hope of Heaven After Husband's Death." She told journalists, "I am a person of faith, and I truly believe that I'm going to see him again someday."[1]

I confess I know little about the couple's relationship with God, but I was glad to hear one of the most famous celebrities in the world had eternity on her mind and was openly speaking about the promise of heaven.

Heaven is on my mind too. It should be on everyone's mind. The Bible says, "Set your mind on things above, not on things of the earth. For you died, and your life is hidden with Christ in God. When Christ who is our life appears, then you will also appear with Him in glory" (Colossians 3:2–4).

So many people only think about things here below, with all the toil and trouble of life. When I'm walking down the street, browsing in a shopping mall, or dining at a restaurant, I study people's faces. I can see the stress. There's not a lot of genuine happiness going around. We're besieged with dreadful world conditions, polarizing political movements, and difficult personal situations. We're too busy and too burdened to enjoy life as God intended. To make things worse, we don't know how long we have on earth.

Yet when we open the pages of God's Word, sunlight bursts out. The Scriptures flash with gold, glisten with glory, and sing of the hope to come. The entire Bible points to the promise of heaven!

That should do something to us. It should change something inside us. Only when our minds are set on "things above" can we properly deal with "things below."

There are lots of reasons to get excited about our eternal home, and I want to give you thirty-one of them in this book. I've written these pages to unleash within you the power of biblical hope. We always need something to look forward to in life, don't we? For those who love Jesus, heaven is our greatest goal and surest outlook.

Heaven is the home we've never visited, the inheritance coming to us, and the consummation of our relationship with Christ. It's closer than we know. Whatever your day looks like today, a better one is on the way, heading toward you at the speed of glory. Jesus is preparing a place for you, a land of many mansions with multitudes of angels and millions of friends.

Don't you want to know about it?

For a lot of Christians, the expectation of heaven is dulled by ignorance and misunderstanding. Hollywood has its portrayals of heaven, and great artists have painted pictures of heaven, which you can see on the walls of the world's museums. A host of people have stories about what they saw or dreamed or experienced. Many religions talk in vague terms about some kind of idealistic future state. Even a lot of Christian believers spout sentimental phrases without much biblical depth.

The world gives us speculation, but the Bible gives us certainty by providing the only authorized version of glory. God's Word is like a mirror at an intersection that shows us what's just around the corner. The Lord has imparted unfailing and infallible information about the city "whose architect and builder is God" (Hebrews 11:10 NIV). The Bible is a future-oriented book in which the King of Glory has given us magnificent glimpses of what's ahead.

In the first section of *The Promise of Heaven*, I'll begin with that very theme—the sense of *anticipation* that should occupy us every morning when we awaken and see the dawn. The apostle Paul used phrases such as "Paradise" and the "third heaven" (2 Corinthians 12:2–4). Jesus also called it Paradise (Luke 23:43), as well as "My Father's house" (John 14:2).

Hebrews 11:10 speaks of "the city which has foundations." What do these terms mean? We'll delve into it.

Then we'll consider the *atmosphere* of heaven. Many people move across the nation and around the world, trying to find the climate that's best for them. What about the climate of heaven? Well, the air is clear there. From Scripture, we even know some of the building materials God has used in crafting the Celestial City. We know something of the citizens who will crowd into Hallelujah Square. We know some of the things we'll be doing, including the worship we'll be rendering.

But if you think we'll just sit around all day listening to sermons, think again. There won't be a dull moment! You'll read about some of the events we will experience (and even the rewards we will receive) in the *appointments of heaven* section.

I also want to provide *answers* to some of the questions I'm frequently asked about heaven, such as that perpetual question, "Will we know each other in heaven?" (Short answer: Of course we will!) What about our loved ones already there—are they watching us? Do they know what's happening in your life? What about marriage? Will there be weddings in heaven? Will there be animals there? All this information will fuel your expectations, but that's not the only reason to study this subject.

Finally, I have an entire section on *application*—how the predictions of our future home should inspire our lives right now. When the truth about heaven permeates our hearts, it brings energy to our steps and encouragement to our minds. It casts a golden glow across every day, even over the roughest moments.

Except for Jesus Christ Himself, I can't think of a subject in Scripture that so encourages me as heaven. The more I've studied this topic, the less I can keep it to myself. If you could glimpse your future in Christ, you'd worry much less about today. Your stress levels would decrease. Your enthusiasm would increase. And you would fall asleep every night thinking of the glories ahead.

These are the blessings God has for the followers of Jesus Christ. But may I also add this truth: Without Him, there is judgment and hell. My ultimate goal is to persuade some of my readers who don't truly have a relationship with Christ to personally acknowledge Him as their Lord and Savior. Without Christ, there's so much to lose. With Him, there's so much to eagerly expect!

Most months have thirty-one days, and we need a word of encouragement from Scripture for every one of them. Two years ago, I wrote a book about the rapture of the church—*The Great Disappearance: 31 Ways to Be Rapture Ready.*

Last year, I advanced the teaching to cover the thousand-year reign of Christ, which follows the rapture and Tribulation—*The Coming Golden Age: 31 Ways to Be Kingdom Ready.*

The book you hold in your hands completes this trilogy—*The Promise of Heaven: 31 Reasons to Get Excited About Your Eternal Home.*

Add them all together, and I have discovered ninety-three different prophetic truths that can saturate your heart with keen anticipation, which is an essential element of our mental and spiritual health. Because remember, we all benefit when we keep heaven on our mind.

The Bible says, "'No eye has seen, no ear has heard, and no mind has imagined what God has prepared for those who love him.' But it was to us that God revealed these things by his spirit. . . . So we can know the wonderful things God has freely given us. When we tell you these things, we do not use words that come from human wisdom. Instead, we speak words given us by the Spirit, using the Spirit's words to explain spiritual truths" (1 Corinthians 2:9–10, 12–13 NLT).

As we move through these pages together, let's make it our goal to become aware of the wonderful things God has freely given us—things not just for tomorrow but also for today.

Let's set our minds on things above, where Christ is.

Let's study what the Holy Spirit has revealed to us in the Bible about the promise of heaven!

PART 1

THE ANTICIPATION OF HEAVEN

These all died in faith, not having received the
promises, but having seen them afar off were
assured of them, embraced them and confessed
that they were strangers and pilgrims on the earth.
For those who say such things declare plainly that
they seek a homeland. And truly if they had called
to mind that country from which they had come
out, they would have had opportunity to return.
But now they desire a better, that is, a heavenly
country. Therefore God is not ashamed to be called
their God, for He has prepared a city for them.
HEBREWS 11:13–16

CHAPTER 1

LONGING FOR HEAVEN

In 2005, there weren't many people on the planet whose futures seemed brighter than Tom Brady's. As an NFL quarterback, Brady had just won his third Super Bowl with the New England Patriots. He'd signed a new contract worth more than $60 million. And he'd been chosen as America's most eligible bachelor by *Entertainment Tonight*.

Most would say he had a perfect life. Which is why many people were shocked when he seemed to question his own success in an interview with *CBS News*.

The interviewer, Steve Kroft, referenced several of Brady's recent accomplishments. Then he asked, "This whole experience—this whole upward trajectory—what have you learned about yourself? What kind of an effect does it have on you?"

Here's how Tom Brady responded:

Why do I have three Super Bowl rings, and still think there's something greater out there for me? I mean, maybe a lot of people would say, "Hey man, this is what [it] is." I reached my goal, my dream, my life. Me, I think: It's gotta be more than this. I mean this can't be what it's all cracked up to be. I mean I've done it. I'm 27. And what else is there for me?

Taken aback, the interviewer asked, "What's the answer?"
"I wish I knew," said Brady. "I wish I knew."[1]
In the two decades since that interview, Tom Brady has continued to live the kind of life most people only dream about. He won a total of seven Super Bowls before finally retiring from the NFL at age forty-four. He experienced both marriage and divorce. He became a father. Recently he became part owner of the Las Vegas Raiders franchise.

I don't know whether Tom Brady has found the answer he was searching for more than two decades ago. But I do know *what* he was searching for. That's because I know what every person is searching for, down deep where it matters most—what every person was designed to long for and seek out.

It's heaven. The answer is heaven.

We're going to learn a lot about heaven in these pages, including many of the details Scripture provides about when we'll arrive there, who we'll find, and what we'll do. But for now, I want to start with that central reality of yearning—that pull we feel toward something that is beyond our current experience. I want to show you that your longing for heaven reveals your desire for more, your desire for home, and your desire for God Himself.

LONGING FOR HEAVEN IS LONGING FOR MORE

Let's go back to Tom Brady for a moment. He said there's "gotta be more than this" to make life meaningful and purposeful and fulfilling, even when "this" includes everything most people believe is important.

He's right! There does need to be "more" for each of us to be satisfied. That's because we were created to experience more than we can in this current age. We were created for more beauty. More blessings. More laughter. More passion. More enjoyment. More contemplation. More love. More everything!

To be more specific (pun intended), we were created for perfection. "Then God saw everything that He had made, and indeed it was very good" (Genesis 1:31).

The reason we feel so disillusioned and so impoverished even when life is going well is because humanity as a whole was cast out from the perfection we were designed to enjoy. These may be the saddest verses in all of Scripture:

> Then the LORD God said, "Behold, the man has become like one of Us, to know good and evil. And now, lest he put out his hand and take also of the tree of life, and eat, and live forever"—therefore the LORD God sent him out of the garden of Eden to till the ground from which he was taken. So He drove out the man; and He placed cherubim at the east of the garden of Eden, and a flaming sword which turned every way, to guard the way to the tree of life. (Genesis 3:22–24)

Ever since that moment, humanity has been like the prodigal son attempting to find sustenance and satisfaction from pig slop. Deep in our history and deep in our hearts, we remember our Father's house, and we miss it. We long for it. We even groan for it, as Paul described in Romans 8: "For we know that the whole creation groans and labors with birth pangs together until now. Not only that, but we also who have the firstfruits of the Spirit, even we ourselves groan within ourselves, eagerly waiting for the adoption, the redemption of our body" (verses 22–23).

Peter Toon captured it well: "The most tragic strain in human existence lies in the fact that the pleasure which we find in the things of this life, however good that pleasure may be in itself, is always taken away from us. The things for which men strive hardly ever turn out to be as satisfying as they expected, and in the rare cases in which they do, sooner or later they are snatched away."[2]

Another writer said it this way:

Here is the surprise: God made us this way. He made us to yearn—to always be hungry for something we can't get, to always be missing something we can't find, to always be disappointed with what we receive, to always have an insatiable emptiness that no thing can fill and an untamable restlessness that no discovery can still. Yearning itself is healthy—a kind of compass inside us, pointing to True North.[3]

We were made for more than this world—and that's what heaven is. It's "more."

LONGING FOR HEAVEN IS LONGING FOR HOME

Imagine you've been on a long trip, and you're almost to your house—just a few minutes away from the end of your journey. You're feeling cramped from the airplane seats. You're sore from heaving heavy luggage and feeling the straps of your bag dig into your shoulder. You're tired and jet-lagged and maybe even a little cranky. When you arrive, you plan to toss your bags by the front door, kick off your shoes, and sit down in your favorite chair.

What's the first word that will come out of your mouth when you finally get the weight off your feet? The first sound?

For me, it would probably be something like, "Aaaaaahhhhhhhhh."

There is a very real sense in which reaching heaven will be like that sound—like that feeling. Because when we get there, we will finally be arriving home. We will finally find ourselves in the place we've always belonged.

On the final day before His crucifixion, Jesus may have been thinking about His own opportunity to return home, because He offered a detailed and beautiful prayer on behalf of His disciples who would remain in this world after His resurrection and ascension to heaven. And not just the disciples then following Jesus—our Lord offered specific prayers for all who would choose to follow Him throughout the centuries.

During that prayer, He spoke about the dissonance we feel in this present world and our longing for our true home:

> "But now I come to You, and these things I speak in the world, that they may have My joy fulfilled in themselves. I have given them Your word; and the world has hated them because they are not of the world, just as I am not of the world. I do not pray that You should take them out of the world, but that You should keep them from the evil one. They are not of the world, just as I am not of the world." (John 17:13–16)

Later in that same prayer, Jesus added, "Father, I desire that they also whom You gave Me may be with Me where I am, that they may behold My glory which You have given Me; for You loved Me before the foundation of the world" (verse 24).

One of the reasons you long for heaven is because you don't belong in this world. None of us belong here. Peter described followers of Jesus as "sojourners and pilgrims" (1 Peter 2:11). The author of Hebrews used the language of "strangers and pilgrims" (11:13). The apostle John instructed us, "Do not love the world or the things in the world" (1 John 2:15). Why? Because "the world is passing away, and the lust of it; but he who does the will of God abides forever" (verse 17).

When you feel out of place in this world—in your country or your community or even your home—don't be alarmed. Don't try to "fix" that feeling by adapting yourself to this world. Instead, allow your longing for heaven to guide you toward home.

LONGING FOR HEAVEN IS LONGING FOR GOD

The pull we feel toward heaven represents a longing for all the "more" we've been missing throughout our lives. It's a longing for a home we've never seen yet always needed. Finally, it's a longing for the God we were always meant to know, love, and serve.

King David described this longing in Psalm 27:

> One thing I have desired of the LORD,
> That will I seek:
> That I may dwell in the house of the LORD
> All the days of my life,
> To behold the beauty of the LORD,
> And to inquire in His temple. (verse 4)

David didn't want more of this world. He wanted more of God's presence, which means he wanted more of God Himself. That is where our deepest satisfaction is found. Only in heaven and only with God will we finally and fully feel the completeness we were created to enjoy.

Now, you might say, "Dr. Jeremiah, I have a personal relationship with Jesus Christ. I have an intimate connection with my heavenly Father." Yes, you do! And I rejoice with you in those blessings—truly, I do.

At the same time, everything you and I experience in our spiritual lives right now is clouded by the reality of sin. We are still tainted by the corruption of sin, which means we don't enjoy God's love and intimacy and fellowship in the way we were intended to enjoy it. That was even true for the apostle Paul: "For now we see in a mirror, dimly, but then face to face. Now I know in part, but then I shall know just as I also am known" (1 Corinthians 13:12).

Once again, don't allow yourself to become satisfied with your current connection to Jesus. You long to know Him better, so allow that longing to draw you closer to Him. Then, one day, revel and rejoice when you return home and see Him face-to-face.

Here is how Mark McMinn said it:

> However messed up our abnormal world may be, the story is not over yet. The Christian story is ultimately a comedy and not a tragedy; it ends as it began. Someday, there will be a new heaven and a new earth. Birds will really sing. Lions and lambs will tumble and play in grass that is truly green. Our bodies won't be riddled with wrinkles, muscle spasms, and cancer. There will be pure joy and beauty and goodness. And God, who longs to be with us, will walk with us in the Garden.[4]

That may sound frightening or intimidating now—but it won't then. No ecstasy in this broken world will ever compare with our joy then, as we walk with God. We will be home. And it won't just be a story about a prodigal son or daughter who could never be good enough to earn God's favor. It will be a story about a loving God who delights in offering lavish, exuberant love. The depth of God's love will be seen everywhere.

Few songs capture our longing for heaven like "Over the Rainbow." It swept the world like a tornado when Judy Garland, playing Dorothy, sang it in the 1939 film *The Wizard of Oz*. In an early scene, Dorothy wonders aloud whether there really is a place out there where she can experience peace instead of trouble. "Do you suppose there is such a place, Toto? There must be. It's not a place you can get to by boat or train. It's far, far away. Behind the moon, beyond the rain."⁵ Then she begins to sing, "Somewhere over the rainbow, way up high."

Decades later, Israel "IZ" Kamakawiwo'ole—known as the "Voice of Hawaii"—revived the song for a new generation. His gentle, ukulele-laced version echoed the same hope for a place somewhere beyond our current reach that not only touches our deepest yearnings but satisfies them.

The songwriters—Yip Harburg and Harold Arlen, both sons of Jewish immigrants—wrote the lyrics in 1939 as war loomed over Europe.⁶ Though safe in America, they felt the ache for something more: peace, safety, and a place to belong. So they gave the world a lyrical appeal that still tugs at our hearts. They helped us picture a world somewhere over the rainbow, somehow above our own experiences, where the skies are blue and the dreams we dare to cling to really can come true.

Aren't you filled with that kind of longing when you read about heaven? When you think about heaven? When you try to imagine heaven? Don't you feel that echo inside you like a comforting lullaby your mother used to sing back when you were just a little baby? It's in our DNA to yearn for a better place—to ache for a home way up high where dreams really do come true.

There's only one place like that. It's heaven. And it's a longing that will be fulfilled!

CHAPTER 2

THE PROMISE
OF HEAVEN

Way back in 1962, Brendon Grimshaw accomplished something most people only dream about: He purchased his own private island in paradise. He bought a tiny spit of the Seychelles in the Indian Ocean, just above Madagascar. The island, called Moyenne, cost him $10,000.

Once the deal was done, the real work began. The island had become overgrown with weeds and choked with invasive fauna. Most days, rats were the only animals he encountered. But Grimshaw was diligent. For decades, he worked his way across the 120,000 square meters of his island, clearing trails, planting more than sixteen thousand trees, and bringing birds and tortoises back to the land.

Brendon Grimshaw died in 2012, which means he spent fifty years in dedicated service to his personal slice of paradise. In the years before his death, he received numerous offers to buy the island for staggering sums. There were even rumors that a Saudi prince offered $50 million for the deed of Moyenne Island. But Grimshaw refused each proposal. Instead, he reached an agreement with the

Seychelles government to turn the island into the world's smallest national park.

When his life came to a close, Grimshaw was buried in a small cave within his beloved island. A simple tombstone reads, "Moyenne taught him to open his eyes to the beauty around him and say thank you to God."[1]

Take a good look around you! The God of the universe has enveloped you with never-ending beauty. Above your head is a swirling mixture of clouds, cobalt, and a canopy of stars that stretches millions of light-years into the depths of the universe. Beneath your feet are meadows and grass—millions of blades in a single acre. Around you are trees, flowers, and sometimes mysterious patches of fog. Birds wing their way through the pathless air, and the spanning oceans rise and fall with the tides.

What a beautiful world! Sometimes the wonders of nature can lift our spirits when little else can. You may be weary or discouraged right now. God has designed His world to help you. When we pause to feel the sunshine on our faces, listen to the singing of the crickets at night, or smell the fragrance of blooming lilacs, it lifts our spirits like a tonic.

Ecclesiastes 3:11 says God "has made everything beautiful in its time." If that's all the verse said, it would be a wonderful truth. But the very same verse goes on to say, "Also He has put eternity in their hearts."

Our God has filled the world with His artistry, and He has placed inside us a desire to enjoy His creation forever. Despite its beauty, our present world is marred with problems, almost all of them caused by us. Even so, God's craftsmanship shines through humanity's haze.

Beauty and eternity! It's an ache built into the human heart. That is the promise of heaven, and that's why the Lord has filled the Bible with information about our everlasting home. Whether we realize it or not, there is a heaven-shaped vacuum in our heart we long to have filled.

C. S. Lewis wrote, "There have been times when I think we do not desire heaven, but more often I find myself wondering whether in our heart of hearts, we have ever desired anything else. . . . It is the secret signature of each soul, the incommunicable and unappeasable want, the thing we desired before we met our wives or made our friends or chose our work, and which we shall still desire on our deathbeds."[2]

This was clearly on the mind of our Lord Jesus Christ on the final night of His earthly life. In the upper room with His disciples around Him, He told them:

> "Let not your heart be troubled; you believe in God, believe also in Me. In My Father's house are many mansions; if it were not so, I would have told you. I go to prepare a place for you. And if I go and prepare a place for you, I will come again and receive you to Myself; that where I am, there you may be also." (John 14:1–3)

The Savior of the world wanted to teach His friends about heaven. Let's take a closer look and see what we can learn from that conversation.

HEAVEN MEANS BELIEVING IN A PERSON

Jesus began His words in John 14 on a note of assurance: "Let not your heart be troubled." The Good News Translation says, "Do not be worried and upset. . . . Believe in God and believe also in me." These words are for you. Imagine the Lord Jesus Christ, standing in all His strength and splendor, looking at you amid the situations of your life and saying: "Don't be worried and upset."

Today we've accumulated an armory of agents to help us combat anxiety—medications, therapies, breathing techniques, coping mechanisms, support groups, mindfulness exercises, religious rituals, playlists, medical professionals, and psychological counselors. Any of these, used wisely, may be helpful. But on that long-ago night amid the flickering torches of the upper room, the Lord Jesus had only one recommendation: Himself.

"Let not your heart be troubled; you believe in God, believe also in Me."

Our discussion of heaven and the mental peace it brings to us always starts with a person—the person of Christ. Our relationship with Him starts when we acknowledge our failures and our need for Him, and then we open our hearts to Him and trust Him as Savior and Lord. But that's only the beginning of our journey in believing Him, trusting Him, and leaning on Him during frightening times.

Jesus' words would be hollow without what happened to Him three days later. He rose physically and literally from the grave following His crucifixion. His body was the same, but different. He was recognizable, but He was now physically equipped to live endlessly without aging and without deteriorating. This is our single greatest biblical clue about heaven. The risen Jesus will be there personally and bodily, letting us know heaven is a real place. We will reside there with Him in our physical, resurrected bodies.

HEAVEN MEANS BELIEVING IN A PLACE

Now, let's drill a bit more into heaven as a place. That's the word Jesus used in John 14: "In My Father's house are many mansions; if it were not so, I would have told you. I go to prepare a *place* for you" (verse 2).

The word Jesus used is the Greek term *topos*, from which we get our word "topography." It refers to a literal location—a particular district, neighborhood, region, or habitat. Hebrews 11:16 calls it "a heavenly country." Revelation describes it as a vast capital city (21:10). The Psalms refer to heaven as "Zion," where God dwells (9:11). During the course of this book, we'll look at all those designations for heaven and many more.

In John 14, Jesus described this place as His "Father's house." The idea could be rendered *household, family, home,* even *palace.* The idea is one of residence.

In short, the Father's house is where God dwells, and there are many mansions there. The Greek word for "mansion" simply means *a place to stay, a dwelling,* or *a home.* But *mansion* is a perfectly good word to describe any dwelling place in heaven!

The key word in this entire section is *Father,* occurring twenty-three times. God the Father is the One who brings peace, perspective, and permanence to our troubled hearts through His Son, Jesus. In this comforting image of the Father's house, we come face-to-face with the closeness, intimacy, and everlasting nature of heaven. Heaven is not a feeling or a fantasy. It is a prepared place for prepared people.

This will be our lasting home. Remember, you are not home yet. This world is passing away, and all of us are passing away from the world. The Bible describes us as pilgrims and strangers on the earth (1 Peter 2:11). We may own homes, even beautiful ones, but they're only temporary because we're not here for long.

Just ask Edward Harriman. He was a preacher's kid who dropped out of school to become an errand boy on Wall Street. In less than ten years, he was a member of the New York Stock Exchange. He later became one of America's leading railroad giants. He was known as "King of the Railroad."

In 1885, he purchased nearly eight thousand acres north of New York City for his forever home—an estate he called "Arden." The one-hundred-thousand-square-foot mansion sat on twenty thousand acres at the top of Mount Orama with breathtaking views. The mansion, which is today an exclusive conference center, boasts wide corridors, sprawling sitting rooms, sweeping courtyards, spewing fountains, and lavish bedrooms. It's one of the largest private homes in America.

Harriman moved into his sprawling mansion in early 1909—and died there on September 9 of the same year. He was sixty-one, and he only enjoyed his version of paradise a few months before death took it all away.[3]

Our earthly homes—whether we live in a cardboard box or a sprawling estate—are temporary. Heaven is your forever home, which you'll enjoy in a resurrected body with a glorious Friend named Jesus Christ.

HEAVEN MEANS BELIEVING IN A PROMISE

That leads us to another truth: Heaven is believing in a promise. Jesus said, "And if I go and prepare a place for you, I will come again and receive you to Myself; that where I am, there you may be also" (verse 3). Within the context of our Lord's impending death, resurrection, and ascension, the only logical interpretation of this promise involves His return and the rapture of the church.

It's incredible to consider how much the Lord wants to be with us—wants us to be where He is. He prayed in John 17:24, "Father, I desire that they also whom You gave Me may be with Me where I am, that they may behold My glory."

Jesus had many things to say on earth, and the Bible has much to say to us as well. Some of the words are truths for us to accept. Some are prayers for us to echo. Some are warnings about things to avoid. Some are words of reassurance. There are long passages devoted to the praise of God's glory, and Jesus offered many teachings about the ethics of life, loving God, and loving one another.

To me, the most wonderful category of biblical teachings is the promises the Lord has made to us. They represent the foundation of our faith. John Piper wrote, "The key that unlocks the treasure chest of God's peace is faith in the promises of God."[4]

As someone has said, "God makes a promise; faith believes it; hope anticipates it; and patience quietly waits for it."

Of all His promises, our Lord's simple words that He is preparing a place for us and will come again and receive us and take us to be with Him for eternity—well, could there be a better promise to believe, anticipate, and wait for?

We all need our Lord's promise. We need it badly. And we have it!

Vaneetha Rendall Risner has learned to rest on that promise. Vaneetha contracted polio as an infant, was misdiagnosed, and lived with widespread paralysis. Things began improving after she found Christ as a young person. She got a dream job in Boston and earned an MBA from Stanford where she met and married a classmate.

Then things unraveled again. She had four miscarriages, and her son died from a doctor's mistake. She was diagnosed with post-polio syndrome, meaning she would likely be a quadriplegic. That's when her husband betrayed her and moved out. Through all this, Vaneetha's walk with God grew stronger, her faith bored deeper into the Word, and she has been a testimony of victory to many.

In her book *Walking Through Fire*, she simply put it like this: "Life is a journey, yes, but only if there's a destination. I'm on my way to my Father's house, and I absolutely cannot wait for the party. When I get there I will jog, run, sprint, race, and finally leap into the arms of my Savior."[5]

She long ago discovered that her suffering was temporary, "and it was preparing me for heaven, where there would be incomparable glory, far greater than my pain."[6]

What better way to celebrate the sure and certain promise of heaven!

HEAVEN MEANS BELIEVING IN A PLAN

That brings us to a final truth in John 14:4–6. Jesus said, "'Where I go you know, and the way you know.' Thomas said to Him, 'Lord, we do not know where You are going, and how can we know the way?' Jesus said to him, 'I am the way, the truth, and the life. No one comes to the Father except through Me.'"

When Thomas asked about the "way," Jesus didn't offer a list of instructions. He offered Himself. That's the heart of the gospel. Jesus is our plan for salvation.

William Barclay illustrated it this way:

> Suppose we are in a strange town and ask for directions. Suppose the person asked says: "Take the first to the right, and the second to the left. Cross the square, go past the church, take the third on the right and the road you want is the fourth on the left." The chances are that we will be lost before we get half-way. But suppose the person we ask says: "Come, I'll take you there." In that case the person to us is the way, and we cannot miss it. That is what Jesus does for us. He does not only give advice and directions, He takes us by the hand and leads us; He strengthens us and guides us personally every day. He does not tell us about the way; He is the way.[7]

That can sound narrow to our culture. Some say it's intolerant. But if we follow Jesus, we don't get to revise His words. We simply repeat them. As one preacher said, "We're only as narrow as Jesus was." The truth doesn't change based on public opinion.

And the Bible is consistent:

- "Nor is there salvation in any other, for there is no other name under heaven given among men by which we must be saved" (Acts 4:12).
- "There is one God and one Mediator between God and men, the Man Christ Jesus" (1 Timothy 2:5).

In our age of tolerance, many reject this truth. But Proverbs warns us that "there is a way that seems right to a man, but its end is the way of death" (14:12).

God doesn't change His method of salvation for each person. Just as every person is physically born the same way—through a mother and a father—every person is spiritually born the same way: through faith in Jesus Christ. That's the only plan that leads to heaven.

Jesus is the way! He wants to take you home to the Father's house, but you can't get there without Him.

D. L. Moody once told the story of a wealthy man who was dying. When the doctor said there was no hope, the man called for his lawyer to make out his will. He had a four-year-old daughter who didn't understand what death meant. Her mother gently explained that daddy was going away. So the little girl tiptoed to her father's bedside, looked into his eyes, and asked, "Papa, do you have a home in the place where you're going?"

That question hit hard. The man had spent his life accumulating properties and possessions, but none of it could go with him. He had many homes on earth, but no home in heaven.

Someday, each of us will leave it all behind. We'll leave our homes, our titles, and our bank accounts. When that moment comes, one question will matter most: Do you have a home in heaven?

I know someone who can take you there.

In fact, He is the way.

CHAPTER 3

THREE HEAVENS

One day, Suzanne Edwards found a deflated blue helium balloon in the backyard of her home in Monroe, Georgia. Attached to it was a picture of a man, woman, and little boy, who all seemed very happy. Also attached, a note scribbled in childlike printing. As she read the words, Suzanne began to cry.

It said: "Dad, I wish you were here so we could have fun together. I wish you a Merry Christmas. I hope you tell God to give me those presents. I hope you are happy in heaven. If you are okay then tell me. I love you, Alejandro."

The author of those plaintive words, as Suzanne learned later, was seven-year-old Alejandro Garcia-Herreros, whose home was about twenty miles away. Three years before, Alejandro had been living with his parents in Cúcuta, Colombia, where his father, Carlos, was a law professor known for his pro–law enforcement views. On December 4, 2013, Carlos was murdered in the street. He was shot to death in front of Alejandro.

Alejandro's mother moved with him to the United States, but Christmas remained a poignant and painful season for the boy.

Toward the end of each year he composed a letter to his dad and sent it upward in a helium balloon, with the belief the balloon would ascend to heaven and take the message to his dad.

Using social media, Suzanne attempted to get in touch with Alejandro's mother by saying, "A helium balloon floated into my yard today and landed on my heart!" Writing a message to be passed on to the boy, Suzanne told him: "I want you to know that heaven is a wonderful place, more amazing than you or I can even imagine. It is a place where there is no pain and no worries. I am certain your daddy didn't want to leave you or cause you to feel lonely or sad. . . . He will always love you and I am sure that you make him proud! Have a Merry Christmas!!"

When his mother relayed the message to him, Alejandro cried—and so did millions of other people when the story was discovered and picked up by major media outlets around the globe.[1]

Stories like that remind us of how much we need a hope that reaches beyond this life. That's why the comfort we find in the true biblical promise of heaven matters so much. Heaven is real and it is more wonderful and amazing than you and I could ever imagine!

With that in mind, I'd like to continue our exploration of eternity by highlighting a few foundational truths about the wonders of heaven—starting with its centrality as a theme in God's Word.

THE CENTRALITY OF HEAVEN

Though some churches neglect the subject, heaven is a prominent theme in Scripture. The word *heaven* is mentioned more than six hundred times in the Bible. Thirty-three of the thirty-nine Old Testament books talk about heaven, along with twenty-one books in the New Testament. In the Old Testament, the primary Hebrew term is *shamayim*, which is a plural word meaning "the heights." The New Testament uses the Greek word *ouranos*, which inspires the name of the planet Uranus. The word refers to something that is raised up or lofty. So the language of the Bible speaks of heaven as a place that is high and lofty and lifted up.

In addition, the Bible presents a galaxy of related terms, such as "the house of the LORD" (Psalm 23:6), "the city which has foundations" (Hebrews 11:10), "Zion" (Zechariah 8:3), "Mount Zion" (Revelation 14:1), and "New Jerusalem" (Revelation 21:2). Heaven plays such a prominent role in Scripture that if you delete all the references to it from the Word of God, the text of the Bible would fall apart in key places and turn to mishmash.

The word *heaven* in its ultimate sense implies the residence of the almighty God. That's hard for us to grasp, because God is omnipresent—that is, He is consciously and literally present everywhere throughout the material (visible) and spiritual (unseen) realms at all times. Theologian Stephen J. Wellum wrote, "God's entire being is simultaneously everywhere so that He fills every part of space."[2]

Yet God localizes His presence as well, and the Bible often speaks of God as dwelling on His throne in heaven, the nerve center of all creation and the epicenter of His power and authority. Job 22:12 asks, "Is not God in the height of heaven?" Jesus taught us to pray, "Our Father in heaven, hallowed be Your name" (Matthew 6:9). Psalm 11:4 says, "The LORD is in His holy temple, the LORD's throne is in heaven."

Heaven is a central theme in the Bible because it is the central zone of God's power, presence, rule, and reign.

THE LOCALITY OF HEAVEN

Young Alejandro instinctively knew one of the simplest truths about heaven: It's up! It's above our heads. Our English word *heaven* comes from an Old English word meaning "sky" or "a canopy, an arched vault." It seems to have originally come from a German term meaning "covering."[3] It first appears in the Bible in Genesis 1:1 where it's contrasted to Earth: "In the beginning God created the heavens and the earth."

Whether we're thinking of heaven as the sky, the universe, or the home of God, it is above us. That's why Jesus looked up when He prayed (Mark 6:41). In the Old Testament book of Ecclesiastes, Solomon wrote, "I have seen all the works that are done under the sun; and indeed, all is vanity and grasping for the wind" (1:14). In other words, if all we have is what's down here under the sun, we are without ultimate hope. We need a God, a heavenly throne, and an eternal home above us.

The phrase *down from heaven* occurs twenty-eight times in the Bible. The prophet Elijah called fire "down from heaven" (2 Kings 1:12). Psalm 14:2 says, "The LORD looks down from heaven." Jesus said, "I have come down from heaven, not to do My own will, but the will of Him who sent Me" (John 6:38).

Whenever you see a beautiful sunrise, a cloudless cobalt sky, or a vast expanse of stars, take a moment and ponder that above and beyond them all is heaven, the city of God, our eternal home!

THE PLURALITY OF HEAVEN

Having said that, I need to point out something else about the use of the word *heaven* in the Bible. When we speak of heaven as God's abiding place, we are using the term in its highest and holiest meaning.

As you work your way through the hundreds of mentions of the word *heaven* in the Bible, you soon realize there is a plurality of heavens. In fact, the Bible specifically speaks of three distinct heavens. When the apostle Paul wrote to the Corinthians about his visions and revelations, he told them of a time when he was "caught up to the third heaven" (2 Corinthians 12:2). That clearly implies there is also a first and second heaven.

THE FIRST HEAVEN

The first heaven is the atmospheric heaven—the sky with its clouds and birds and life-giving oxygen. Genesis 1:20 says, "Birds fly above the earth across the face of the firmament of the heavens." Psalm 104:12 talks about the "birds of the heavens," meaning birds flying through the pathless air. Referring to God's ability to send rain clouds across the land, Job asked, "Who has the wisdom to count the clouds? Who can tip over the water jars of the heavens?" (Job 38:37 NIV). Isaiah 55:10 talks about how "the rain and the snow come down from heaven" (NIV).

In these passages, the word *heaven* refers to the atmosphere that sends its rain and snow down to the earth. We live on a privileged planet, surrounded by a thin layer of gases—mainly nitrogen and oxygen—that make life possible. The first heaven is the place within that atmosphere where clouds form, birds fly, and lightning flashes.

THE SECOND HEAVEN

The second heaven is the vast universe beyond our atmosphere—outer space, filled with billions of stars, planets, constellations, meteors, and galaxies. The book of Psalms praises God for the lavish display of His glory in the universe around us. Psalm 8:3–4 says, "When I consider your heavens, the work of your fingers, the moon and the stars, which you have set in place, what is mankind that you are mindful of them?" (NIV).

Psalm 19 begins, "The heavens declare the glory of God; and the firmament shows His handiwork" (verse 1).

Jesus predicted a coming day when "the sun will be darkened, and the moon will not give its light; the stars will fall from heaven" (Matthew 24:29). These are all references to the second heaven, the stellar skies.

Most of us can't appreciate the evening expanse of stars because of light pollution. One special place you can visit is Joshua Tree National Park in California. It's an "International Dark Sky Park" and a favorite destination for "astrotourism."[4] That's when people travel to places where they can best see the glories of the nocturnal skies. In ancient times, everyone was an "astrotourist," because the evening skies were plainly visible.

All of us should search out some times and places, when possible, to simply lie on our backs or in lounge chairs and soak in the celestial heavens. Doing so leads to spiritual worship of our glorious God. The Bible says, "For since the creation of the world God's invisible qualities—his eternal power and divine nature—have been clearly seen, being understood from what has been made" (Romans 1:20 NIV).

THE THIRD HEAVEN
The third heaven is the one Paul had in mind when he wrote,

> I know a man in Christ who fourteen years ago—whether in the body I do not know, or whether out of the body I do not know, God knows—such a one was caught up to the third heaven. And I know such a man—whether in the body or out of the body I do not know, God knows—how he was caught up into Paradise and heard inexpressible words, which it is not lawful for a man to utter. (2 Corinthians 12:2–4)

Paul was not referring to the atmospheric heaven or to the stellar heaven. He was referring to the highest heaven, the very dwelling place of God. King Solomon spoke of this in 1 Kings 8:27, when he prayed, "But will God indeed dwell on the earth? Behold, heaven and the heaven of heavens cannot contain You. How much less this temple which I have built!"

Moses called this the "highest heavens" in Deuteronomy 10:14. Other Bible writers described it as God's holy temple. The prophet Habakkuk wrote, "But the LORD is in His holy temple. Let all the earth keep silence before Him" (Habakkuk 2:20).

Hebrews 11:14 calls this place "a homeland." Jesus referred to it as the "Father's house" in John 14:2.

This heaven—the heaven of heavens, the highest heaven, the Father's house—is the locale of the throne and the dwelling place of God. It is Paradise. It is our eternal home. This is where we will soon live side by side with God and with the angels and with the redeemed of all the ages.

As I was writing this, a story came across the news about the recovery of a World War II pilot. U.S. Army Air Force 1st Lt. Herbert G. Tennyson, twenty-four, of Wichita, Kansas, has finally been accounted for. He was last seen as the pilot on board a Liberator bomber during a bombing mission along the northern coast of New Guinea. Crew members from other aircraft saw flames shooting from the tail of his plane, apparently the result of anti-aircraft fire. The plane plummeted into the Pacific Ocean. After the war, the army searched for the remains of the plane and its victims, but without success. Only recently have renewed efforts located the remains of Tennyson's body, which will be returned to Wichita for burial.

The thing that caught my eye was the name of Tennyson's airplane: *Heaven Can Wait*. Those words were painted in white stencil lettering on the front of his plane along with the image of an angel.[5]

The thing is—heaven *can't* wait. We never know when Jesus will return or death will call. Everyone on earth is subject to sudden death at any moment, day or night. Whether we're engaged in a high-risk assignment like a military pilot or sleeping in a soft bed within a guarded mansion, we don't know if we'll be alive tomorrow.

That's why I can't wait to tell you that the heaven above your head should be on your mind right now. It's in your future, and what you need to know about heaven is within the Scriptures. Pondering these things assuages the uncertainty of life, comforts us at the moment of death, and brightens our pathway from here to eternity.

CHAPTER 4

THE TREASURES OF HEAVEN

Did you know the most expensive engagement ring in the world ended up in a backpack, lugged through the African wilderness for three weeks, while the would-be groom mustered his nerves to propose? It was a sapphire and diamond ring that originally belonged to Princess Diana. Prince Charles purchased the ring from the British jeweler Garrard because it reminded him of a sapphire brooch passed down from Queen Victoria. After Charles and Diana divorced and Diana was killed in a Paris car crash, the ring had no one to wear it.

Prince William wanted to pass it on to his girlfriend, Kate Middleton. "It's my mother's engagement ring," he said, "so I thought it was quite nice because, obviously, she's not going to be around to share in any of the fun and excitement of all this."[1]

When he and Kate took a vacation in Kenya, William tucked the ring into his backpack. He later admitted he was a nervous wreck every day for three weeks, afraid he'd lose the keepsake. Finally, in a rustic cabin on a wildlife reserve, William knelt on one knee and gave Kate the twelve-carat oval sapphire, which is surrounded by a halo of fourteen solitaire diamonds.

Imagine if William had lost the ring in Africa. People would still be slashing though the brush looking for it! How wonderful that this world—this old earth—still thrills us with the diamonds, sapphires, rubies, emeralds, and other precious stones that sparkle with all the colors of the universe.

Now think ahead. According to the Bible, there will one day be a new earth. Everything in our current universe will be reforged and restored, which will include a mingling of the spiritual world and the physical world—the new heaven and new earth. The beauty and preciousness of this new, eternal home will be far greater than that of the old earth. We will explore these concepts in more detail in later chapters.

For now, let's look at this description of New Jerusalem (the capital city of the new earth) from John's vision as described in Revelation:

> The construction of its wall was of jasper; and the city was pure gold, like clear glass. The foundations of the wall of the city were adorned with all kinds of precious stones: the first foundation was jasper, the second sapphire, the third chalcedony, the fourth emerald, the fifth sardonyx, the sixth sardius, the seventh chrysolite, the eighth beryl, the ninth topaz, the tenth chrysoprase, the eleventh jacinth, and the twelfth amethyst. The twelve gates were twelve pearls: each individual gate was of one pearl. And the street of the city was pure gold, like transparent glass. (21:18–21)

Our eternal home will stun us with its unparalleled wealth and beauty. But it's not just material prosperity and external beauty that make heaven precious for all God's people. There's far more! Here are several treasures we'll enjoy for eternity when we enter our Father's house.

OUR REDEEMER IS IN HEAVEN

The first thing that makes heaven precious is the presence of Jesus. Our Redeemer will be there. Our Savior. Our King. Hebrews 9:24 says, "For Christ has not entered the holy places made with hands, which are copies of the true, but into heaven itself, now to appear in the presence of God for us."

I have a feeling that when we get to heaven and see the golden streets and the gates of pearl and every other visual marvel, they will all fade into insignificance when compared with Christ. Imagine the moment we see Jesus! Right now we don't see Him with our eyes. We don't have the privilege of standing in the presence of Christ, "whom having not seen you love. Though now you do not see Him, yet believing, you rejoice with joy inexpressible and full of glory" (1 Peter 1:8).

If we rejoice with joy inexpressible and full of glory now, when we cannot see Him with visible eyesight, think of our joy and glory when we can see Him! Think of the wonder when at last we focus our eyes on Him who, though He was God, became a man and paid the penalty for our sins on the cross. What a moment that will be! Everything else will pale in comparison.

We'll be like Stephen, who said, "Look! I see the heavens opened and the Son of Man standing at the right hand of God!" (Acts 7:56). We'll be like the apostle John who turned and saw "One like the Son of Man, clothed with a garment down to the feet and girded about the chest with a golden band. . . . And when I saw Him, I fell at His feet as dead. But He laid His right hand on me, saying to me, 'Do not be afraid; I am the First and the Last. I am He who lives, and was dead, and behold, I am alive forevermore. Amen'" (Revelation 1:13, 17–18).

I remember hearing someone say that if he could be in heaven and peek through a keyhole and see Jesus for a single second every thousand years, it would be worth it. That's true, but that's also underselling reality. I'm not sure how it will work on a practical level, but every individual soul in heaven will enjoy fellowship with Jesus in a way that is deeply personal and far beyond our knowledge of Him now.

That's what Scripture tells us: "The throne of God and of the Lamb shall be in it, and His servants shall serve Him. They shall see His face" (Revelation 22:3–4).

OUR RELATIONSHIPS ARE IN HEAVEN

In June 2024 Lorraine Williams boarded a plane from British Columbia, Canada, headed to the United Kingdom. This wasn't an ordinary trip; it was the journey of a lifetime. Waiting for her in Liverpool were two people: her brother James and her sister Josephine. What made the reunion interesting was all three siblings had never met. They'd been separated from each other for more than seventy years.

Lorraine, James, and Josephine had each signed up for a genetic testing service. That's how they discovered they were siblings, with all three sharing the same father. Prior to that moment, they'd been unaware of each other's existence. James and Josephine had never met their father but instead grew up in orphanages and foster homes.

There was a lot of pent-up hope and anticipation when the siblings finally got together in Liverpool—and the end result more than lived up to the hype.

"It's been nothing but positivity and happiness," said Lorraine. Josephine experienced "an explosion of emotions." James added, "Although we've only just met each other, it's like we've known each other our whole lives."[2]

Chances are good you've experienced the sting of separation from loved ones over the course of your life. Maybe you've lost parents. Or siblings. Or children. Or close friends. Maybe you're dealing with the stress of strained relationships or the disappointment of being physically distant from those you care about. Maybe you've been carrying those feelings for years—or decades.

The pain of that separation is real. But for followers of Jesus, the pain is not permanent.

That's the second reason why heaven is precious for the children of God: because it allows us to enjoy our most important relationships for eternity. That means so much to me. At this point in my life, I've lost people who were dear to me—my parents, my sister, my friends. How awful to think I'd never see them again. Instead, because of heaven, I will, and I can't wait!

OUR RESIDENCE IS IN HEAVEN

Heaven is also precious to us because that's our place of residence. I'm not just talking about where we will live; I'm talking about our citizenship. When we experience the salvation offered through the gospel of Jesus Christ, we legally become residents of heaven.

Philippians 3:20 says, "For our citizenship is in heaven, from which we also eagerly wait for the Savior, the Lord Jesus Christ." That means we are not citizens of earth who are going to heaven; we are citizens of heaven who are traveling through earth.

Have you ever applied for a passport? You have to state where you were born, where you currently live, your birthdate, and so forth. If approved, the government issues you a passport to let other governments know you are a citizen of the United States or Germany or Mexico or wherever. I was born in Toledo, Ohio, and I live in Southern California. I have a U.S. passport. But my real residence is in heaven. I'm a citizen of that land, and I'm currently here on earth on an ambassadorial mission. That's true of every believer. We are "ambassadors for Christ" (2 Corinthians 5:20).

But there's more! It's one thing to be a citizen of a country. It's another to be part of the royal family. We've been *born again* into the kingdom of God, but we've also been *adopted* into the family of God. Scripture says:

But when the fullness of the time had come, God sent forth His Son, born of a woman, born under the law, to redeem those who were under the law, that we might receive the adoption as sons.

And because you are sons, God has sent forth the Spirit of His Son into your hearts, crying out, "Abba, Father!" Therefore you are no longer a slave but a son, and if a son, then an heir of God through Christ. (Galatians 4:4–7)

This is an incredible honor, privilege, and blessing. The angels, for example, are citizens of the kingdom but not sons and daughters like those of us for whom Jesus died. I love the old song that says, "I'm a child of the King!"

We long for a world without conflicts, misunderstandings, hurt feelings, or strained friendships. Well, it's just around the corner. Our residence is in heaven, and we will return there soon.

OUR RICHES ARE IN HEAVEN

I said earlier that material wealth is not what makes heaven precious to God's children, and that's true. But it's also true that heaven is filled with many types of wealth—many kinds of riches and rewards that comprise an incredible inheritance for the children of God.

That's a key word: *inheritance.*

As we just read from Galatians 4:4–7, God became your Father and made you an heir when you accepted the salvation offered by Jesus. Christians are children of God in a legal sense, and the Bible is filled with information about our inheritance. The book of Ephesians says, "In Him also we have obtained an inheritance" (1:11). Colossians 1:12 says we are qualified in Christ "to be partakers of the inheritance of the saints in the light." Hebrews 9:15 says we are called in Christ to "receive the promise of the eternal inheritance." Revelation 21:7 says about the glories of heaven: "He who overcomes shall inherit all things."

The apostle Peter expressed that same concept in these stunning words: "Blessed be the God and Father of our Lord Jesus Christ, who according to His abundant mercy has begotten us again to a living hope through the resurrection of Jesus Christ from the dead, to an inheritance incorruptible and undefiled and that does not fade away, reserved in heaven for you" (1 Peter 1:3–4).

Inheriting money and possessions here on earth can be a life-changing event, especially if the windfall is a surprise. Some years ago, a man died in Portugal. His imposing name—he was an aristocrat—was Luis Carlos de Noronha Cabral da Camara. He was a childless bachelor when he died at the age of forty-two. Prior to his death and in the presence of two witnesses, he picked people at random from the Lisbon telephone directory to be his heirs. When these people were given their share of da Camara's estate, they were so shocked some thought they were being scammed.[3]

One lady said, "I thought it was some kind of cruel joke. I'd never heard of the man."[4]

You and I, as children of the Lord, are due to receive an inheritance beyond anything we can comprehend. It's not because our names are in the phone book but because they are in the Lamb's Book of Life.

You have an inheritance in Christ that will never be touched by inflation. It won't be lost in an economic crash. Its value will never decline or decrease, and it is both reserved and preserved for you. Your name is on it, and your eternal resources are there in heaven.

In the summer of 2022, experts at the National Galleries of Scotland were examining a painting called *Head of a Peasant Woman* when they made a shocking discovery. They found a second, entirely new painting on the back of the canvas. It was largely covered by layers of cardboard and glue, and it was only visible by using advanced scanning techniques—but it was there.

Closely examining those scans revealed the second painting to be a self-portrait of the artist. It was a bearded man sitting down and wearing a wide hat and a neckerchief tied loosely at the throat. In the portrait, the artist gazed out toward the viewer with his trademark intensity.

That artist's name is Vincent van Gogh.

Not surprisingly, this discovery sent shock waves through the art community. Professor Frances Fowle, who is a senior curator at the gallery, called it a "sensational find," noting that "moments like this are incredibly rare."[5]

Think about that for a moment. Art enthusiasts, students, and professors have studied van Gogh's *Head of a Peasant Woman* for well over a hundred years. (The original painting dates back to 1885.) Yet even after such a long time of intense scrutiny and contemplation, this precious work of art still had more to offer.

Heaven is the same way!

The more we study heaven, the more we will discover about God's precious gift of eternity and eternal life. The more we saturate ourselves in the truth of heaven, the more precious those truths and that gift will become to us.

CHAPTER 5

A BODY FOR HEAVEN

There aren't many normal days on the site of Camp 3 near the summit of Mount Everest. The camp is usually set up at an elevation of around 24,500 feet, which is within the "death zone" caused by frigid temperatures and significantly reduced oxygen. So, every person there is literally taking their life in their hands.

On a particular day in 2007, everyone stood in slack-jawed amazement as a singular climber entered the camp. That climber's name was Wim Hof, and in many ways he was similar to the other adventure-seekers looking to summit the world's highest mountain—bold, courageous, and open to risks others preferred to avoid.

There was one key difference between Wim Hof and everyone else, however: clothing. While every other climber and every member of the support staff was decked out in the latest cold-weather gear—including performance jackets, gloves, the latest boots, and many other layers—Hof wore only a pair of shorts and open-toed sandals. He had no shirt. No hat. No socks. Nothing to stand between his body and the merciless cold.

Known throughout the world as the "Iceman," Hof has become a legend for his ability to thrive in severe cold. Scientists are baffled by Hof's ability to endure extremes that would mean certain death for any other person. The Iceman attributes his extraordinary feats to what he calls the "Wim Hof Method," which seems to be a combination of breathing techniques, exposure, meditation, and chutzpah.[1]

I have no idea whether Hof is a once-in-a-lifetime physical specimen, a motivational genius, a charlatan, or something completely different. But I do know that his ideas remind me of a truth I have been pondering a long time: Human beings are destined for more than we currently experience.

I'm talking about the physical transformation all followers of Jesus will experience at the moment of our resurrection and transition to heaven. That resurrection is more than resuscitation. It's more than simply coming back to life. It is a moment of transformation during which we will become something new.

Three people rose from the dead in the Old Testament, and Jesus raised three people from death during His ministry—a boy in the town of Nain, a girl in Capernaum, and His friend Lazarus. Both Peter and Paul brought someone back from death. But all of those were temporary resurrections because each of those people died again.

Christ arose in a different way. The essence of His physical body was changed—it was glorified and rendered everlasting, imperishable, and improved with various skills and abilities to enjoy forever. He would not and could not die again.

The resurrection of Jesus Christ from the dead provides the proof and the pattern for what's ahead for all God's children. In Philippians 3:21, we're told that Christ "will transform our lowly body that it may be conformed to His glorious body." John wrote in 1 John 3:2, "It has not yet been revealed what we shall be, but we know that when He is revealed, we shall be like Him, for we shall see Him as He is."

Let's look together at what the Bible teaches about our heavenly bodies. What will they be like? And what can we look forward to?

OUR BODIES WILL BE INCARNATE

On one occasion when Jesus appeared to His disciples after His resurrection, He told them, "Behold My hands and My feet, that it is I Myself. Handle Me and see, for a spirit does not have flesh and bones as you see I have" (Luke 24:39).

This tells us we aren't going to be some kind of ghostlike phantom that floats around forever. We're going to have our same literal, physical bodies, but they will be risen, resurrected, and glorified—equipped for eternity. Just as Jesus took on flesh at the incarnation, so our heavenly bodies will be incarnate.

During two of His post-resurrection appearances, Jesus ate with His disciples, which shows us our glorified bodies will be capable of eating. I consider that good news, don't you? People seem to be curious about this, because I've often been asked if we will need to eat in heaven. Well, I don't know if we will need to eat, but we certainly will enjoy eating and drinking, since Jesus did.

The body of Christ was also touchable. It could be held. In John 20:27, Jesus told Thomas, who had a hard time believing that Jesus had really risen from the dead, "Reach your finger here, and look at My hands; and reach your hand here, and put it into My side. Do not be unbelieving, but believing."

OUR BODIES WILL BE IDENTIFIABLE

Next, our bodies will be identifiable. You will still be you in heaven, and everyone will recognize you. You'll instantly know your loved ones.

I realize that on two occasions after His resurrection, people were confused about our Lord's identity. The first was at the tomb, when Mary Magdalene thought Jesus was the gardener. But her eyes were filled with tears. She quickly recognized Him (John 20:16). The other was on the Emmaus Road, when the two travelers thought He was a stranger. But that's because "their eyes were restrained, so that they did not know Him" (Luke 24:16).

On every other occasion, people identified Jesus and called Him by name. They will call you by name, too, as soon as they see you. The apostle Paul said of that day, "Now I know in part, but then I shall know just as I also am known" (1 Corinthians 13:12).

In describing the moment of our resurrection in 1 Thessalonians 4, Paul told the people not to grieve beyond measure over those who had passed away, for we would see them again and be caught up in the heavens with them. "And thus we shall always be with the Lord" (verse 4:17).

The three men in Jesus' story about the afterlife—Abraham, the beggar Lazarus, and the rich man in hades—all recognized each other (Luke 16:22–31).

At the transfiguration of Christ in Matthew 17, Peter, James, and John recognized Elijah, Moses, and the brilliantly illuminated Jesus. Here we have men whose earthly lives were separated by centuries, yet they all knew each other. They were standing there physically, fellow-shipping and talking together. Moses and Elijah were known by their same names, but they were glorified, energized, and wrapped in light.

Perhaps the best answer is the one I heard years ago. An old lady approached her pastor and said, "Will I know my daughter when I get to heaven? She's there waiting on me."

The pastor replied, "My dear, did you recognize her on earth? Yes? Well, we aren't going to be less aware in heaven than we are on earth, are we? We'll actually be smarter and our memories will be keener. Yes, you will instantly recognize your sweet daughter."

OUR NEW BODIES WILL BE INDESTRUCTIBLE

In 1 Corinthians 15, Paul wrote, "The body is sown in corruption, it is raised in incorruption" (verse 42). The word *sown* refers back to an argument Paul made earlier in the chapter. Specifically, he chided the Corinthians for being afraid of death. He said in verse 36, "Foolish one, what you sow is not made alive unless it dies." The picture is of a seed being planted in the soil, then germinating, then sprouting into something new—something much better and much more significant.

This is the same path we follow when we die. We are sown in corruption, then raised in incorruption. What is corruption? It is what happens to our current bodies that suffer strokes, heart attacks, cancer, diabetes, arthritis, asthma, migraines, and all the rest. The Bible says, "Our outward man is perishing" (2 Corinthians 4:16).

From the instant of our resurrection, our new bodies will never wear out nor grow old. They will be totally resistant to deterioration or decay. Your new body will be designed for eternity. It will not be subject to accidents, diseases, aging, or death. It will be pain-free and disease-free. It will never wear out and never die.

The exclamation point to this truth is found in Romans 6:8–9, which describes the resurrection body of Jesus: "Now if we died with Christ, we believe that we will also live with him. For we know that since Christ was raised from the dead, he cannot die again; death no longer has mastery over him" (NIV).

Notice those words about our Savior: He cannot die again. His glorified body is imperishable and indestructible. And this is the model for our own eternal bodies.

OUR NEW BODIES WILL BE ILLUMINATED

Let's move to 1 Corinthians 15:43, which says the body "is sown in dishonor, it is raised in glory." We could accurately translate the word *glory* as "brilliance," which means our new bodies may actually have a luminescent quality to them.

In Exodus 34:29 something unusual happened to Moses after he spent time with the Lord. His face became radiant and began to shine.

THE PROMISE OF HEAVEN

The same thing happened to Jesus on the Mount of Transfiguration (Luke 9:28–30). In Revelation 21 we're told the entire city of New Jerusalem will be luminescent, brightly illumined by the light that radiates from the resurrected Christ. Daniel 12:3 says the resurrected saints "shall shine like the brightness of the firmament."

Our bodies will shine with light, just like Moses' face did after being with God. Just like Jesus did on the mountain. When we are raised in glory, we'll shine like the sun. Psalm 34:5 says, "They looked to Him and were radiant."

By the way, shouldn't our faces exhibit a foretaste of that now? The Scripture says, "And we all, who with unveiled faces contemplate the Lord's glory, are being transformed into his image with ever-increasing glory, which comes from the Lord, who is the Spirit" (2 Corinthians 3:18 NIV).

Does your face reflect your anticipation for heaven, even now?

OUR NEW BODIES WILL BE INCREDIBLE

Here's another truth about our resurrected bodies: They will be incredible. As Paul declared in 1 Corinthians 15:43, "It is sown in weakness, it is raised in power."

For most of my life, I've made it a point to visit the gym regularly. As the decades have passed, I've switched the types of exercises I perform during a given week to accommodate the physical changes of age. Yet no matter how hard I work at maintaining my physical health, I can't deny that my body today is weaker than when I was in my twenties and thirties. I'm older and more fragile. A little worn down.

Do you know what comes to mind when I ponder the reality of my resurrection body? Thank God I won't have to drag my current frame into eternity! I'm ready for something new. Something powerful. Something incredible.

Our resurrection bodies will be astonishing, full of energy, bursting with enthusiastic power, and perhaps capable of extraordinary functions. If the glorified body of Christ could pass through walls and travel by impulses of thought, perhaps the same will be true for us. Without being dogmatic on the specifics, I'm convinced our glorified bodies will not have the same limitations we have today. We will certainly be mobile and able to move, which means we can travel from place to place. So, at the very least, how wonderful to contemplate traveling around the new earth without the fatigue or stress of airport security and seats made for tiny people!

OUR NEW BODIES WILL BE INFINITE

Our resurrection bodies will be incarnate, identifiable, indestructible, illuminated, incredible—and also infinite. Paul wrote in 1 Corinthians 15:44–45, "It is sown a natural body, it is raised a spiritual body. There is a natural body, and there is a spiritual body. As so it is written, 'The first man Adam became a living being.' The last Adam became a life-giving spirit."

What did Paul mean by a "spiritual" body? I've already indicated my firm belief that our heavenly bodies will be literal, physical, touchable, identifiable, and powerful. I do not believe the word *spiritual* in verse 44 implies that our bodies will be incorporeal or mere apparitions. Instead, our new bodies will exist on a higher plane.

The basic difference between a natural body and a spiritual body is that the former is suited for life on earth, while our spiritual bodies will be suited for life in heaven for eternity with God. In our current bodies, we couldn't function in the realm of heaven. But God is going to give us new bodies like in kind to the ones we have now, only completely made over and transformed and capable of living in both the seen and unseen realms, which will have been brought together and united in Christ.

In Hollywood, actors often try to create a new body for themselves to get a role. Kumail Nanjiani wanted to star in a superhero movie called *Eternals*. He worked out every day for a solid year and avoided every bit of pizza, donuts, and refined sugar. He ate very few carbs. In the end, he became ripped, with killer muscles, a rock-solid body, and the physique of a superhero.

But after filming ended, Nanjiani said, his relationship with food worsened, so he forced himself to devour "unhealthy amounts of unhealthy food."[2]

There's a better way to get a new body and star in something eternal! I've described it as best I can in this chapter, but now I'm going to ask the apostle Paul to sum it all up. He had a truly inspired way of putting things:

And if the Spirit of him who raised Jesus from the dead is living in you, he who raised Christ from the dead will also give life to your mortal bodies because of his Spirit who lives in you. (Romans 8:11 NIV)

CHAPTER 6

BEING WITH JESUS

Master Sgt. Daniel Redman was deployed to Korea for a solid year, and he missed his family. They missed him, too, especially his two sons—Jacob in fifth grade and Jason in seventh. "He's been gone for a while and I've been missing Him," Jacob said.

When Redman found out he was coming back home to Maine, he told his wife, but they decided to surprise the boys. Television cameras followed Master Sgt. Redman as he entered the fifth-grade classroom—where Jacob jumped out of his chair and hugged his dad. Redman looked down at his boy and said, "Did you miss me?" Jacob, crying, nodded his head, not willing to let go of his dad. Then it was on to the seventh-grade classroom, where Jason spotted his dad, raced across the room, and grabbed his dad so hard that Redman said, "Holy smokes!" The classroom cheered—there wasn't a dry eye in the place.

"You see them on FaceTime and Facebook Messenger and you know they are growing and getting bigger," Redman said. "But it's a lot different when you finally get to see them in person."[1]

We've all seen videos and television reports of these surprise reunions, and we can't watch them without our eyes watering. Perhaps one of the reasons they touch us has to do with something deeper—our innermost longing to be reunited with our Lord Jesus Christ. Like Jacob, we can't help saying, "He's been gone for a while and I've been missing him."

We see Jesus in the pages of the Bible. We have His Spirit in our hearts. But it will be a lot different when we finally get to see Him in person. As we used to sing, "It will be worth it all when we see Jesus!"

In this chapter I want to explore why that is true, and why being with Jesus will be such a foundational part of our experiences in heaven.

CHRIST'S LONGING TO BE WITH US

As I immersed myself in all the biblical passages I could find about our eternal home, one truth jumped off the pages of Scripture and into my heart. The main thing about heaven is not the streets of gold, the gates of pearl, or even our reunion with our loved ones. As wonderful as those things are, the main thing is our Lord Jesus Christ.

Heaven is heaven because that's where Jesus is.

The Bible says, "We love Him because He first loved us" (1 John 4:19). In a similar way, we can say, "We want to be with Him because He first wants to be with us." I do not have the eloquence or vocabulary—nor the depth of understanding—to explain how and why Jesus so longs to be with us. With you. But Scripture tells me it's true.

We see this most vividly in the sacred prayer Jesus offered to His Father in John 17, just before He entered the garden of Gethsemane on His way to die for us. He prayed, "Father, I desire that they also whom You gave Me may be with Me where I am, that they may behold My glory which You have given Me; for You loved me before the foundation of the world" (verse 24).

"I want My followers to be with Me and see My glory!"

The apostle Paul reflected on this when he prayed that we "may be able to comprehend with all the saints what is the width and length and depth and height—to know the love of Christ which passes knowledge" (Ephesians 3:18–19).

Paul was teaching us to ask God for a greater ability to know something that transcends knowledge—how much Christ truly loves us. How much He really loves *you*! This is the entire gospel in its most personal form. Jesus so wanted you to be with Him in heaven that He paid the greatest imaginable price to make it happen. He became human, endured the brutality of crucifixion, and shed His blood so that you may have a life that's forgiven and a life that's forever.

OUR LONGING TO BE WITH HIM

Jesus wants to be with us so much that it causes us to want to be with Him. As I said, we love Him because He first loved us. In John 14:3 He said, "And if I go and prepare a place for you, I will come again and receive you to Myself; that where I am, there you may be also." He told the dying thief on the cross, "Assuredly, I say to you, today you will be with Me in Paradise" (Luke 23:43).

Can you imagine hearing those words directly from the Savior's lips? "You will be with Me."

Paul explained death in similar terms, saying, "We are confident, yes, well pleased rather to be absent from the body and to be present with the Lord" (2 Corinthians 5:8). When Paul was writing to the Philippians about his own death, he declared, "For I am hard-pressed between the two, having a desire to depart and be with Christ, which is far better" (Philippians 1:23).

In his most definitive explanation of the rapture of the church, the apostle said, "Then we who are alive and remain shall be caught up together with them in the clouds to meet the Lord in the air. And thus we shall always be with the Lord" (1 Thessalonians 4:17).

After all is said and done and all the explanations are made, there is only one thing that really matters when it comes to heaven: Jesus is there, and we will be with Him. He longs to be with us, and He plants in our hearts the eternal desire to be with Him.

Often when we talk about a believing loved one who passed away, we say, "He is in heaven." Perhaps we should say, "He's with Jesus." Or, "She's with the Lord."

There's a hunger in every heart for the kind of love and permanence that only Christ can give. Whitney Houston, the American singer and actress, lived a troubled life and died at the age of forty-eight. She accidentally drowned in a bathtub at the Beverly Hilton Hotel in Beverly Hills. She was one of the best-selling artists in history.

On the night before her death, she performed a heartfelt rendition of "Jesus Loves Me." She told the crowd she had given her heart to Jesus. She told friends she thought the end was near, and in the days leading up to her death, she began quoting the Bible, singing hymns, and talking about Christ and heaven and the afterlife. On the morning of her death, she read about the baptism of Jesus by John the Baptist, and she told a friend, "I'm gonna go see Jesus. I want to see Jesus."[2]

Deep within us, we all have that same desire—though we don't always realize it.

Dr. R. T. Kendall was thinking about heaven one day, and he pondered all the people he wanted to meet. "I want to meet Paul the apostle. I will ask him, 'Did I faithfully interpret what you said about the faith of Christ?' I want to ask James, 'Did I really get it right on your epistle in James 2:14?' I want to meet Martin Luther—my hero. John Calvin—my favorite theologian. Charles Wesley and John Newton—my favorite hymn writers. Martyn Lloyd-Jones—my chief mentor."

Kendall continued:

One of the things I expect to be true is the reunion with my loved ones. My mother has been there since 1953, my father since 2002. I have friends I want to see there. All my mentors who have shaped my mind and my preaching style.

But first and foremost—words fail me to put this as I would wish . . . I only know . . . I want to see Jesus! The wonderful thing is that we will get to see Him before we see anyone else. I want to worship Him. To thank Him for leaving heaven, to become nothing, to make Himself of no reputation, to become an embryo in the virgin Mary's womb. I want to thank Him for fulfilling the law. For never sinning. For dying on the cross. For saving me. I will thank Him for His infinite patience with me.[3]

What is it that makes you most excited about seeing Jesus? What do you want to tell Him? What do you want to hear from Him? What emotions do you expect to flood your mind and heart when you finally stand before Him face-to-face?

Such questions are worth thinking about. Heaven and Jesus are worth thinking about. Because as we will see in page after page throughout this book, the more we set our minds on the wonders of tomorrow, the more we are encouraged and inspired today.

UNTIL THEN

But until we reach the place where Jesus dwells, we can still enjoy His presence by means of His abiding Holy Spirit. On the night before His death, Jesus told His disciples, "I shall ask the Father to give you someone else to stand by you, to be with you always. I mean the Spirit of truth. . . . I am not going to leave you alone in the world" (John 14:16–18 PHILLIPS).

We are hindered now, in a way. We love the Lord Jesus Christ, and we can communicate with Him in prayer. We can read His Word. We can sense His presence within us and around us by His Spirit. Yet we do not actually see Him.

Peter said, "You love him even though you have never seen him. Though you do not see him now, you trust him; and you rejoice with a glorious, inexpressible joy" (1 Peter 1:8 NLT).

After Jesus rose from the dead, He said to Thomas, "Thomas, because you have seen Me, you have believed. Blessed are those who have not seen and yet have believed" (John 20:29).

The Bible says, "While we are at home in the body we are absent from the Lord. For we walk by faith, not by sight. We are confident, yes, well pleased rather to be absent from the body and to be present with the Lord" (2 Corinthians 5:6–8).

One day we'll see the One whom we love, and we'll see Him up close. Even close enough to hug! But until then, we "practice His presence." We offer ourselves to Him as living sacrifices (Romans 12:1–2). We spend time with Him each day in prayer and Bible study. We talk with Him throughout the day as we pray without ceasing (1 Thessalonians 5:17). We do His work, knowing He is with us, even to the end of the age (Matthew 28:20). We enter God's presence with other believers as we worship and sing and partake of Communion in church (1 Corinthians 11:23–26). Even now we are seated with Christ in the heavenly places (Ephesians 2:6).

But, oh, to see Him face-to-face. The old hymn "When We All Get to Heaven" has a line that says, "Just one glimpse of Him in glory will the toils of life repay."

Another old gospel song on the same subject says:

> When my lifework is ended and I cross the swelling tide,
> When the bright and glorious morning I shall see;
> I shall know my Redeemer when I reach the other side,
> And His smile will be the first to welcome me.

That song was written by Fanny Crosby, one of the greatest hymn writers in Christian history. She was blinded in infancy because of a wrongly prescribed medication for her eyes, but she lived independently and joyfully until her death at the age of ninety-four. One day a pastor told her how sorry he felt for her blindness. She surprised him by saying, "Do you know that, if at my birth I had been able to make one petition to my Creator, it would have been that I should be made blind?"

"Why?" exclaimed the pastor.

"Because when I get to heaven, the first face that shall ever gladden my sight will be that of my Savior."[4]

Imagine being blind all your life, then getting to heaven where the first face you see is the sweet, smiling face of our Lord! Yes, we shall see His face (Revelation 22:4). Jesus longs to be with us, and we long to be with Him—to see His smile, to hear His voice, to have His attention, to enjoy His friendship, and to worship His glory.

As Fanny Crosby said in another of her hymns:

> And I shall see Him face to face,
> And tell the story—Saved by grace.[5]

PART 2

THE ATMOSPHERE
OF HEAVEN

Now I saw a new heaven and a new earth, for the
first heaven and the first earth had passed away.
Also there was no more sea. Then I, John, saw
the holy city, New Jerusalem, coming down out of
heaven from God, prepared as a bride adorned
for her husband. And I heard a loud voice from
heaven saying, "Behold, the tabernacle of God is
with men, and He will dwell with them, and they
shall be His people. God Himself will be with them
and be their God. And God will wipe away every
tear from their eyes; there shall be no more death,
nor sorrow, nor crying. There shall be no more
pain, for the former things have passed away."

Then He who sat on the throne said,
"Behold, I make all things new."
REVELATION 21:1–5

CHAPTER 7

HEAVEN AND
EARTH RESTORED

With the flourish of a pen, it was done. Larry Silverstein had just signed an agreement he hoped would be the capstone on a legendary career in New York real estate. The deal, which cost $3.2 billion, had been struck with New York's Port Authority and allowed him to manage and develop a critical property in Lower Manhattan for ninety-nine years.

At the time, this was the most expensive real-estate transaction in New York history and the culmination of a decades-long dream. Silverstein was seventy years old, and when the deal went through he decided he was ready to step away from the hustle and bustle. Maybe not full retirement, but certainly a chance to rest.

He said to his wife, "Now that we've got the brass ring . . . whatever you want to do that we delayed all these years doing, we can do."

Now he adds, "It didn't turn out that way. Such is life."[1]

The property Silverstein purchased was the World Trade Center. The deal was signed in July 2001—just weeks before the terrorist attacks of September 11. In less than two months, everything Silverstein had purchased literally came crashing to the ground.

In the year that followed, a number of politicians, business associates, and insurance adjusters suggested Silverstein simply abandon the site. They told him the Twin Towers could not be rebuilt. They told him New Yorkers wouldn't want to return to the spot where so many had been killed in such a hateful attack. They told him there was no future for his old dreams.

But Silverstein saw things differently. "I've been a New Yorker all my life. You expect me to just walk away from my obligation to New York? I can't do that." Instead, he informed the world of his intention to "get on with the rebuilding and do it as quickly as possible."[2]

It took longer than anticipated, but in the end Silverstein accomplished his goal—and once again achieved his dream. On November 3, 2014, a new tower opened to the public on the same site where the Twin Towers once stood. Officially called One World Trade Center, the building is also referred to as the Freedom Tower. A magnificent combination of geometrical steel and glass, the new tower rises to a height of 1,776 feet, making it the tallest building in the western hemisphere.

The reconstruction of the World Trade Center accomplished more than simply replacing a building—it transformed a community. "Before 9/11, there was nothing here," says Silverstein. "After six o'clock at night, it was dead. You could roll a bowling ball down Wall Street and hit nothing. . . . Now, it's bustling with human beings."[3]

It sounds strange to say, but our world is following a similar trajectory to that of the World Trade Center plaza. During the very first moments of human history, this world was broken and corrupted by sin—a spiritual terrorist attack masterminded by Satan. But God, our Creator, has not abandoned us. For ages now, God has revealed Himself to us, first through the Jewish people and ultimately through the incarnation of Jesus Christ. When He has completed His work of redeeming humanity, He will rebuild our earthly home.

Out of the brokenness of our current system, a new heaven and a new earth will be born. Let's see what Scripture says about God's incredible promise, our incredible place, and the universe's incredible promotion.

GOD'S INCREDIBLE PROMISE

As we've seen already in this book, the promise of heaven is pervasive throughout God's Word. Over and over again, Scripture reminds us that our current world is not the only world—that when our life on earth comes to an end, our fullest life will begin with God in heaven. That guarantee is foundational for the Christian faith.

At the same time, the Bible is also salted with promises of a *new* heaven. Not only that, but a new earth. For example, take a look at these intriguing words from Psalm 102:

> Of old You laid the foundation of the earth,
> And the heavens are the work of Your hands.
> They will perish, but You will endure;
> Yes, they will all grow old like a garment;
> Like a cloak You will change them,
> And they will be changed.
> But You are the same,
> And Your years will have no end. (verses 25–27)

The psalmist didn't understand all the details of God's plan for eternity, but he certainly foresaw a future time when our current reality would "grow old like a garment." Haven't we felt that as a people? As a civilization? So much of our world these days seems worn out and threadbare. Now, I don't think the same is true of the third heaven in its current form—God's dwelling place isn't wearing thin. Yet the psalmist perceived a day when God would transform even the glories of heaven into something new and more glorious in almost the same way a man swaps out one coat for another.

In the New Testament, Peter expanded on and amplified this promise:

> But the day of the Lord will come as a thief in the night, in which the heavens will pass away with a great noise, and the elements will melt with fervent heat; both the earth and the works that are in it will be burned up. Therefore, since all these things will be dissolved, what manner of persons ought you to be in holy conduct and godliness, looking for and hastening the coming of the day of God, because of which the heavens will be dissolved, being on fire, and the elements will melt with fervent heat? Nevertheless we, according to His promise, look for new heavens and a new earth in which righteousness dwells. (2 Peter 3:10–13)

What a description! What a promise! These verses almost feel like the opening scenes of a Hollywood blockbuster in which an alien race launches an attack against earth—something so powerful that even "elements will melt with fervent heat."

The Bible gives us the timeline for when these events will take place. First will come the rapture, in which Jesus will rescue His church. Then the Tribulation, where God will pour out His judgment and wrath against all evil. At the end of those seven years, Christ will physically return to earth as our conquering King, and all the saints will join Him. He will set up a preview of heaven on earth that will last for a thousand years—the Millennium. That era will come to an end with a new rebellion, or a new repetition of the fall from Genesis 3, followed by the Great White Throne Judgment.

That is the moment when "the heavens will pass away with a great noise." What we know and perceive as the universe will be disbanded and dissolved. Time itself will come to an end. The old version of creation will be consumed, and God will establish something new in its place: a new heaven and a new earth to be enjoyed for eternity.

God has made that promise to you.

OUR INCREDIBLE PLACE

Would you like to know what the new heaven and new earth will be like? You can! At the end of the vision that became the book of Revelation, God supernaturally revealed to the apostle John several scenes, or snapshots, of our eternal home. Those visions were recorded within the final two chapters of Revelation, and they start with these critical words: "Now I saw a new heaven and a new earth, for the first heaven and the first earth had passed away" (21:1).

Unfortunately, we don't have space in these pages to review with a fine-tooth comb everything John recorded about the eternal state. But there are several important details that are worth highlighting.

First, John saw "the holy city, New Jerusalem, coming down out of heaven from God, prepared as a bride adorned for her husband" (v. 2). New Jerusalem is not the entirety of heaven in our eternal state. Rather, it is the capital city of heaven. According to verse 2, that city will be joined with the new earth after God remakes the universe, and we will be able to dwell there with God. Importantly, we will not be confined to that location. The Celestial City will be the launching point for our exploration of a new and perfect universe.

Let's stop there for a moment because this is an important concept. When God remakes creation, what we currently think of as "heaven" and "earth" will be joined together. There will no longer be a distinction between the kingdom of the world and the kingdom of God—between earth as a planet and heaven as a spiritual dominion. No, heaven and earth will become one, joined in perfect harmony.

No wonder verse 3 is packed with so much joy: "And I heard a loud voice from heaven saying, 'Behold, the tabernacle of God is with men, and He will dwell with them, and they shall be His people. God Himself will be with them and be their God.'"

What else can we learn about the new heaven and new earth? There is a large section in Revelation 21 that describes the beauty of New Jerusalem (verses 9–21), and then John makes a specific point about telling us what will *not* be there: no temple (verse 22), no sun or moon or night (verse 23), and no sin (verse 27).

That last one is easy to understand—of course there will be no evil present in God's perfect Paradise. But what about the other two absences? First, there will be no temple because God will be physically, emotionally, and relationally present among His people. We will commune with Him in perfect intimacy at every moment, which means there will be no need for a holy, set apart "house of the Lord." Second, there will be no sun or moon because God will suffuse eternity with His own light. In our current world, darkness occurs when there is an absence of light. But in our eternal home, there will never be an absence of God (nor will our eternal bodies need to rest for the night). We will exist in God's healing light as fish exist in water. (Note: chapter 15 offers a deeper exploration of other things that won't be present in our eternal home.)

John's vision of eternity continued into Revelation 22 with a final, delightful picture that is packed with emotional weight. Let yourself feel that emotion as you read these words:

And he showed me a pure river of water of life, clear as crystal, proceeding from the throne of God and of the Lamb. In the middle of its street, and on either side of the river, was the tree of life, which bore twelve fruits, each tree yielding its fruit every month. The leaves of the tree were for the healing of the nations. And there shall be no more curse, but the throne of God and of the Lamb shall be in it, and His servants shall serve Him. They shall see His face, and His name shall be on their foreheads. There shall be no night there: They need no lamp nor light of the sun, for the Lord God gives them light. And they shall reign forever and ever. (verses 1–5)

This is what your eternal home will be like.

CREATION'S INCREDIBLE PROMOTION

When I first began studying the concept of a new heaven and earth, I understood Scripture to say that God will completely destroy what is old before recreating the new out of nothing. It's easy to get that impression from 2 Peter 3:10 when it says the heavens will "pass away with a great noise" and the earth will be "burned up."

Over time, however, I have grown in my understanding of this eternal transition. Instead of creation being annihilated, the present heaven and earth will be cleansed, glorified, and equipped for our eternal use. Rather than being destroyed, creation will be refined and promoted to a renewed perfection without the stain of sin.

Let's look again at those two phrases to show you what I mean. Peter said the old heaven and earth will "pass away," which is a euphemism for death. When we say someone we care about has passed away, we don't mean they have ceased to exist or that they were annihilated. Instead, they have moved from one phase of existence to another.

Similarly, Peter's use of the phrase *burned up* in the original Greek actually means to be "laid bare" or "exposed." This isn't a matter of utter destruction but of stripping everything away and getting back down to the original elements. The great universal conflagration Peter described will be a purification of the cosmos—a burning away of everything associated with sin, death, the curse, and the temporal.

Dr. W. A. Criswell put it this way: "God someday shall purge this earth and this universe of all of its sin and unrighteousness and darkness and death. . . . Out of this purged mass of God's creative work,

He will reshape, He will remake, He will re-create all of the heavens and this earth. There will be no destruction of what God has made. It is a renewal. It is a renaissance. It is a regeneration. It is a re-creation (Revelation 21:1–5)."[4]

By reforging the cosmos in this way, God will deny Satan the satisfaction of having marred creation through sin. Remember, when God created the heaven and the earth in the book of Genesis, He was very pleased with His handiwork. Genesis 1:31 says, "Then God saw everything that He had made, and indeed it was very good." There is no evidence the Lord ever changed His mind about that, and His purpose for redeeming the world was not to abandon His creation but to restore it.

Speaking of masterpieces, several years ago a man named Julian Baumgartner received a William Merritt Chase painting from a client. Baumgartner is an art conservator, which means he restores paintings and other works of art through a detailed and painstaking process—one that often stretches over several months.

This particular painting was badly damaged. The subject was a young girl in a white dress, with a blue ribbon in her hair. But the canvas was torn in several places. The colors had faded. The paint was cracked and marred. Worst of all, the painting had undergone an attempted restoration from an amateur. "It's really frustrating to receive a painting that has been worked on in the past, and the work isn't good or the materials are incorrect," says Baumgartner. "I have to undo that just to get to a point where we can start to properly address the issues at hand."

On a whim, he decided to make a video of his restoration work on the Chase painting, which he posted on YouTube. The response was overwhelming—Baumgartner Restorations now has close to two million followers.

Baumgartner credits his growing popularity at least in part to the charmed nature of restoration itself. "I might be the first person in over 200 years to see a painting as the artist saw it. There's kind of a little magical moment where I get to see the piece as it was originally intended."[5]

What a sentiment! And what a window into our own eternal future. For thousands of years, humanity has been clumsily and inexpertly attempting to fix the corruption caused by sin. Thankfully, we are in the hands of a true Master. When the time is right, He will restore creation to His own original intention where we will thrive as His living masterpieces. Forever.

CHAPTER 8

THE CELESTIAL CITY

At the northern region of the Red Sea, a new city is rising from the desert, so extravagant and innovative it may bankrupt Saudi Arabia. Neom is the brainchild of crown prince Mohammed bin Salman (known as MBS). He broke ground of the project in 2017, hoping the city would be finished by 2039.

The whole metropolis will be powered by renewable energy, with underground railroads, a huge canal to the Red Sea, a floating business district, and a gigantic palace for the royal family with sixteen buildings, four swimming pools, an extensive garden, a marina, ten helipads, and a private golf course. The most innovative structure will be "The Chandelier," a glass building thirty stories tall that will hang upside down from a giant steel bridge. The highlight of the city will be two side-by-side buildings higher than the Empire State Building with an unbelievable length of 110 miles.

Nothing is going as planned with Neom. Costs have soared, planners have downsized the project, corruption has drained some of the funds, and the city's estimated cost now stands at twenty-five times the annual budget of oil-rich Saudi Arabia.[1]

There's not enough money or genius on earth to build a perfect city. But almighty God can do it. The city MBS dreams about is only a shadow of what is to come. The capital city of the universe, the sensational municipality of New Jerusalem, is already being prepared in heaven by God Himself.

According to Scripture, this city will be far larger than any presently on earth. It will be taller, happier, and more exquisite. The Bible delights in telling us about this place. The final two chapters of Scripture use the word *city* twelve times to describe our eternal home, and I don't believe it's a figure of speech. It is an actual physical place—a real city. Our resurrected bodies will be physical, real, and tangible, so they will need an actual home—a literal city.

THIS CITY IS HOME

God's men and women of faith have been excited about this city since the days of Abraham because they instinctively know it's the headquarters of our eternal home. According to Genesis, Abraham grew up in the great city called Ur of the Chaldeans, a stunning metropolis in the ancient world. But at the call of God, he left Ur and never returned. He became a pilgrim and nomad, living in tents and herding animals. Still, according to the book of Hebrews, Abraham was eager to resume city life in eternity.

> By faith Abraham, when called to go to a place he would later receive as his inheritance, obeyed and went, even though he did not know where he was going. By faith he made his home in the promised land like a stranger in a foreign country; he lived in tents, as did Isaac and Jacob, who were heirs with him of the same promise. For he was looking forward to the city with foundations, whose architect and builder is God. (11:8–10 NIV)

He was looking forward to it! When he lay down in his camel-hide tent in the desert, his day's work finished, he thought of this city—the one God had told him about. That's the only way Abraham could have known about New Jerusalem. He often talked with God, and in this way he undoubtedly learned of his eternal home. He was eager to get there!

He must have told his son and grandson about it, because six verses later, we read this statement regarding all the patriarchs in Abraham's family: "Therefore God is not ashamed to be called their God, for he has prepared a city for them" (Hebrews 11:16 NIV).

The writer of Hebrews didn't stop there. In the next chapter, he wrote about all of us who claim Christ as our Savior: "But you have come to Mount Zion, to the city of the living God, the heavenly Jerusalem. You have come to thousands upon thousands of angels in joyful assembly, to the church of the firstborn, whose names are written in heaven" (12:22–23 NIV).

Hebrews draws to a close by telling us: "For here we do not have an enduring city, but we are looking for the city that is to come" (13:14 NIV). Abraham looked forward to that city, and so do we! We share his excitement. It's our home!

The book of Revelation gives us the fullest glimpse of this city, starting with a glorious promise from Jesus: "He who overcomes. . . . I will write on him the name of My God and the name of the city of My God, the New Jerusalem, which comes down out of heaven from My God" (3:12).

The climactic description of New Jerusalem is appropriately found in the final two chapters of God's Word, Revelation 21 and 22. Here we learn God will create a dazzling new universe and a stunning new earth. Then, at just the right moment, like a bride floating down the aisle, the great city of New Jerusalem—the dazzling city with its foundations—will descend from the sky to its preplanned spot on the new earth and become the capital city of God's eternal kingdom. The Bible says:

Now I saw a new heaven and a new earth, for the first heaven and the first earth had passed away. Also there was no more sea. Then

I, John, saw the holy city, New Jerusalem, coming down out of heaven from God, prepared as a bride adorned for her husband. And I heard a loud voice from heaven saying, "Behold, the tabernacle of God is with men, and He will dwell with them, and they shall be His people. God Himself will be with them and be their God. And God will wipe away every tear from their eyes; there shall be no more death, nor sorrow, nor crying. There shall be no more pain, for the former things have passed away." (Revelation 21:1–4)

THIS CITY IS HUGE

Mohammed bin Salman envisions the city of Neom to cover more than ten thousand square miles, but that's nothing compared with New Jerusalem. Revelation 21:15–16 says, "And he who talked with me had a gold reed to measure the city, its gates, and its wall. The city is laid out as a square; its length is as great as its breadth. And he measured the city with the reed: twelve thousand furlongs. Its length, breadth, and height are equal."

In today's terms, New Jerusalem will be about fifteen hundred miles wide, fifteen hundred miles long, and fifteen hundred miles high. One way of visualizing its footprint is simply to think of the entire eastern half of the United States stacked fifteen hundred miles high. I know this is mind-boggling, but we have a mind-boggling God, don't we?

F. W. Boreham was a brilliant pastor and essayist who carefully considered the size and capacity of the great city. In one of his writings he tells of discussing this with a man named Tammas, who was an Australian engineer and a member of Boreham's church. Boreham shared the dimensions of the Celestial City with Tammas, asking him, "Did you ever think about the size of the city God has prepared?" Tammas replied:

Man, it's amazing; it's astounding; it beats everything I ever heard of! John says that each of the walls of the city measures twelve thousand furlongs. Now, if you work that out . . . it will give you an area of 2,250,000 square miles! . . . The only "city foursquare" that I ever saw was Adelaide in South Australia. The ship that brought me out from the Old Country called in there for a couple of days, and I thought it a fine city. But, as you know very well, the city of Adelaide covers only one square mile. Each of the four sides is a mile long. London covers an area of one hundred and forty square miles. But this city—the City Foursquare! It is 2,250,000 times as big as Adelaide! It is 15,000 times as big as London! It is twenty times as big as all New Zealand! It is ten times as big as Germany and ten times as big as France! It is forty times as big as all England! It is ever so much bigger than India! Why, it's an enormous continent in itself.

But Tammas wasn't done.

Wait a minute—I've been going into the matter of population, and it's even more wonderful still. Look at this! Working it out on the basis of the number of people to the square mile in the city of London, the population of the City Foursquare comes out at a hundred thousand millions—seventy times the present population of the globe.[2]

To reemphasize, I interpret these last two chapters of the Bible literally. I see no reason to spiritualize these words. When the Bible talks about the walls of the city, I believe it means literal walls. When we read about the crystal river, I believe we will dip our toes in it and feel the splash.

How will God drop a city like that out of heaven? How can that happen?

He will do it with the same power He used when He spoke a word and the world came into being in Genesis 1:1. He will do it with the same power He exerted when Jesus burst from the tomb. This is easy for Him who created the vastness of space, reversed the processes of death, and raised His sleeping children to incorruptible life.

If God wants to build a dazzling home for us that will descend to a new earth, He can do it. And He will do it, for it is one of the climactic promises of His Word. In my studied opinion, that's the most natural way to understand Revelation 21.

After all, this is His eternal capital. It is the location of His throne!

In a city this large, will there be congestion and traffic jams? I don't want to be dogmatic about this, but the resurrected Jesus was able to travel by telepathy. That's been a major concept in science fiction, but maybe it will be a reality on the new earth. Perhaps we'll have the ability to travel instantly by the impulses of thought. When I sit and ponder these things, I can easily become overwhelmed with excitement at what's ahead.

The Bible also tells us about a vast, high, broad wall surrounding New Jerusalem, punctuated by twelve gates, each of which is made of pearl. Revelation 21:17–21 says, "Then he measured the walls and found them to be 216 feet thick (according to the human standard used by the angel). The wall was made of jasper, and the city was pure gold, as clear as glass. The wall of the city was built on foundation stones inlaid with twelve precious stones. . . . The twelve gates were made of pearls—each gate from a single pearl! And the main street was pure gold, as clear as glass" (NLT).

This is way beyond exciting! The city walls are made of jasper, which in biblical times was a crystal stone like a diamond, and the gigantic gates are made of solid pearl. Imagine seeing this from afar. It will sparkle and shine as it rotates down to the earth, and all the hues of the glory of the city will be overwhelming. It will take our breath away.

The foundation will be layered stones of solid emerald, diamond, sapphire, topaz, amethyst, and all the rest. These will be the most massive and beautiful stones in the universe. Imagine these layers as massive enough to serve as the foundations for a city that's fifteen hundred miles in every direction! Imagine approaching heaven's capital and seeing it from afar!

We'll witness this magnificent city, soaring fifteen hundred miles into the atmosphere, built upon gemstone foundations, with each gate brilliantly crafted from a single pearl. We'll walk into this holy city with jaws dropped and eyes widened in absolute wonder, for even the most beautiful places on earth don't hold a candle to what God has prepared for us.

THIS CITY IS HOLY

Let's assume MBS completes his futuristic megalopolis in Saudi Arabia. Will it be free from crime? Will people avoid getting sick there? Will there be no tragedies? Do you think jails, police officers, and emergency responders will be unneeded? No, that city will have the same problems as any other city—maybe more—because it will be inhabited by people with a fallen, human nature. People will get sick and die every day. Corruption will seep into the government, and laws will be imperfect and occasionally unjust.

But not in God's great city! This will be a holy city. John wrote, "Then, I, John, saw the holy city, New Jerusalem" (Revelation 21:2). A few verses later, he wrote, "And he carried me away in the Spirit to a great and high mountain, and showed me the great city, the holy Jerusalem, descending out of heaven from God" (21:10). Shortly afterward, he added, "And if anyone takes away from the words of the book of this prophecy, God shall take away his part from the Book of Life, from the holy city" (22:19).

The chief characteristic of this city is its holiness.

Donna and I have visited some of the greatest and most beautiful cities of the world, but none of them have been holy. My own city of San Diego is a lovely place with an almost perfect climate, tucked like a gem between desolate mountains and the gleaming Pacific. But it's far from holy. All the great cities of the world have an underside to their beauty. They are polluted, corrupt, filled with vice, brimming with immorality, riddled with crime, plagued by death and disease, and struggling with every known human sin.

Not so in New Jerusalem. The *Wycliffe Bible Commentary* says, "A holy city will be one in which no lie will be uttered in one hundred million years, no evil word will ever be spoken, no shady business deal will ever even be discussed, no unclean picture will ever be seen, no corruption of life will ever be manifest. It will be holy because everyone in it will be holy."[3]

Without sin, there will be no death. There will be no jails, courtrooms, prisons, hospitals, or funeral homes in heaven. This is a holy place for holy people, for those who have been made holy by God's infinite grace through the blood of Jesus Christ. Holiness brings happiness, and what joy we'll experience!

Again, John described the city in the shape of a cube—fifteen hundred miles long, high, and wide. The holy of holies inside the tabernacle and, later, inside the temple was also in the shape of a cube. Many people believe the city of New Jerusalem is the true and actual holy of holies, which serves as the dwelling place of God in the temple of His new universe. In fact, Revelation 21:3 says of this city, "Behold, the tabernacle of God is with men, and He will dwell with them, and they shall be His people. God Himself will be with them and be their God."

I have a friend whose wife passed away. During their final conversation on earth they agreed to meet by the Crystal River in New Jerusalem and walk hand in hand alongside its banks. He often goes to sleep at night visualizing this great diamond city descending from the highest heaven to the new earth. "I know I can't fully envision it," he said, "but the Bible gives me a lot to imagine. It's perhaps the most peaceful and exciting thought I ever have, short of seeing Jesus Himself."

I hope you share his excitement, and mine, for this heavenly city for which we yearn. It's huge; it's holy; and it's our eternal home!

CHAPTER 9

A TOUR OF NEW JERUSALEM

Do you know the first city in the world was built by the first murderer in history?

Genesis 4 tells the story of Cain's jealousy toward his brother Abel. "While they were in the field, Cain attacked his brother Abel and killed him" (verse 8 NIV). The Lord placed Cain under a curse, and Cain went to the land of Nod, east of Eden. Genesis 4:17 says, "And Cain knew his wife, and she conceived and bore Enoch. And he built a city, and called the name of the city after the name of his son—Enoch."

We don't know where this place was, but in those days when people lived for hundreds of years, Cain apparently used his descendants to populate the city he built. The city of Enoch, established by Cain, marks the beginning of civilization and the development of towns and cities.

As far as we know, that city is long gone, as are many of the great cities of antiquity. Pompeii was destroyed by the eruption of Mount Vesuvius. Carthage was destroyed by Rome. Persepolis was wiped away by Alexander the Great. Nineveh, once the greatest city on earth, is now a pile of rubble in the Iraqi desert. Who knows how long today's great cities will survive?

In the previous chapter we started to explore New Jerusalem, which Scripture calls "the city that is to come" (Hebrews 13:14 NIV). As we've seen, the final two chapters of God's Word provide a sort of biblical brochure of New Jerusalem. Here, in this chapter, I'd like to take you on a little tour. I want to point out five glorious features I'm excited to describe about the Holy City: the street, the light, the tree, the river, and the throne.

THE STREET

First is the grand boulevard that traverses the city. Revelation 21 says, "The construction of its wall was of jasper; and the city was pure gold, like clear glass. . . . And the street of the city was pure gold, like transparent glass" (verses 18, 21). The entire city and its major thoroughfare is a unique gold that conveys some kind of transparent quality.

One commentator said,

Both the buildings and the streets of the city are made of gold. In the present world, gold is the most precious of metals, the standard of all currencies and the greatest of all objects of human greed and conflict. In the new Jerusalem, however, the very streets are paved with gold and the buildings are plastered with gold. The most beautiful and valuable of metals is now the most abundant of metals! . . . The gold of heaven is so good and so flawless that, like the Jasper stone, it is crystal clear, reflecting golden beams of brilliance from every surface.[1]

The gold of heaven will be so pure that we will seem to look into it and through its clear depths even as we walk upon it.

THE LIGHT

The transparent nature of the gold will enhance the shimmering light that radiates throughout the city. The source of that light? The person of Jesus Christ. He Himself will be the city's power plant, and the glory of God will be her generator. Four different verses describe this:

- "Her light was like a most precious stone, like a jasper stone, clear as crystal" (Revelation 21:11).
- "The city had no need of the sun or of the moon to shine in it, for the glory of God illuminated it. The Lamb is its light" (verse 23).
- "And the nations of those who are saved shall walk in its light" (verse 24).
- "There shall be no night there: They need no lamp nor light of the sun, for the Lord God gives them light" (22:5).

There will be no lampposts in New Jerusalem, no lanterns, no floodlights or flashlights or table lights. A constant presence of brilliant light will emanate throughout the city from the throne of God and of the Lamb. The brilliance of that light will beam forth from the Lord Jesus in His glorification, and it will fill the city with radiance.

Were it not for our new glorified eyesight, we would be blinded like Saul of Tarsus on the Damascus Road when he saw Christ (Acts 9:3–9). But the glory of the Lord won't hurt our eyes at all; in fact, our new eyes will be perfectly made for such light. I can't imagine that, but I can anticipate it.

Try again to picture what you will see as you approach the Holy City—the shimmering, translucent gold, the precious substrata of the foundation stones, the gigantic pearls at the gates, and the brilliance of light radiating from the throne. This is the New Jerusalem described in Scripture, and it's the fulfillment of a prophecy made hundreds of years before the birth of Christ, in Isaiah 60:19: "The sun shall no longer be your light by day, nor for brightness shall the moon give light to you; but the LORD will be to you an everlasting light, and your God your glory."

It's vital to carry these images in our minds because people who understand where they're headed live with greater purpose. In a sense, we are all real estate agents going out into our world and inviting people to reserve their place in the new heavens, the new earth, and the city of light.

THE RIVER

The beauty of the city will be enhanced by the gushing river of crystal waters flowing through it. Revelation 22:1 says, "And he showed me a pure river of water of life, clear as crystal, proceeding from the throne of God and of the Lamb."

I believe this is the same river mentioned in Psalm 46:4: "There is a river whose streams shall make glad the city of God, the holy place of the tabernacle of the Most High."

Most of the great cities of the world have the ribbon of a river running through them—Cairo has the Nile; Baghdad, the Tigris; Budapest, the Danube; London, the Thames; Paris, the Seine; Rome, the Tiber. Visit New York and you can take a boat trip up and down the Hudson and East Rivers. If you're in Washington, D.C., you can walk along the Potomac.

If you visit the city of Jerusalem right now, you'll be visiting one of the few great world cities without a river. But one day the new city of Jerusalem—the heavenly Zion—will have a river of waters that are clear as crystal flowing from the throne of God. It will be the most beautiful river ever created in time or eternity.

THE TREE

Revelation 22:2 says, "In the middle of its street, and on either side of the river, was the tree of life, which bore twelve fruits, each tree yielding its fruit every month. The leaves of the tree were for the healing of the nations."

On both sides of the Crystal River are the trees of life—not just one tree but multiple trees. Notice that verse 2 refers to "each tree." The Greek term indicates a plurality of trees, such as we'd find in an orchard. These trees will bear fruit every month, and it will be like eating fruit from the garden of Eden.

Notice the phrase that speaks of the leaves being used "for the healing of the nations." The word "healing" in the Greek language is *therapeia*, from which we get "therapeutic." We'll be able to eat the leaves of the tree, and those leaves will somehow give us a greater sense of our lives and our presence in heaven. This "therapy" will not enhance our holiness, because we will already be perfectly holy, but somehow it will give us a greater sense of enjoyment and fulfillment. It will be heaven's therapy for our ever-increasing well-being.

THE THRONE

In the center of it all will be the throne of God. The final chapter of the Bible says, "And he showed me a pure river of water of life, clear as crystal, *proceeding from the throne of God and of the Lamb*" (Revelation 22:1).

The longer you study the Bible, the more you're drawn to the "throne scenes" of Scripture. In Exodus 24, Moses and the elders of Israel hiked up Mount Sinai to confirm Israel's covenant with God. The passage says, "And they saw the God of Israel. And there was under His feet as it were a paved work of sapphire stone, and it was like the very heavens in its clarity" (verse 10). They saw the vast platform on which God's throne rests!

In chapter 6 of his book, Isaiah "saw the Lord sitting on a throne, high and lifted up, and the train of His robe filled the temple" (verse 1). A category of angels known as seraphim were flying around the throne, crying, "Holy, holy, holy" (verse 3).

Daniel saw the throne of God and he wrote, "His throne was a fiery flame, its wheels a burning fire. . . . Ten thousand times ten thousand stood before Him" (Daniel 7:9–10).

Psalm 103:19 says, "The LORD has established His throne in heaven, and His kingdom rules over all."

In Acts 7, Stephen became the first Christian murdered for his faith, and he cried, "Look! I see the heavens opened and the Son of Man standing at the right hand of God!" (verse 56).

In Revelation 4, John wrote, "Behold, a throne set in heaven, and One sat on the throne. And He who sat there was like a jasper and a sardius stone in appearance; and there was a rainbow around the throne, in appearance like an emerald" (verses 2–3).

Oh, to finally see it for ourselves! The throne of glory, the throne of grace, the throne of God!

THE WARNING

This is our destination, our eternal home. New Jerusalem is a city foursquare, the capital city of the new heavens and the new earth, the holy of holies for God's presence. It will have plenty of room to house His children, all the people who have ever trusted God from the beginning of time, including those who have died before the age of accountability—all the children who have died without having an opportunity to receive Christ and all those mentally incapable of understanding the gospel.

Its atmosphere will sparkle. It will glow with shimmering light reflecting off its crystal towers, its multicolored foundations, its golden streets, and its gates of pearl. It will have a sense of drawing you into itself. I wish I had a greater vocabulary to describe it.

But the last two chapters of the Bible also reiterate a grave warning. All the way through Revelation 21 and 22 we see caution signs about the danger of being denied access to this city.

Revelation 21:7-8 says, "He who overcomes shall inherit all things, and I will be his God and he shall be My son. But the cowardly, unbelieving, abominable, murderers, sexually immoral, sorcerers, idolaters, and all liars shall have their part in the lake which burns with fire and brimstone, which is the second death."

A few verses later you'll find this: "Its gates shall not be shut at all by day (there shall be no night there). And they shall bring the glory and the honor of the nations into it. But there shall by no means enter it anything that defiles, or causes an abomination or a lie, but only those who are written in the Lamb's Book of Life" (21:25–27).

In the final chapter of Scripture, the warning is flashed again: "Blessed are those who do His commandments, that they may have the right to the tree of life, and may enter through the gates into the city. But outside are dogs and sorcerers and sexually immoral and murderers and idolaters, and whoever loves and practices a lie" (Revelation 22:14–15).

All of us are sinners. We have all practiced lying. Many Christians have episodes of sorcery or immorality or idolatry or even murder in their pasts. These verses do not imply that those sins will keep us out of heaven if the blood of Christ has redeemed us. But if we have not repented of our sins and placed our faith in Christ, those sins will certainly prevent us from walking the streets of gold.

If you're living in sin without any regard for the forgiveness of God, and if you are failing to respond to His gracious invitation found in the gospel, you will have no part in the new heaven, the new earth, or the city of New Jerusalem. The only people allowed there are those whose names are written in the Lamb's Book of Life. There are no exceptions.

You won't be able to argue your way into that city or con your way in or sneak in or bribe your way in. If you have not accepted God's plan for your life and received His forgiveness for your sin, when the moment comes, you will be denied entrance into heaven and into the city we have described. I don't want that to happen to you!

Have you made your reservation for the heavenly city? If not, I urge you to do that now! The last invitation in the book of Revelation says, "And the Spirit and the bride say, 'Come!' And let him who hears say, 'Come!' And let him who thirsts come. Whoever desires, let him take the water of life freely" (22:17).

A few decades ago, a comedian named Sam Kinison became very popular on the stand-up circuit. Sam grew up with some Christian influences, but he went another route as an adult. He once summed up his own story by saying, "I have lived a carnal life. My view of life is, 'If you're going to miss heaven, why miss it by two inches? Miss it!'"[2]

Not very long after, Kinison was driving from California to Nevada to perform when his sports car collided with a pickup truck. He staggered from the car, sat on the side of the road, and died at the age of thirty-eight.[3]

I don't want anyone reading this book to miss heaven by two inches, two feet, or two miles. Jesus gave His life on Calvary to provide forgiveness for the sins that separate you from God. He rose from the dead to give you a resurrection like His so that where He is you may be too. Don't gamble with your soul. Trust Christ as your Lord and Savior today!

CHAPTER 10

THE CITIZENS OF HEAVEN

Fred Rogers dreamed of starting a television show for children based around the theme of a lovely, loving neighborhood. Mr. Rogers majored in music composition at Rollins College, so he wrote the lyrics and composed the tune to his theme song. But he wanted it to sound just right, so he hired a classically trained pianist, John Costa, to arrange and perform the song. Both men felt children could appreciate fine music, and the song's opening notes were inspired by a Beethoven sonata.

Costa took his mission seriously. He said, "Children have ears, and they're people, and they can hear good music as well as anybody else. So I started right from the beginning playing for them as I would for any adults."

"Won't You Be My Neighbor?" became one of the most recognizable children's songs in history, and the concept of "neighbors" occurs eight times in its brief lyrics. That song opened each show during the lifetime of the program. From 1968 to 2001, Mr. Rogers asked us all: "Won't you be my neighbor?"[1]

All of us dream of an idyllic neighborhood where everyone is pleasant, crime is absent, smiles abound, complaints are never heard, and every contact with our fellow citizens is enjoyable. This inborn feeling is actually an intrinsic desire for heaven.

It's always a wonderful day in *that* neighborhood, and you'll love your fellow citizens. Philippians 3:20–21 says, "For our citizenship is in heaven, from which we also eagerly wait for the Savior, the Lord Jesus Christ, who will transform our lowly body that it may be conformed to His glorious body, according to the working by which He is able even to subdue all things to Himself."

Wow! There's so much in those verses—the Second Coming of Christ, the transformation and glorification of our bodies, our likeness to Jesus, and His power to subdue everything under His feet. But I simply want you to see that word *citizenship* and notice the opening phrase is in the present tense: "For our citizenship is in heaven."

If you know Christ as Lord and Savior, your heavenly citizenship is active. It's current. Think of it like this: Right now, by making a significant donation, you can become a citizen of a country you've never actually visited. Several nations have citizenship investment programs. They include Malta, Cyprus, St. Kitts, Dominica, and Turkey. That means some people are citizens of, say, Turkey, because of a sizable investment there, though they have yet to set foot in the country.[2]

The same is true of heaven. Jesus made a sizable investment—what an understatement!—for you, and you are now a citizen of heaven while traveling through earth. How wonderful to ponder that heavenly neighborhood where all is as it should be, and where you belong!

If we think back to Mr. Rogers and his famous question, we might wonder: Who will be our neighbors in heaven? The Bible answers that question for us in one remarkable passage—Hebrews 12:18–24:

For you have not come to the mountain that may be touched and that burned with fire, and to blackness and darkness and tempest, and the sound of a trumpet and the voice of words, so that those who heard it begged that the word should not be spoken to them anymore. (For they could not endure what was commanded: "And if so much as a beast touches the mountain, it shall be stoned or shot with an arrow." And so terrifying was the sight that Moses said, "I am exceedingly afraid and trembling.")

But you have come to Mount Zion and to the city of the living God, the heavenly Jerusalem, to an innumerable company of angels, to the general assembly and church of the firstborn who are registered in heaven, to God the Judge of all, to the spirits of just men made perfect, to Jesus the Mediator of the new covenant, and to the blood of sprinkling that speaks better things than that of Abel.

Earlier the writer of Hebrews had exhorted us to "run with endurance" the earthly race God has assigned us (12:1–2). We do this by keeping our eyes on Jesus (verse 2) so that we'll not become weary and give up (verse 3). The hardships we face are God's way of helping us grow in spiritual discipline (verses 5–11). We should encourage others in their race (verse 13), live at peace with our neighbors, and practice personal holiness (verse 14). We must exhort each other to avoid immorality and godlessness (verses 14–17).

The reason for all those exhortations is because we aren't living in fear and kept at a distance from God like the children of Israel at Mount Sinai. No, because of Christ we have already become citizens of heaven, Mount Zion, the city of the living God, and the heavenly Jerusalem. We are documented residents of our eternal home.

Then the author of Hebrews listed those who will be living with us in the same neighborhood. He said, "You have come to Mount Zion and to the city of the living God." He again used the present tense because we are all citizens of that place, with our passports issued the moment we came to Christ by grace through faith. Commentator David Allen wrote, "The author is using these references in a spiritual sense to refer to a heavenly state and to the spiritual place of God's presence and his people's home."[3]

Let's take a deeper look at that wonderful paragraph and learn more about our current and future neighbors in heaven.

ANGELS

The first set of neighbors is described as "an innumerable company of angels." The New International Version says, "But you have come to Mount Zion, to the city of the living God, the heavenly Jerusalem. You have come to thousands upon thousands of angels in joyful assembly" (verse 22). These are happy and holy angels in a festive mood, celebrating and worshiping.

We learn three distinct things here. First, we will see the angelic host and be among them. That's implied by the words "you have come." Yes, the angels are around us now in the unseen realm, but in eternity we'll be among them as friends, neighbors, and fellow servants.

Second, there are thousands upon thousands of angels. In various English translations this assembly is called "the gathering of countless happy angels," or "innumerable angels in festal gathering," or "millions of angels gathered for the festival." In Psalm 68:17, David said, "The chariots of God are twenty thousand, even thousands of thousands." In one of Daniel's visions in Babylon, he saw God (whom he called "the Ancient of Days") on a flaming throne surrounded by angelic beings: "A thousand thousands ministered to Him; ten thousand times ten thousand stood before Him" (Daniel 7:10). The same language is echoed in John's vision of God's throne in Revelation 5:11: "Then I looked, and I heard the voice of many angels around the throne, the living creatures, and the elders; and the number of them was ten thousand times ten thousand, and thousands of thousands."

Third, this vast multitude has a joyful attitude; they are in a jovial frame of mind. The phrase *joyful assembly* was used for the feasts of Israel in the Old Testament. It implies happiness and celebration.

In his book *All the Angels in the Bible*, Herbert Lockyer listed seven known categories of heavenly beings: Angels, Seraphim, Cherubim, Sons of God, Morning Stars, Watchers—and then Thrones, Powers, Rulers, and Authorities, which he grouped together.

Lockyer's son, Herbert Lockyer Jr., compiled this book after Lockyer's death, based on his father's notes and research. In the preface, he told a fascinating story. During World War I, British soldiers had to retreat from the Battle of Mons in France. The date was August 25, 1914. Later, many of the men and their officers testified to the appearance of heavenly guardians who aided the British army. They declared that without the help of angels, the British would have been annihilated by the pursuing German army. So many British soldiers spoke of this secret army that many of the men became Christians.[4]

As I read that story, it came to my mind that some of these angels, or all of them, were saving the lives of the men who would one day be their next-door neighbors!

BELIEVERS

The next group of heavenly citizens is the "church of the firstborn who are registered in heaven" (Hebrews 12:23). These are all the Christians who have followed Jesus Christ during the past two thousand years. You and I are in this category! When the Holy Spirit descended on the Day of Pentecost, He began working alongside the church to bring about a continuous harvest of souls for the kingdom. The gospel has penetrated every generation, and the flame of evangelism has never gone out. Every era of history can record remarkable stories of God's work through His expanding church.

Jerry Horn of Texas told a friend of mine about his experience during the Vietnam War. He was a career Air Force officer and spent several years in Southeast Asia. Because there were so many airmen during the war, he lived off-base in Saigon. The region was rife with wartime tension because the enemy was prone to set off remote-controlled explosives in places frequented by Americans. He said, "There might be one hidden near the old woman cooking rice on the street. A soldier would walk by, and the thing would explode, killing everyone in sight. One never knew when an attack would come. When we were in the city, we always stayed near walls, with our backs to the wall, so no one could sneak up behind us."

"But there was one place where the tension and fear were absent," Jerry said.

He attended a church in Saigon, and it had a mingling of Vietnamese and American servicemen and women. "Somehow," he said, "when we walked in that church all nervousness and strain left us. We felt safe there, and it was a haven from fear. As we sang and worshipped and fellowshipped and studied the Bible, we knew that somehow in that place we were safe, and we felt it."

The number of similar stories throughout Christian history rivals the number of angels in heaven. God is moving on earth, working through His church, and constantly increasing the citizenship census of New Jerusalem.

GOD

Hebrews 12:22–23 continues with, "You have come to thousands upon thousands of angels in joyful assembly, to the church of the firstborn, whose names are written in heaven. You have come to God, the Judge of all" (NIV).

Moses told the Israelites in Deuteronomy 4:39, "Therefore know this day, and consider it in your heart, that the LORD Himself is God in heaven above and on the earth beneath; there is no other." Joshua told them, "The LORD your God, He is God in heaven above and on earth beneath" (Joshua 2:11). King Jehoshaphat prayed, "O LORD God of our fathers, are You not God in heaven, and do You not rule over all the kingdoms of the nations, and in Your hand is there not power and might, so that no one is able to withstand you?" (2 Chronicles 20:6).

Jeremiah called on us to lift our hearts and hands "to God in heaven" (Lamentations 3:41). Daniel told King Nebuchadnezzar, "But there is a God in heaven who reveals secrets" (Daniel 2:28). And Jesus taught us to pray, "Our Father in heaven" (Matthew 6:9).

God the Father dwells in heaven; it is His home. When we go there, He will welcome us into His own home. We will dwell in His house (Psalm 23:6; John 14:2). I'm not certain we will physically see God the Father, even with the eyes of our new glorified bodies. He dwells "in unapproachable light, whom no man has seen or can see" (1 Timothy 6:16). John 1:18 says, "No one has seen God at any time. The only begotten Son, who is in the bosom of the Father, He has declared Him."

This is a bit of speculation, but it seems to me God the Father is enveloped in impenetrable light; God the Holy Spirit is invisible, being spirit; and it is Jesus—God the Son—who manifests the Godhead for us to see. But we'll have no doubt the Trinity—Father, Son, and Holy Spirit—is filling heaven with the divine presence.

FAITHFUL SAINTS

The fourth group of heavenly citizens is the "spirits of just men made perfect" (Hebrews 12:23). I believe this refers to the Old Testament saints—those whom Jesus took with Him when He ascended to heaven.

When godly men and women died before the resurrection of Christ, they went to an intermediate place called Paradise. When

Jesus ascended to heaven, He took Paradise up to the third heaven. He led His people there, all who had died in faith before the ascension. That includes all of the Old Testament saints—Abraham, Isaac, Jacob, Moses, Solomon, Elisha, Micah, and so on.

Now when believers die, their bodies go in the grave to sleep, but their souls don't remain here on earth. When we pass away in Christ, our souls go to be with Him in the third heaven. Instantly, at the moment of death, the angels transport us to be with Abraham and with Lazarus and with all the departed saints and with Christ in Paradise.

We're going to take a deeper look at Paradise in a later chapter, but for now it's important to know that all those heroes from the Old Testament will be our neighbors in heaven. They will live with us in New Jerusalem—the spirits of just men and women made perfect. I confess I'm especially eager to meet my namesakes, David and Jeremiah.

JESUS

The passage in Hebrews climaxes with the name of Jesus! "To Jesus the Mediator of the new covenant, and to the blood of sprinkling that speaks better things than that of Abel" (12:24). Every human being in heaven arrived there through the blood of the great Mediator, who, through His death, made peace for us with God. Because of Him, we will have an incredible neighborhood—the new heavens, the new earth, and the city of New Jerusalem.

News outlets across the nation picked up the story of a one-in-a-million happenstance for Hillary Davis. She lived with her husband, Lance, in a simple house that sat so close to another house that the two homes shared a common driveway. One day, a new woman moved into the house beside Hillary. Because Hillary and Lance hadn't gotten along very well with their former neighbors, they kept their distance. But their young daughter, Stella, made friends with the new woman, whose name was Dawn.

"I was annoyed by it to be honest," said Hillary. "I'm like, 'Stella, just stop. What if they don't even like little kids?'" But Stella enjoyed her new friend. As Hillary and Dawn slowly became acquainted, they came to an incredible discovery. They were actually long-lost sisters. Hillary had been adopted in infancy, and she had always longed to know something about her birth family.

Since then, the two sisters have been busy making up for lost time—sharing birthdays, holidays, meals, and lots of laughs.[5] What a story! A woman who wanted to find her lost family discovered her sister was living right next door.

When you get to heaven, you're going to find a lot of long-lost brothers and sisters from all the ages living right next door. They will be fellow citizens, along with the angels and with the Lord God Himself—Father, Son, and Holy Spirit. I'm looking forward to being there, and I hope you would, well . . . won't you please . . . will you please be my neighbor?!

CHAPTER 11

THE CURRENCY
OF HEAVEN

Antonio Lopes Siqueira was a simple farmer in Brazil, raising cattle in an area that put him squarely in the center of South America. One day he spent eighty-three cents to buy a ticket in Brazil's largest lottery, where the odds of winning the jackpot were one in fifty million. He had been doing this for years without success.

But this time he won, and the prize was $32 million! You can imagine Antonio's euphoria. What to do with all that money?

Antonio immediately scheduled an appointment with his dentist to treat himself to some much-needed oral surgery. Brazil's newest multimillionaire showed up on time at the dentist's office and was in the waiting room when pain struck his chest. He collapsed to the floor. Attempts to resuscitate him failed, and when emergency responders arrived, they pronounced him dead at age seventy-three, apparently from a heart attack.

The lottery shop manager said, "He always joked that he was going to win the prize. It's very sad, everyone dreams of earning that kind of money. It's a shame he can't enjoy it."[1]

That's a lesson for all of us. We don't have much time to enjoy the things of this earth. The Bible repeatedly reminds us that our lives here are brief. The patriarch Job said, "My days are swifter than a weaver's shuttle . . . my life is a breath!" (Job 7:6–7).

Psalm 144:4 agrees: "Man is like a breath; his days are like a passing shadow."

King David said, "LORD, remind me how brief my time on earth will be. Remind me that my days are numbered—how fleeting my life is. You have made my life no longer than the width of my hand. My entire lifetime is just a moment to you; at best, each of us is but a breath" (Psalm 39:4–5 NLT).

That's why the Bible tells us to focus our attention on eternal things that will endure forever. Jesus said, "Do not lay up for yourselves treasures on earth, where moth and rust destroy and where thieves break in and steal; but lay up for yourselves treasures in heaven" (Matthew 6:19–20).

We know what kinds of treasures we can find on earth. But what are the treasures of heaven? What does it mean on a practical level to "lay up" or invest our lives in ways that produce those treasures? After all, if we're going to focus on things that are eternal, we need to know what they are.

One of my professors in seminary, Howard Hendricks, used to put it this way: "Only two things in this world are eternal—the Word of God and people. It only makes sense to build your life around those things that will last forever." The only things you can take to heaven are the Word of God and the lives of those you help win to Christ. In this chapter, I'd like to explore both—and to show how both impact our lives today.

THE WORD OF GOD

There's no doubt God's Word is eternal. Psalm 119:89 says, "Forever, O LORD, Your word is settled in heaven." The apostle Peter wrote,

"All people are like grass, and all their glory is like the flowers of the field; the grass withers and the flowers fall, but the word of the Lord endures forever" (1 Peter 1:24–25 NIV).

In what way is the Bible eternal? After all, those blessed books we read and study every day aren't going up with us in the rapture, are they? No. The biblical descriptions of the rapture in 1 Thessalonians 4 and 1 Corinthians 15 don't picture us flying upward with Bibles in our hands. The verses we've memorized—now, those we will have! We'll take them to heaven with us inside our minds and souls.

But don't you think we'll have copies of Scripture waiting for us? I believe every word of God is true. It's eternally true, and we'll be studying His truth forever. After all, we know there are other books in heaven. Moses once asked God to forgive the Israelites for their sins, adding, "But if not, I pray, blot me out of Your book which You have written" (Exodus 32:32).

Malachi 3:16 says, "Then those who feared the LORD spoke to one another, and the LORD listened and heard them; so a book of remembrance was written before Him for those who fear the LORD and who meditate on His name."

Think of that! The Lord is so delighted when we speak about Him that He notates our words in a special book in heaven. The apostle Paul talked about his fellow workers whose names were written in the Book of Life (Philippians 4:3).

One of the angels in heaven had a special book he wanted the apostle John to eat, which meant he wanted him to read and digest its contents (Revelation 10:1–11). Several times in Revelation, we read about the Book of Life, which was written before the foundation of the world (13:8; 17:8; 22:19). And Revelation 20:12 tells us that on the Day of Judgment, the books will be opened, revealing the attitudes and actions of all humanity.

I don't think those will be the only books in heaven. We will not be omniscient or all-knowing there. We will not possess total knowledge as God does. So we'll be capable of learning. We'll certainly be literate and able to read and eager to learn. I expect there will be many books in heaven; and if you've ever wanted to be an author, perhaps you'll add to the books in the libraries of New Jerusalem.

If there is learning, if there is creativity, if there are books in heaven, I cannot imagine we'd be missing the most famous, and only, book almighty God gave to us on earth—the Bible.

Korean pastor Daniel Kim wrote, "We will be students for an eternity. Get used to it! But there are no student loans in this school. We could not ask for a more perfect and wonderful textbook, one that stands forever, the Bible!"[2]

I can't wait to open the Bible to one of Paul's difficult sentences and ask him to personally explain what he meant—although I might have to wait in line behind Augustine, Luther, Tyndale, Calvin, Spurgeon, and you! Imagine attending a lecture and having Jonah read his book and personally describe his experiences. Yes, I'm speculating a bit. But my impressions are based on some solid assumptions—we will be literate but not all-knowing; the original authors of the Bible will be among us; God's truth is eternal; there are books in heaven; and we'll be able to understand everything God has said to us in Scripture better and more fully than ever we did on earth.

That's why I encourage you to fall in love with God's Word now. Let it enlighten your mind and empower your personality. Read it, memorize it, meditate on it, obey it, and share it with others.

OTHER PEOPLE

That leads to the other thing we can take with us to heaven: those whom we help win to the Lord. This is important and urgent. We need to help others find salvation now—by the testimonies we share, the tasks we pursue, and the treasures and offerings we invest in the kingdom.

THE TESTIMONIES WE SHARE

Mary Hart was a twentieth-century medical missionary who devoted her life to winning people to Christ in China. She married fellow worker Walford Hart, who died nineteen days later from dysentery. Sometime afterward Mary herself came down with dysentery, and she grew weaker and weaker. When she realized she was dying, she had all the mission employees and workers come to her room. "I am going to die," she said. "I am not afraid; I want to see you in heaven."

She called each worker by name and thanked them. Then, with nearly her last words, she told them, "Thank you for all you have done for me. I am going to heaven; my husband is there. I want you to trust my Savior, and I want to meet you all in heaven."[3]

Who says things like that anymore? Well, *we* should! We must let our friends and loved ones know we're going to heaven and we want to see them there too. I cannot think of anything that will comfort your family more, should you pass away, than to remember your testimony of knowing Jesus and anticipating heaven. Our testimonies can make a difference in the lives of others, if we'll simply voice them.

THE TASKS WE PURSUE

The Lord also gives us all tasks and personal ministries to pursue. I'm a steadfast follower of Christ today as a result of the combined influence of many people. That starts with my parents, but it also includes Sunday school teachers, vacation Bible school workers, youth group leaders, and coaches—all of whom served the Lord faithfully without always seeing immediate results.

The Bible says, "Be steadfast, immovable, always abounding in the work of the Lord, knowing that your labor is not in vain in the Lord" (1 Corinthians 15:58). Paul wasn't writing those words to pastors and bishops, but to the ordinary members in the sometimes-troubled church in Corinth.

He told them, "I planted, Apollos watered, but God gave the

increase" (1 Corinthians 3:6). Whatever God calls you to do, do it faithfully, prayerfully, and cheerfully! Those three attitudes cannot fail to produce results for the kingdom.

Russell E. Gehrlein (Master Sergeant, U.S. Army Retired) grew up in a churchgoing family, but he never heard the gospel preached clearly enough for him to grasp. In the mid-1970s, his dad and sister took him to see a couple of gospel-related plays, which piqued his interest. During his senior year in high school, a friend invited him to a Youth for Christ club near his school.

At the Christmas meeting, the speaker shared the gospel so clearly that Russell bowed his head and accepted Christ as his Lord and Savior. He has served the Lord faithfully ever since, through his years of military service and beyond. His eternal destiny was assured because of his dad, sister, best friend, and a speaker whose name is forgotten. But it's not forgotten to God! We are all commissioned to serve the Lord as He assigns our work for the expansion of the kingdom.[4]

THE TREASURES WE INVEST

We also have the joy of expanding the kingdom through investing our treasure—our tithes and gifts and offerings—to the Lord. I believe this was what Jesus meant when He talked about laying up treasures for ourselves in heaven (Matthew 6:19–20). He wasn't telling us to neglect our futures or our families. We need to be wise and faithful providers. But utmost in our thoughts should be the privilege of using our funds to further the population of heaven.

You've probably never heard of Humphrey Monmouth, but he has touched your life. He was a successful businessman in sixteenth-century England. When the Protestant Reformation broke out, Monmouth embraced the gospel. He met preacher William Tyndale and let him stay in his home. Tyndale longed to translate the Bible into English, but he was reckoned an outlaw by the British government. Monmouth contributed the funds needed for Tyndale's translation project, funds to help Tyndale escape to continental Europe, and funds for copies of the new translations to be smuggled back into England. He used his shipping connections to hide the Bibles among bales of hay and cotton.

Tyndale's Bible became the basis for the King James Bible and many of our newer translations, bringing the gospel to the English-speaking world. We can't begin to calculate the number of souls in heaven because of Monmouth's generosity. Even today there is a group known as the Monmouth Society encouraging people to use their funds to pave the way for multitudes to hear the gospel and become citizens of heaven.[5]

Whether we can give a billionaire's bequest or a widow's mite, the Lord Jesus is able to convert our earthly finances to salvation experiences as we faithfully support our local churches and the ministries He lays on our hearts. Chuck Bentley wrote, "True biblical stewardship is not ordering your finances in such a way that you can freely spend money however you want; rather, it is ordering your finances in such a way that God can freely spend you however He wants."[6]

I don't think we can study heaven without gaining a corresponding burden to do all that's possible to ensure that our loved ones, friends, neighbors, and earth's multitudes hear the good news of the Lord Jesus Christ.

Your testimony, tasks, and treasures don't have to be perfect. Just available. In his book *Transforming Bible Study*, Bob Grahmann said that when he was in college, he wanted to start a Bible study in his dorm. He had never done anything like that before.

So after much prayer and with much fear, I decided that. . . . I would gather some of my friends and lead the study right then, as a 19-year-old student. . . .

That first evening was the worst Bible study ever. I asked the guys on my floor if they would come, but I did it in such an ineffective way that only one guy showed up, and I think he came out of pity. I was nervous. I was sick. I was shaking. But I did lead the Bible study, just for that one fellow. At the end of four weeks, I asked him what he thought, expecting to hear an honest assessment that this was indeed the worst Bible study in the history of Christendom. But instead he said, to my amazement, "I want to accept Jesus." I was shocked! I was amazed! I saw again the power of God's word to bring new life.[7]

God's Word and human souls are eternal. We can't take much with us to heaven, but may God fill our hearts with His Word—and with that message let's determine to take as many people as possible to heaven with us!

CHAPTER 12

THE ANGELS OF HEAVEN

Pastor John Boston was driving on Airport Road in Columbus, Ohio, when he swerved to avoid a car that crossed the center line and veered toward him. Boston crashed into a utility pole, causing a live transformer to fall onto his vehicle. Thousands of volts of electricity began frying the car. The windshield started melting and the passenger window folded inward. The driver's side door was jammed, and no one could touch the car without getting electrocuted.

Suddenly a man appeared out of nowhere, easily opened the door, helped Pastor Boston out, and led him away just as the car exploded. "He said his name is Johnny," Boston recalled. The man told Boston, "The police are almost here, and I can't be here when they get here, but you're going to be okay." Then the man was gone. When rescue workers showed up, electricity was still surging through the vehicle, and firefighters couldn't explain how Boston had gotten out. "It gives me goosebumps," said one emergency responder.

As for Pastor Boston, he had only one explanation—he believes he was rescued by an angel.[1]

I've heard stories like that all my life. In fact, a very similar incident recently happened to my doctor. Without being dogmatic about any one experience, I do believe angels exist, they are present around us, and they are often God's agents in helping us. As Hebrews 1:14 explains, angels are "ministering spirits sent forth to minister for those who will inherit salvation."

I've preached and written about angels throughout my ministry. They populate the Bible, and we can study them in about three hundred passages from Genesis to Revelation. In this chapter I want to address a specific issue: How will we relate to angels in eternity? Will we see them? Visit with them? Labor alongside them? Worship beside them? Live under their authority? Or could we even rule over them?

In short, how will we interact with angels in heaven?

Before going further, let me dispense with one idea. We will not *be* angels. Sometimes when a child dies, we hear someone say, "Well, he's an angel with God now." Occasionally someone says something about our passing away and growing wings. No. Angels are angels, and humans are humans. There is nothing in the Bible that indicates we'll take on an angelic nature.

What the Bible says is even better!

WALKING ALONGSIDE ANGELS

First, we'll live and walk among angels, which means we will be able to see them, fellowship with them, and enjoy their company. Right now, we're living in the midst of two realms—the visible and the invisible, the physical and the spiritual. Colossians 1:16 says, "For by Him all things were created that are in heaven and that are on earth, visible and invisible." The apostle Paul advised us to "fix our eyes not on what is seen, but on what is unseen, since what is seen is temporary, but what is unseen is eternal" (2 Corinthians 4:18 NIV). We cannot literally see into the spiritual realm, unless the Lord occasionally allows us to entertain an angel unaware (Hebrews 13:2).

All this will change when eternity dawns. Paul wrote, "He made known to us the mystery of his will according to his good pleasure, which he purposed in Christ, to be put into effect when the times reach their fulfillment—to bring unity to all things in heaven and on earth under Christ" (Ephesians 1:9–10 NIV). The New Living Translation renders verse 10 like this: "And this is the plan: at the right time he will bring everything together under the authority of Christ—everything in heaven and on earth."

Revelation 21 tells us about the moment when God will create the new heavens and the new earth, and when the Holy City will descend. A loud voice will cry: "Behold, the tabernacle of God is with men, and He will dwell with them" (verse 3).

Randy Alcorn wrote, "The marriage of the God of Heaven with the people of Earth will also bring the marriage of Heaven and Earth. There will not be two universes—one the primary home of God and angels, the other the primary home of humanity. Nothing will separate us from God, and nothing will separate Earth and Heaven. Once God and mankind dwell together, there will be no difference between Heaven and Earth. Earth will become Heaven—and it will truly be Heaven on Earth."[2]

With our glorified bodies, we will see, hear, smell, feel, and taste the joys of heaven.

We'll see the Lord Jesus, and I believe we'll see all the various ranks and echelons of angels, including seraphim, cherubim, archangels, and those occupying thrones, dominions, and powers.

Look again at Hebrews 12:22: "But you have come to Mount Zion, to the city of the living God, the heavenly Jerusalem. You have come to thousands upon thousands of angels in joyful assembly" (NIV). That verse clearly indicates the tangibility of our association with angels in heaven.

According to Revelation 21:12, an angel will be stationed at each of the twelve gates going into New Jerusalem. They will not be there for defensive purposes, since all evil and danger will be forever banished. They must be there to greet us as we come and go from the city. Surely we'll be able to see them, don't you think?

I don't want to speculate beyond the teaching of Scripture, but angels and humans carried out conversations in the Bible. I see no reason why we won't do the same in heaven. Will they live in homes as I believe we will? Could they be our next-door neighbors? Can you imagine walking down a golden street while chatting with an angel? Is it possible angels will come up to us and say, "Do you remember that time you almost drowned when you were eleven years old? Guess who saved you?!" Yes, it's possible. Angels have names, such as Michael and Gabriel. Don't you think we'll learn their names and be at home with them?

That's my sense of it. It's not hard for me to believe we'll walk alongside angels in glory.

WORSHIPING ALONGSIDE ANGELS

If we walk alongside angels, we will most certainly worship alongside them. Isaiah saw the angels at worship and described it in chapter 6 of his book. Flying around God's glorious throne was a group of angels called seraphim, and one cried to the other, "Holy, holy, holy is the LORD of hosts; the whole earth is full of His glory!" Isaiah said the entire temple trembled, the doorposts shook, and the house was filled with smoke (verses 1–4).

The apostle John had a similar vision in Revelation 4 when he saw God's throne surrounded by cherubim, crying, "Holy, holy, holy, Lord God Almighty, who was and is and is to come!" (verse 8). Alongside the angels were a group of twenty-four elders, which, as I've often explained, likely represent the saints of all the ages, the collected body of believers from both the Old and New Testament eras.

Revelation 4:10–11 describes how we'll worship side by side with the angels, falling down before Him who sits on the throne, casting our crowns before Him, and singing, "You are worthy, O Lord, to receive glory and honor and power; for You created all things, and by Your will they exist and were created."

Let me suggest something. Don't you think we are worshiping side by side with angels every time we stand in church and sing words like, "Holy, holy, holy, Lord God Almighty, early in the morning our song shall rise to Thee"?

Or newer songs like the one that says, "You are lifted high, holy—holy forever"?

The apostle Paul makes a strange comment in Ephesians 3:10, that the "principalities and powers in the heavenly places" learned about God's plan to establish His church by listening to the apostles explain it. Peter said something similar in 1 Peter 1:12. And 1 Corinthians 11:10 seems to indicate that we should worship properly and reverently "because of the angels." In 1 Corinthians 4:9, Paul implied the apostles and their ministries were well known to angels. Psalm 34:7 tells us the angels of God encamp around us.

Many times as the choir and orchestra at our church have filled the room with glorious music in praise to God, I've wondered if I could hear the whisper of angel wings, so to speak. The difference is that right now, they worship among us as invisible creatures. In heaven, we'll see our co-worshippers visually. But should it not make us sing more sincerely and listen to the Word more carefully if we remember angels are fluttering among the pews?

Charles Spurgeon said, "You can be like the angels now by being always in a state of praise. Let no murmur escape your lips; let no complaining dwell on your heart. Praise God, though the sun shines not; praise him though the mists and fog are thickening; praise him though the winds should howl and the rain descend. You are not to be ruled by circumstances. Angels praise him in the night as well as in the day: do you the same."[3]

WORKING ALONGSIDE ANGELS

Finally, we'll not only be walking and worshiping beside angels, we will be working alongside them too. I have sound biblical authority for telling you this. On two occasions in the book of Revelation, the apostle John was so overcome by the presence of an angel that he bowed down to worship him. On both occasions, the angel gave the same response: "Don't do that! I am a fellow servant with you" (19:10; 22:9 NIV). In the first passage, the angel continued to say, "I am a fellow servant with you and with your brothers and sisters who hold to the testimony of Jesus."

We humans are fellow servants with God's angels, which means we'll be working alongside our angelic friends for eternity. Elsewhere in this book, I have a chapter about the meaningful work and service that will occupy us in heaven. For now, just consider how wonderful it will be to fulfill our responsibilities with angelic helpers beside us.

I want to mention one other passage in the Bible that causes me to raise an eyebrow. In 1 Corinthians 6:1–3, the apostle Paul discouraged believers from suing one another or taking one another to court. He said we should be able to work out these issues for ourselves. And he added, "Do you not know that we shall judge angels? How much more, things that pertain to this life?"

What does that mean? Some scholars believe it refers to our taking part in what Christ will do when He judges and condemns the fallen angels at the end of the age. Other commentators point out that the Greek word translated "judge" could mean to "rule" or "govern." They believe it indicates that in the future we may have authority even over angels.

Elsewhere the Bible says, "If we endure, we shall also reign with Him" (2 Timothy 2:12).

In his commentary on 1 Corinthians, David E. Garland suggested that Paul wanted "to remind the Corinthians of their glorious end-time destiny when they will be given dominion even over the angels. In that day, the current state of affairs will be radically reversed."[4]

Sometimes the Lord gives us glimpses of truths that will only be fully revealed later. But of this I have no doubt: At the dawning of eternity, the spiritual and physical realms of reality will merge into one glorious reality under Jesus Christ. And we will meet the angels! We'll walk beside them, worship beside them, and work beside them. I have a feeling it will be like meeting old friends.

As I worked on this chapter, I read about a group of five girls who grew up in the same community in California in the 1940s. They were as close as sisters, and their favorite song back then was "(How Much Is That) Doggie in the Window." After the eighth grade, they all went different ways. That was in 1951. But they didn't forget each other and they recently reunited in Las Vegas. It was the first time they've seen each other in seventy-four years. During that span of time, each one had lost a husband and had to navigate grief on her own. Now they poured out their hearts to one another.

They also laughed a lot. They remembered the time they had all gotten into trouble at school for wearing jeans, which was a no-no back then. And the time they had snuck into a drive-in theater. They reminisced about the hours they spent in their local milkshake shop, feeding nickels into the jukebox.

The women spent five days together and could hardly stop talking and catching up with each other. One of the women said they didn't seem like friends but like long-lost family.[5]

Maybe that's a tiny example of how we'll feel in eternity. Heaven is going to be a glorious reunion with a long-lost family—believers from all the ages and angels from all the ranks, together with our Lord Jesus Christ. I don't want to miss it, do you?

CHAPTER 13

HEAVENLY WORSHIP

After a lifetime of waiting, Derek Lew stood in front of a door he never really thought he would open. It wasn't fancy by any particular measure—just a bluish-gray, nondescript door with a metal knocker in the center, a doorbell off to one side, and the number "33" stenciled into the frosted glass above the frame.

But that "33" was everything.

You see, he was standing in front of the entry to the famous Club 33 at the Walt Disney World theme park in Orlando, Florida.

If you're not familiar with that name, don't feel bad—that's actually the point. Club 33 is a secret dining area found inside most Disney theme parks that is as exclusive as it is expensive. Membership in Club 33 costs tens of thousands of dollars and must be renewed each year. The reward is access to a secret haven within a sea of tired tourists.

When Derek stepped through that door, he was greeted by an attendant who confirmed his reservation and welcomed him with cold towels and cucumber water. He was ushered to a well-appointed dining room where even the plates are emblazoned with the "Club 33" logo. There Derek ordered from a menu packed with delicacies such as "Grilled BBQ Quail with Figs and Corn Velvet," "Iron Seared Fish," "Royal Red Shrimp in a Sungold Tomato Broth," and "Organic Chocolate Marquise, Passion Fruit Sorbet, and Pecan Brittle." After the delicious food, he purchased souvenirs available only to Club 33 members and their guests.

According to Derek: "[My] experience at Club 33 is something I will never forget. From the kindness we were shown to the gorgeous dining room to the incredible food, every minute was nothing short of perfect."[1]

In case you're wondering, I'm not turning this chapter into a Disney commercial. Instead, I'm excited to look together at an altogether different type of secret door—one that was revealed to the apostle John near the end of his life and recorded in Revelation 4. There was nothing nondescript about this door. It was both supernatural and surprising, and it unveiled a kingdom literally defined as "nothing short of perfect."

Here's what John wrote: "After these things I looked, and behold, a door standing open in heaven. And the first voice which I heard was like a trumpet speaking with me, saying, 'Come up here, and I will show you things which must take place after this'" (Revelation 4:1).

Are you ready to take a peek through that door and see what worship will be like in heaven?

THE CONTEXT OF WORSHIP IN HEAVEN

Revelation 4 and 5 provide a glimpse into heaven at the great worship service that will occur around the throne of God during the final events in world history—events that will lead to the return of Christ. Many commentators believe these are the two greatest chapters on the subject of worship in the Bible, for they take us up to heaven and let us see celestial worship as it unfolds before God's throne.

There has never been a time in my life when I've drifted away from the practice of public worship, and I suppose I know the rituals and routines as well as anyone. In most of our worship services today, we have three parts: We praise God, we pray to God, and we preach His Word. Other things take place, too, but these are the core elements.

Interestingly, those elements were actually developed in the Jewish synagogue. When the Jews were scattered across the ancient world and unable to worship in Jerusalem, they built synagogues wherever they were and met each Sabbath for praise, prayer, and the proclamation of Scripture. These were the things Jesus did as He visited the synagogues of Galilee during His earthly ministry.

Yet as I read Revelation 4 and 5, I'm struck with the fact that the worship we see in heaven is different. It rises to a higher level. As far as I can tell from these two chapters, only one of those three elements will survive in heaven.

I do not think we will have prayer in heaven, at least not as we practice it on earth. There will be no need to pray as we do now. We will live in the very presence of almighty God, and we will commune with and have an ongoing relationship with Him much more intimately than we do now. Even so, our prayer requests will all have been answered. There will be no need to pray in terms of supplication, no need to pray for others, no need to confess our sins, and no need to ask for healing. Our conversations with the Lord will be immediate and in person, so we will not need to go into our closets, shut the door, and pray to our Father in secret, as Jesus taught us to do on earth in Matthew 6:6.

Nor will there be a need for preaching. The Bible says, "For now we see in a mirror, dimly, but then face to face. Now I know in part, but then I shall know just as I also am known" (1 Corinthians 13:12). We will still enjoy poring over God's Word, for Psalm 119:89 says, "Forever, O LORD, your word is settled in heaven." But we will not have to exhort anyone to trust it or to obey it, for we'll be living in a state of perfect spirituality, and we will certainly not have to make evangelistic appeals, for everyone will be saved and forever safe.

That leaves only one great element dominating heavenly worship: praise! Praising our God is the only one of the three aspects of our common worship practices that will survive into eternity. Scripture reveals that truth many times, including these psalms:

- "In God we boast all day long, and praise Your name forever" (Psalm 44:8).
- "So I will sing praise to Your name forever" (Psalm 61:8).
- "My mouth shall speak the praise of the LORD, and all flesh shall bless His holy name forever and ever" (Psalm 145:21).

THE CENTER OF WORSHIP IN HEAVEN

Let's see what happened when John walked through the door in his heavenly vision: "Immediately I was in the Spirit; and behold, a throne set in heaven, and One sat on the throne. And He who sat there was like a jasper and a sardius stone in appearance; and there was a rainbow around the throne, in appearance like an emerald" (Revelation 4:2–3).

God's throne is the center of heaven, and it serves as the central focus of heavenly worship. The term *throne* appears forty-two times throughout the book of Revelation, with several of those instances coming in chapters 4 and 5. Each reference is a reminder of God's sovereignty, authority, reign, and absolute power.

These visions of God's throne remind us that while events on earth seem chaotic and often meaningless, the King of the universe is seated upon His throne, sovereign and in control. Hallelujah!

I understand that life sometimes *feels* out of control. Sometimes it *seems* like the darkness is winning and the light is nowhere to be found. Maybe that's how you're feeling now.

If so, take courage from John's example—because he was feeling pretty low himself before he received this heavenly vision. Remember,

John was the last living apostle. His closest friends had been martyred for their faith, and it had been many decades since he'd physically walked with Jesus. Now John found himself exiled to the island of Patmos and forced to face an uncertain future alone.

It was at that moment he looked and saw a door, heard a voice like a trumpet, and stepped through to see this glorious vision of a celebration service in heaven.

Here's a different translation of that scene: "And instantly I was in the Spirit, and I saw a throne in heaven and someone sitting on it. The one sitting on the throne was as brilliant as gemstones—like jasper and carnelian. And the glow of an emerald circled his throne like a rainbow" (Revelation 4:2–3 NLT).

As John gazed at the majesty and beauty of the throne of his Creator, all he could comprehend was its diamond-like brilliance, fiery beauty, and stormy grandeur. If the door to heaven were to open for you today and you could see the throne in heaven, it would look the same now as then. It would thrill you with a joy that would never die. God is still seated on His throne, and His throne is a seat of glory and of grace. It's the heart and hub of all our worship both now and forevermore.

THE CHORUS OF WORSHIP IN HEAVEN

That brings us to the chorus of praise we will hear around the throne. The apostle John actually eavesdropped on a worship celebration in heaven. Here is what he saw and heard:

Around the throne were twenty-four thrones, and on the thrones I saw twenty-four elders sitting, clothed in white robes; and they had crowns of gold on their heads. . . . Whenever the living creatures give glory and honor and thanks to Him who sits on the throne, who lives forever and ever, the twenty-four elders fall down before

Him who sits on the throne and worship Him who lives forever and ever, and cast their crowns before the throne, saying: "You are worthy, O Lord, to receive glory and honor and power; for You created all things, and by Your will they exist and were created." (Revelation 4:4, 9–11)

I believe the twenty-four elders represent the church of the living God. They represent the redeemed of all the ages—including you and me! John saw us all there in heaven before the throne, singing God's praises while beholding the most jaw-dropping setting of grandeur in the entire universe.

The vision continues in Revelation 5:8–10, and here we see not only God the Father but God the Son, who is the object of great interest and praise:

Now when He had taken the scroll, the four living creatures and the twenty-four elders fell down before the Lamb, each having a harp, and golden bowls full of incense, which are the prayers of the saints. And they sang a new song, saying: "You are worthy to take the scroll, and to open its seals; for You were slain, and have redeemed us to God by Your blood out of every tribe and tongue and people and nation, and have made us kings and priests to our God; and we shall reign on the earth."

Oh, I wish I could hear that audibly right now—to hear the voices, to ascertain the melody, to grasp the power of the decibels as all of heaven sings the praises of the Lamb! One day we'll be there, but until then we can tune our hearts to heaven's frequency and use this as our model of praise and worship.

Outside of the words of the Bible, the most famous definition of *worship* I've read comes from the pen of William Temple, who served as Archbishop of Canterbury during the difficult days of World War II. He wrote, "To worship is to quicken the conscience by the holiness of God, to feed the mind with the truth of God, to purge the imagination by the beauty of God, to open the heart to the love of God, to devote the will to the purpose of God."[2]

This describes the worship in heaven, and it should be the goal of every worshiper on earth.

THE CRESCENDO OF WORSHIP IN HEAVEN

One of the interesting observations I've made while studying worship in the book of Revelation involves what I'm calling the crescendo of worship in heaven. Now, *crescendo* is a musical term that refers to a gradual, steady increase in volume and force. The music grows louder and stronger until it reaches a climactic finish.

In the worship songs of Revelation, there is an obvious crescendo, and we can see this in the doxologies we encounter. The word *doxology* comes from the Greek term *doxa*, meaning "honor" or "glory." It's a declaration of the glory of God, and the doxologies of Revelation expand like a telescope as you progress through the book. Let me show you.

- Revelation 1:6 has a twofold doxology: "To Him be *glory* and *dominion* forever and ever. Amen."
- Revelation 4:11 contains a threefold doxology: "You are worthy, O Lord, to receive *glory* and *honor* and *power*; for You created all things, and by Your will they exist and were created."
- Revelation 5:13 proclaims a fourfold doxology: "*Blessing* and *honor* and *glory* and *power* be to Him who sits on the throne, and to the Lamb, forever and ever!"
- Revelation 7:12 gives us a sevenfold doxology: "Amen! *Blessing* and *glory* and *wisdom*, *thanksgiving* and *honor* and *power* and *might*, be to our God forever and ever. Amen."

You can feel the movement of worship through the book of Revelation building until there is a massive crescendo of praise to the Lord.

I love the feeling we have in church when the musicians plan crescendos into the worship services. You've probably noticed it in your church. The musicians start small and change keys and get louder and bigger and mightier. Such a buildup in the tone of our worship is biblical. That's what the Bible says will happen in heaven, and we're just rehearsing down here—getting ready for what we'll experience above.

Speaking of rehearsing, have you heard about the largest gospel choir ever assembled? It happened in May 2016 when the Iglesia Ni Cristo gathered 21,262 singers together in a huge arena in the Philippines. Led by a conductor and accompanied by a massive pipe organ, the choir sang several hymns together as an act of worship.[3]

Can you imagine yourself there in that stadium? Even before the music started, you would be overwhelmed by the sight of rank upon rank of worshipers standing together in matching robes, backs straight and heads up. Then you would hear the swell of the pipe organ, and then the deeper, soul-nourishing swell of more than twenty-one thousand human voices all joined together and all lifted upward in praise.

I wish I had been there to hear it!

At the same time, the largest gospel choir on earth will pale in comparison to even the most casual worship services in heaven. When we reach our eternal home, tens of millions of believers will lift perfect voices in a perfect song, glorifying the perfection of our God.

No, worship in heaven will never be dull or half-hearted. Instead, it will be continuous, righteous, vigorous, thundering, and magnificent. It will set the atmosphere for the new heaven and the new earth, and it will make New Jerusalem pulsate with praise.

CHAPTER 14

THE HAPPINESS
OF HEAVEN

Some people pursue happiness. Scott Thompson planted it.

Scott runs Thompson Strawberry Farm just outside of Bristol in the Dairy State of Wisconsin. For years, the farm has been a popular place for local residents to come and pick their own seasonal produce. Typically that produce has included strawberries and raspberries in the summer, plus pumpkins in the fall. There are also a number of family-friendly activities designed to make sure every visitor has a good time.

But with the pandemic gripping the nation in the early months of 2020, Thompson made the decision to go in a new direction: sunflowers.

"We had kind of been planning to do it for the last couple years and never got around to it," Thompson told reporters. "We said if there was ever a year the world needed more sunflowers, this was it. We just needed some extra happiness this year."[1]

The idea started with a single small field, but the notion soon blossomed (pun intended) until an astounding two million sunflowers had been planted. Yes, two million sunflowers! Thompson added another field planted with zinnias. Then another with Mexican wildflowers. The result was a shining tapestry of natural wonder in rural Wisconsin.

As you might expect, customers visited the farm in droves. They brought blankets and picnic baskets, with many choosing to spend entire afternoons wandering through the blooms or resting quietly among the trails and the flowers and the birds and the butterflies.

"One of the things that's so cool about this is everyone is so happy," Thompson said. "We get all these comments on Facebook, or if I'm out in the field, everybody is like, 'Thanks for doing this.' 'This is what I needed.' People are so happy to be out there and have a place to go."[2]

I've seen some beautiful things in nature, but I've never walked through a field abounding with two million sunflowers. Doesn't that sound amazing? Doesn't that sound so peaceful? I don't think you could encounter something like that without experiencing an overwhelming sense of joy.

Now take that happiness and multiply it by a million. That's heaven! It's a place so filled with happiness that you won't be able to stop smiling.

By the way, what brings a smile to your face and laughter to your soul? Keep that image in mind as you read these words from Psalm 16, written by King David:

> Therefore my heart is glad, and my glory rejoices;
> My flesh also will rest in hope.
> For You will not leave my soul in Sheol,
> Nor will You allow Your Holy One to see corruption.
> You will show me the path of life;
> In Your presence is fullness of joy;
> At Your right hand are pleasures forevermore. (verses 9–11)

We're going to use this passage, and verse 11 in particular, as our guide to exploring and understanding the happiness of heaven.

HAPPINESS IS ENJOYING JESUS' FELLOWSHIP

King David had a special connection with God that sustained him through a life filled with glorious highs and heartrending lows. No matter what David was experiencing externally, he maintained a sense of optimistic happiness because of that deep and abiding connection with his Creator.

"My heart is glad," David wrote, "and my glory rejoices." Why? Because he anticipated his eternal future in God's presence. He understood God would not allow his soul to languish in Sheol, or what we often call "hades," the place of the dead. Instead, David had a strong faith that God would return him to "the path of life."

Most importantly, David knew he would spend eternity in God's presence. He declared, "In Your *presence* is fullness of joy; at Your right hand are pleasures forevermore" (verse 11).

Now, let's take a moment to explore a misunderstanding that has developed within the church in recent years. I have heard several people proclaim something along these lines: "Happiness is external, which means it is dependent on our circumstances going well. Joy, on the other hand, is internal, which is why we can experience joy even in the midst of suffering."

In reality, the Bible doesn't make a distinction between "happiness" and "joy." Those terms are used as synonyms throughout Scripture. So David was not communicating that we will have joy in the presence of God, but we are limited to happiness here on earth—or any other separation between those terms. In truth, heaven will be a place filled with both happiness and joy. And every other good thing we can imagine!

That happiness begins with the incredible privilege of fellowship with Jesus. As Christians, we can be happy because our sins are forgiven. Not one of our sins or some of our sins—but all of them. Every one of our mistakes, failures, offenses, and iniquities have been covered by the blood of Jesus Christ shed on the cross.

David knew that kind of happiness that accompanies such incredible mercy: "Happy are those whose transgression is forgiven, whose sin is covered. Happy are those to whom the LORD imputes no iniquity and in whose spirit there is no deceit" (Psalm 32:1–2 NRSV).

According to Jesus, that kind of forgiveness creates happiness not only for us as individuals here on earth but also for the citizens of heaven: "Likewise, I say to you, there is joy in the presence of the angels of God over one sinner who repents" (Luke 15:10).

The apostles are another illustration of enjoying happiness in the presence of Jesus. In most cases, they spent several years living, traveling, and serving in the footsteps of the Savior. They saw His face. They heard His voice.

Did that mean they avoided all problems and lived in a perpetual state of bliss? No. But they did receive a foundation of happiness and joy that enabled them to endure uncertainty, persecution, and even the loss of their lives—and do so with rejoicing. Indeed, it was the early Christians' incredible effusion of joy in the face of suffering that helped the church spread so rapidly and so explosively throughout the Roman Empire.

Jesus had promised they would experience that kind of joy. After teaching about abiding in Him as the true vine, He declared, "These things I have spoken to you, that My joy may remain in you, and that your joy may be full" (John 15:11).

Even when predicting His own death and resurrection, Jesus assured the disciples that suffering would not derail their happiness. "Most assuredly, I say to you that you will weep and lament, but the world will rejoice; and you will be sorrowful, but your sorrow will be turned into joy. . . . Therefore you now have sorrow; but I will see you again and your heart will rejoice, and your joy no one will take from you" (John 16:20, 22).

HAPPINESS IS ENJOYING JESUS' FULLNESS

Jesus told His disciples that they would experience His joy, and that their joy would be "full." That echoes a similar sentiment from Psalm 16:11. David wrote, "In Your presence is *fullness* of joy."

We often think of heaven as the absence of sin and its consequences, which is true. In his vision of our eternal home, John heard a loud voice from heaven that cried, "Behold, the tabernacle of God is with men, and He will dwell with them, and they shall be His people. God Himself will be with them and be their God. And God will wipe away every tear from their eyes; there shall be no more death, nor sorrow, nor crying. There shall be no more pain, for the former things have passed away" (Revelation 21:3–4).

Heaven will be a home without tears and fears, without pain and strain, without sorrow and sadness.

But heaven will also be a place where joy and happiness are experienced in "fullness." Meaning, living in Jesus' presence is more than the absence of negative circumstances; it is also the active, chock-full, saturated presence of countless blessings.

Some of our happiness there will reflect what we appreciate about our current home on earth—yet perfected and amplified. For example, there will be beauty in heaven that is much deeper and much more poignant than even the loveliest sunrise in our present atmosphere. There will be love in heaven, but fully refined and free from all selfishness. There will be friendship in heaven, but all the barbs and misunderstandings will be removed. There will be work in heaven that is bursting with meaning and purpose and fulfillment.

Yet much that makes us happy in heaven will be unlike anything we've experienced here on earth. That's because heaven itself is unlike anything we have experienced here on earth. Heaven is a new world, bursting with new possibilities and new encounters that will make our hearts glad and our faces shine.

As Paul told us, "Eye has not seen, nor ear heard, nor have entered into the heart of man the things which God has prepared for those who love Him" (1 Corinthians 2:9).

Here's one last thought on the fullness Christ has promised us in heaven. Actually, a series of questions: Can you or I put any limit on God? Can any person or thing limit God in any way? Is there any way for God to reach an end—an end to Himself or an end to what He experiences?

The answer is no. God has no limits. Therefore, there are no limits to God's happiness—nor are there limits to our enjoyment of God. Because God is infinite, there is no point at which our delight in Him will cease or grow stale.

Our happiness in heaven will have no limit. No boundary. No end. Which also means . . .

HAPPINESS IS ENJOYING JESUS FOREVER

We will experience unbounded happiness in heaven because of our fellowship with Jesus, because of the fullness of our eternal home—and because that fullness has no end. Heaven is a place bursting with happiness in part because all who dwell there know the joy and the peace and the pleasure and the comfort and the worship and all the rest of it that will never stop.

Look again at David's words from Psalm 16:11: "At Your right hand are pleasures *forevermore*."

Have you ever enjoyed a gathering or an event so much that you started feeling sad about it ending while it was still going on? Maybe a family reunion where all your children (and possibly grandchildren) gathered together for a time of joy and fellowship. Maybe a party that was especially fun. Maybe a season where your favorite team won game after game. Whatever the actual event was, you were enjoying yourself so much that the impending end of your joy became a source of grief or sadness.

That won't happen in heaven, because there will be no end to our eternal home. No shadow of parting from those we love, including Christ.

Remember what John heard in his vision of eternity: "And He said to me, 'It is done! I am the Alpha and the Omega, the Beginning and the End. I will give of the fountain of the water of life freely to him who thirsts. He who overcomes shall inherit all things, and I will be his God and he shall be My son'" (Revelation 21:6–7).

Think of the happiness inherent in those words. God is "the Beginning and the End," which means He controls the very concept of beginnings and endings. When we reach the eternal state of the new heaven and new earth, there will be no conclusion to our fellowship with God. No finale to our fellowship with one another. No end to the wonders and mysteries of creation.

And no end to joy. *Our* joy—yours and mine.

As we've seen, the primary source of our happiness will be intimate fellowship with the Creator of all things. We will be His sons and daughters—His dearly loved children. And like any good father, He will lavish us with good gifts for the entirety of that connection. We will "inherit all things" and drink freely from the water of life.

Will there be anything in the eternal state that could possibly steal our joy? Lessen it? Dull its impact in our lives? No. "Nothing impure will ever enter it, nor will anyone who does what is shameful or deceitful, but only those whose names are written in the Lamb's book of life" (Revelation 21:27 NIV).

I like the way D. L. Moody described the happiness of our future home:

Think of a place where temptation cannot come. Think of a place where we shall be free from sin; where pollution cannot enter, and where the righteous shall reign forever. Think of a city that is not built with hands, where the buildings do not grow old with time; a city whose inhabitants are numbered by no census, except the Book of Life, which is the heavenly directory. Think of a city through whose streets runs no tide of business, where no hearses with their nodding plumes creep slowly with their sad burdens to the cemetery; a city without griefs or graves, without sins or sorrows, without marriages or mournings, without births or burials; a city which glories in having Jesus for its King, angels for its guards, and whose citizens are saints![3]

Can you imagine it? A world where shame has no voice and sin doesn't get a seat at the table. No one will experience the inner tug-of-war between right and wrong. There will be no regrets or secret struggles. Just hearts filled with gratitude and gladness. There will be no hearses or funerals and no need to lock the door at night.

Lee Horton got a taste of that happiness. After being incarcerated for twenty-five years, he was finally released. And instead of rushing past the little things, he soaked them in. His first trip to the DMV to get his driver's license was magical.

"We heard all the stories that everybody tell us, the bad things about the DMV," he said. "We had the most beautiful time. And all the people were looking at us because we were smiling and we were laughing, and they couldn't understand why we were so happy. . . . Just being in that line was a beautiful thing. It was a wonderful thing."

Not many of us would connect two and a half hours at the DMV with words such as "beautiful" and "wonderful"! Only someone who is truly free can say that and mean it. And Lee meant it! Now every day feels like a gift.

"Every morning . . . I send a message of good morning to every one of my contacts. And that's, like, 42 people. Family members, I send them 'good morning, good morning, good morning. Have a nice day.' And they're like, how long can I keep doing this? But they don't understand that I was deprived. And now, it's like I have been released, and I've been reborn into a better day, into a new day."[4]

Don't you love that phrase? *Reborn into a better day.* Don't you want that experience? A day with no more bad news, emergency rooms, or even DMVs! That day is coming because heaven is coming. And now, while you look forward to that day, why not send a happy text to a friend or family member. Or smile at a stranger.

And if you ever find yourself waiting in line at the DMV—well, choose to laugh like Lee Horton.

CHAPTER 15

ABSENT FROM HEAVEN

Yeonmi Park was born in the North Korean town of Hyesan, only a mile away from the Chinese border. As a young girl, she used to look out across the landscape at night and wonder why cities on the horizon were illuminated by electric light while her own town was plunged into almost total darkness.

"Maybe if I could go where the lights were, I could have a bowl of rice," she told herself. Yet for many years, it seemed like escape was impossible. North Korean guards patrolled the border, and Chinese authorities were known to quickly deport any refugees rounded up in China. Being captured during or after an escape attempt meant guaranteed torture and eventual death in a labor camp.

Still, when Park was only thirteen years old, her mother decided they had to try for freedom. Unfortunately, the woman who promised to help them escape sold them to human traffickers as soon as they crossed into China. After two years of abuse, Park and her mother joined a group of defectors who walked across a portion of the Gobi

Desert at night in order to reach Mongolia. This was a desperate gambit involving frigid temperatures and punishing terrain—but it worked. After surviving the journey against monumental odds, Park and her mother found Christian missionaries who helped them reach South Korea, and ultimately America.

The vision of freedom in America was a driving factor that helped Park keep going despite so many setbacks. In her words, "There's this country called promised land. It's a land of opportunity. It doesn't matter where you come from; it doesn't matter what ancestors you had; it doesn't matter how you look . . . as long as you're willing to work hard and respect others."[1]

Can you imagine how different life must have been for that young girl when she first set foot on American soil? Of course she would have encountered many things unavailable in North Korea, including people of different ethnicities and supermarkets stocked with food. But it must have been shocking how many "normal" elements of North Korean life were entirely absent from her new home. No socialist government, for example. No supreme leader. No menacing guards carrying rifles. No starving children lying in the streets.

I think Christians may experience a similar shock when we first enter the eternal state. Yes, much of that shock will come from the incredible splendor and majesty of God Himself. Hallelujah! But I also think we will be astounded by how much of our "normal" way of life on earth is completely absent from our new home in heaven.

It might surprise you to learn that the apostle John specifically highlighted many of those elements in Revelation 21 and 22—things we will *not* experience as part of our eternal life with Christ.

NO CHAOS IN ETERNITY

Since we're thinking about absences, let's go back to the very beginning of creation when much of what we recognize in our world (and even our universe) was absent from physical reality. The Bible tells us, "In the beginning God created the heavens and the earth. The earth was without form, and void; and darkness was on the face of the deep. And the Spirit of God was hovering over the face of the waters" (Genesis 1:1–2).

At some point near the commencement of our world, only three things existed: God, darkness, and the waters of "the deep."

Emphasizing those three elements may seem strange to modern readers, but that would not have been the case for the original audience of Genesis. Within ancient Jewish culture, both the ocean and darkness were primary symbols for chaos. Those images represented fear and danger because they were forces that could not be controlled by people.

Thankfully, God stepped in. His Spirit was present within the darkness and hovered over the surface of the oceans, which means God was in control. And then God demonstrated His control—His sovereignty and power—through the process of creation. He merely spoke, and in doing so He created light in the midst of darkness, land in the midst of the seas, and life in the midst of lifelessness.

Keep that in mind when you read this description of eternity from the second-to-last chapter of God's Word: "Now I saw a new heaven and a new earth, for the first heaven and the first earth had passed away. Also there was no more sea" (Revelation 21:1).

Does this mean there will be no ocean beaches in eternity? No ocean cruises? No ocean sunsets? I don't think so. Instead, what's likely being communicated in this verse is the absence of chaos in our eternal home. The sea was a source of danger and fear and volatility for the original readers of Genesis 1. John's vision assures us that those chaotic emotions will no longer be present in heaven.

The same is true for darkness, which John also addressed. Later in chapter 21 he wrote this of the New Jerusalem: "The city had no need of the sun or of the moon to shine in it, for the glory of God illuminated it. The Lamb is its light" (verse 23). He added this in chapter 22:

"There shall be no night there: They need no lamp nor light of the sun, for the Lord God gives them light. And they shall reign forever and ever" (verse 5).

Can you imagine a world with no sun? It's coming, but that won't produce a place of darkness. Far from it! No sun or moon means there will be no night. We will live constantly in the light of heaven—the light produced by God Himself. Think what that means for our lives: continual, uninterrupted fellowship and activity. Likewise, the depression and discouragement that often accompany darkness will be gone.

NO CHURCHES IN ETERNITY

If it seems strange to think of heaven without a sun, wait until you read the next "absence" John identified for the New Jerusalem: "But I saw no temple in it, for the Lord God Almighty and the Lamb are its temple" (21:22).

Talk about another surprise! Remember, the early church grew out of the Jewish faith, and many of the earliest Christians were Jews who rightfully recognized Jesus as the Messiah. For them, the temple in Jerusalem was not just a building; it was an institution. It was a foundational element of religious life. To imagine eternity without a temple would have been mind-boggling, to say the least.

John explained why there would be no temple back at the beginning of the chapter: "And I heard a loud voice from heaven saying, 'Behold, the tabernacle of God is with men, and He will dwell with them, and they shall be His people. God Himself will be with them and be their God'" (21:3).

When we reach eternity, God will dwell directly in the midst of His people, just as He started off doing in the garden of Eden. Therefore, there will be no need for a temple or a sanctuary—or a church! I know that statement may make many of my readers feel anxious. After all, lots of Christians today are used to attending church once, twice, or even three times a week. The idea of life without church services may seem as strange to us as life without the temple would seem to the early church.

But God does not dwell in buildings even during this age; He dwells in His people. Right now, we cannot see His presence as a physical manifestation. Instead, He lives in us through His Spirit. In eternity, however, God will dwell "among" us, in our very presence! No building or structure could improve on His very presence in our midst.

The same Jesus who healed the sick, raised the dead, fed the multitudes, died on Calvary, was raised from the dead, and ascended into heaven will be walking among us in heaven. We will have unbroken, personal fellowship with Him forever.

Here's something else. Just as there will be no churches in heaven, there will also be no "churchiness." I'm talking about the empty rituals of routine religious expression. There will be no church congregations that function more like country clubs than embassies for the kingdom of heaven. There will be no legalistic hypocrites who judge the speck in their neighbor's eye while ignoring the log in their own eye. There will be no wolves in sheep's clothing who manipulate God's people in search of financial gain.

All of that will be gone. What will remain is pure worship and pure fellowship between God and humanity.

NO CURSE IN ETERNITY

Are you ready for the especially good news? Some of the absences in heaven will be so wonderful that we can hardly imagine it. John tried to explain them for us on several occasions, including these:

- "And God will wipe away every tear from their eyes; there shall be no more death, nor sorrow, nor crying. There shall be no more pain, for the former things have passed away" (Revelation 21:4).

- "But the cowardly, unbelieving, abominable, murderers, sexually immoral, sorcerers, idolaters, and all liars shall have their part in the lake which burns with fire and brimstone, which is the second death" (21:8).
- "But there shall by no means enter it anything that defiles, or causes an abomination or a lie, but only those who are written in the Lamb's Book of Life" (21:27).
- "And there shall be no more curse, but the throne of God and of the Lamb shall be in it, and His servants shall serve Him. They shall see His face, and His name shall be on their foreheads" (22:3–4).

That final passage offers the key absence that will define our eternal home: "There shall be no more curse."

When Adam and Eve rebelled against God, all creation fell under a curse resulting from sin (Genesis 3:17–19). But because Christ redeemed us from the curse of the law when He died on Calvary, we enter heaven free from the propensity (ability) to sin, the proclivity (tendency) to sin, and the penalty (continual sinning and ultimate death) of sin.

The curse will be lifted. It will be completely removed.

What will that mean for our experiences in heaven? For starters, there will be no more death. Scripture tells us, "The wages of sin is death, but the gift of God is eternal life in Christ Jesus our Lord" (Romans 6:23). Without sin, then, we will no longer be touched by death. Instead, we will fully receive eternal life and everlasting renewal. Death itself will be dead.

Likewise, sickness and pain, which are consequences of sin's influence in our world, will be completely removed. Think of it. Those today who are blind, deaf, lame, mute, congenitally impaired, or deformed—all will receive completely whole resurrection bodies for their eternal stay in heaven. All doctors, nurses, pharmacists, and undertakers will be out of business forever!

The same is true for therapists and psychologists, because there will be no sadness in heaven. No emotional pain nor spiritual malaise. No separation from the people we love. No tears nor sorrow of any kind.

We've been focused on absences in this chapter, which reminds me of an astronaut named Butch Wilmore, who experienced the kind of absence encountered by almost no other person in human history—the absence of earth!

You see, Butch and his teammate Sunita Williams were scheduled for a short mission at the International Space Station in 2024. They planned to conduct several experiments and be part of the station's regular crew rotation for several weeks. Unfortunately, technical issues on their intended spacecraft made it necessary for NASA to pilot the ship remotely back to Earth, which meant Wilmore and Williams remained behind.

Both astronauts spent an incredible 286 days on the ISS before a repurposed SpaceX Dragon capsule allowed them to return home. Almost a full year in outer space!

After their return, Butch Wilmore gave an interview that I found fascinating. One of the reporters had learned that Wilmore continued to attend church during his time in space. He participated in his home congregation's online services. The reporter wanted to know why that was important, and Wilmore was more than willing to give an answer.

Here's what he said:

Well, goodness, the Word of God continually in-filling me—I need it. My pastors are the finest pastors on (or off, in this case) the planet. And to tie in and to worship with my church family was vital. It's part of what makes me go. . . . It was invigorating. It's part of what I need as a believer in Jesus Christ to continue that focus day in and day out. Even though it's fellowship from afar, and it's not like having fellowship up close, still I need it.[2]

There will be many absences when we reach our eternal home—many parts of our current life that we will no longer experience. But one thing we will always experience is fellowship. That includes fellowship with God and fellowship within the community of God. The good news is that we will never again have to settle for that fellowship from afar; not from God and not from those we love. Instead, our experiences worshiping God and communing with our fellow believers will be as intimate as a heartbeat and as close as our next breath.

That fellowship will be vital. It will be invigorating. And it will be a key part of what makes us go throughout eternity.

PART 3

THE APPOINTMENTS
OF HEAVEN

*And I heard, as it were, the voice of a great
multitude, as the sound of many waters and as the
sound of mighty thunderings, saying, "Alleluia!
For the Lord God Omnipotent reigns! Let us
be glad and rejoice and give Him glory, for the
marriage of the Lamb has come, and His wife has
made herself ready." And to her it was granted
to be arrayed in fine linen, clean and bright, for
the fine linen is the righteous acts of the saints.*

*Then he said to me, "Write: 'Blessed are
those who are called to the marriage
supper of the Lamb!'" And he said to me,
"These are the true sayings of God."*

REVELATION 19:6–9

CHAPTER 16

THE JUDGMENT SEAT OF CHRIST

On August 14, 2016, in Rio de Janeiro, the greatest Olympic athlete in history stood atop the medal podium for the final time. He listened as the loudspeakers played "The Star-Spangled Banner." Overwhelmed with emotions, he began to weep long before the song came to an end. When the music did conclude, he gathered his teammates in a final embrace.

I am referring, of course, to Michael Phelps.

As a swimmer representing the United States, Phelps won a staggering twenty-eight Olympic medals, which is more than any person in history. Twenty-three of those medals were gold, which is also a record. The person with the second-most Olympic golds has nine.

What did Michael Phelps do on that night in August 2016 to merit such a prestigious award? He swam 100 meters, which was two lengths of the pool. He was the third leg of a relay team, which means he watched two of his teammates swim, then he dove in and swam, then he watched another teammate swim the final lap and secure the gold.

If we didn't know better, we might take offense at someone being lavishly rewarded for an act that seems so simple. *I can swim two lengths of the pool,* we might think. *I could swim four lengths. Probably eight lengths. So why should he receive such prestigious recognition just because he can swim a little faster than me?*

But of course we do know better. We know that medal ceremony in Rio de Janeiro was the culmination of a lifetime of consistent, rigorous training. As a boy, when other kids his age were watching cartoons, Phelps was in the pool perfecting his strokes and building his speed. As a teenager, when his friends were playing video games or chasing girls, he was in the weight room building his strength. He invested thousands of days and tens of thousands of hours into becoming the very best at his chosen sport.

For that reason—for that lifetime of discipline and dedication—Michael Phelps has stood on medal podium after medal podium to receive the awards he earned.

You and I will experience something similar during our first moments in heaven. At some point, Jesus will come for His followers with a shout, with the voice of an archangel, and with the trumpet call of God (1 Corinthians 15:15–17; 1 Thessalonians 4:13–18). This is the rapture, which is the moment Christ will rescue the church from the impending chaos and terror of the Tribulation.

Immediately after the rapture, every person whose sins have been washed in the blood of Jesus will appear before their Savior at a vast and magnificent ceremony. Scripture refers to this ceremony as "the Judgment Seat of Christ." Theologians often describe this moment as the *Bema* Judgment for reasons we will explore in the next pages.

As with most truths about heaven, the *Bema* Judgment has application both for the future and the present. We will not experience this essential ceremony until Christ rescues His church, which will turn the page on the Age of Grace our world has experienced for the past two thousand years and initiate the Age of Judgment. At the same time, the reality of the *Bema* Judgment provides incredible motivation for the choices we make today. The more we understand what will happen in that critical moment, the more we will be encouraged and inspired to make every second count for the kingdom of God.

Let's learn more by exploring both the atmosphere of the *Bema* Judgment and the assessment it will represent for followers of Christ.

THE ATMOSPHERE OF THE *BEMA* JUDGMENT

I've noticed a lot of confusion today—both inside and outside the church—when it comes to the concept of judgment after death. People believe they will be "judged" at the gates of heaven immediately after their final earthly breath, at which time a decision will be made regarding their eternal future. The idea is that God will wait until that moment to review their lives and determine whether they qualify for heaven or for hell.

I don't know exactly how this misconception came to be. Maybe it's partly due to jokes about conversations with St. Peter at the pearly gates. Or maybe it's due to misinterpretations of the Scripture passages connected with the judgment seat of Christ or the Great White Throne Judgment.

Whatever the source of confusion may be, let me take a moment to add some clarity: The judgment seat of Christ is not a moment of judicial punishment, nor is it a moment where decisions are made about whether a person is permitted to enter heaven.

Instead, the judgment seat of Christ will carry an atmosphere altogether different from the courtroom scenes or sentencing hearings we are familiar with today. That difference has everything to do with the word *bema*.

Writing to the Christians in Corinth, the apostle Paul declared, "For we must all appear before the judgment seat [*bema*] of Christ, that each one may receive the things done in the body, according to what he has done, whether good or bad" (2 Corinthians 5:10).

Throughout the Roman Empire of Paul's day, athletic competitions were commonplace. Some were brutal, as in fights between gladiators. But many other competitions were similar in spirit to our modern Olympic games. Contestants gathered in arenas to compete at various activities—racing, wrestling, feats of strength, tests of agility, and so on. Spectators filled the viewing gallery, cheering on their favorites.

A typical arena of that day contained a raised platform called the *bema*. Often there was an official umpire for each specific arena who sat upon the *bema* to watch the games. From that exalted vantage point, the umpire could evaluate each of the competitors and take note of anyone who demonstrated special prowess or achieved significant success.

In Paul's day, then, being called before the *bema* seat was a positive experience. For a participant in the games, visiting the *bema* to be "judged" meant receiving both recognition and reward.

The same will be true when we as Christians stand before the judgment seat of Christ. For most, that will be a day of celebration and appreciation. Although there will be some unfortunate exceptions.

THE ASSESSMENT OF THE *BEMA* JUDGMENT

As we've seen, only believers will be present at the judgment seat of Christ. Only those who have been saved by God's grace through faith in Him. Therefore, the *bema* will not be a "judgment" in terms of punishment, wrath, or condemnation.

However, it will be a judgment in terms of evaluation. As each one of us stands before our Lord and Savior, we will be assessed based on how we lived our lives and how we invested the resources God gave us—including our time, talents, and treasures. The primary purpose for that evaluation will be for Christ the King to determine what kinds of rewards each person should receive.

Remember 2 Corinthians 5:10: "We must all appear before the judgment seat of Christ, that each one may receive the things done in the body, according to what he has done, whether good or bad."

Critically, it will be Christ Himself who serves as our Judge on that day. This is a truth affirmed throughout Scripture:

- Solomon wrote, "God will bring every work into judgment, including every secret thing, whether good or evil" (Ecclesiastes 12:14).
- Jesus said, "Nothing is secret that will not be revealed, nor anything hidden that will not be known and come to light" (Luke 8:17).
- And the writer of Hebrews added, "There is no creature hidden from His sight, but all things are naked and open to the eyes of Him to whom we must give account" (Hebrews 4:13).

I like how George Sweeting, the former president of Moody Bible Institute, described Christ's unique qualifications to sit on the *bema* seat and assess each of His followers:

God gives Jesus Christ the right to judge all men because of who He is. Jesus is uniquely qualified to judge because He is God and has existed from eternity (John 1:1). As God, He knows everything, can be everywhere at once, and has unlimited power and authority. He knows everything we think and sees everything we do. Thus He can judge perfectly, and with wisdom and full understanding and without error or partiality. Christ is also uniquely qualified to judge because of what He has done. He demonstrated perfect love for all men. Thus, when He judges, His perfect righteousness is balanced by His perfect love.[1]

In his epistle to the Christians in Rome, Paul indicated that we will not be passive observers while Jesus conducts this assessment of our lives. Instead, we will participate in that evaluation by giving an account of everything we've done:

> But why do you judge your brother? Or why do you show contempt for your brother? For we shall all stand before the judgment seat of Christ. For it is written:
> "As I live, says the LORD,
> Every knee shall bow to Me,
> And every tongue shall confess to God."
> So then each of us shall give account of himself to God. (Romans 14:10–12)

Do you see the motivational power inherent with the *Bema* Judgment? The Christians in Rome were busy chastising each other about eating food sacrificed to idols and other minor doctrinal concerns. Paul basically told them to knock it off. Instead of spending so much time judging other believers, they should visualize the future moment when they would stand before Christ and give an account for every thought, every word, every action, and every missed opportunity.

The same is true for believers today, including you and me.

That leads to the next question: On what basis will we be judged at the *bema* seat? What criteria will Jesus use when He evaluates our lives?

Paul answered that question in his first epistle to the Corinthians:

> For no other foundation can anyone lay than that which is laid, which is Jesus Christ. Now if anyone builds on this foundation with gold, silver, precious stones, wood, hay, straw, each one's work will become clear; for the Day will declare it, because it will be revealed by fire; and the fire will test each one's work, of what sort it is. If anyone's work which he has built on it endures, he will receive a reward. If anyone's work is burned, he will suffer loss; but he himself will be saved, yet so as through fire. (1 Corinthians 3:11–15)

In this illustration, Paul envisioned Jesus as an inspector reviewing a house after it's been burned with fire. The "fire" is the burning power of Christ's omniscient gaze (Revelation 1:14). As He examines our lives from His exalted place on the judgment seat, everything that is worthless or sinful will be burned away. Yet everything we have done to invest our resources in God's eternal kingdom will remain—and will shine forth as gold, silver, and precious stones.

Once again, do you see the incredible motivational power of the *Bema* Judgment? Everything we do matters! Every day is an opportunity to invest in the quality of the "house" we are building for Jesus—every hour, every minute, every second. Even when it seems like no one notices what you're doing and nobody will ever appreciate your service, take heart! Because Jesus sees. Jesus notices. And He will commend you on that day.

What determines whether our lives are built from material that endures or that which is burned up? Here is the best explanation I've found in my research:

> I observe that gold, silver, and costly stones are those things which God Himself creates and plants in the earth, and man can do no more than reap the bounty of the provision of God. The wood, the hay, and the stubble are those things that man plants, cultivates, harvests, manufactures, and uses according to his will. And so the suggestion we make is that which God is permitted to do in and through the child of God is that which is gold, silver, and costly stones, and that which the individual does by his own power, for his own glory, because it suits his own will, because it promotes his own purpose, is the wood and the stubble.[2]

I mentioned Michael Phelps—history's greatest Olympian—at the beginning of this chapter. So it's only appropriate that I conclude the chapter by focusing on the greatest gymnast in Olympic history.

Her name is Simone Biles, and she has dominated gymnastics on the world stage for more than a decade now.

As I write these words, Biles has earned eleven Olympic medals, including seven gold. She has thirty world-championship medals, including twenty-three golds. And she's won six all-around gymnastic world championships, which is more than any other female gymnast.

Needless to say, Simone Biles is at the top of her game. She is very familiar with the *bema* seat at Olympic and world-championship events. Yet, importantly, Biles has learned the value not only in *receiving* awards but also in *using* those rewards to give back.

During a recent Christmas season, for example, Biles joined forces with Dick's Sporting Goods to raise money for youth sports organizations in the Houston area, where she grew up.

"Giving back to the community is a given," said Biles. "They've supported me throughout my entire career. At the end of the day, if I can do something to support them—to help uplift and to bring some holiday cheer, especially around some hard times like this—that's what I'm going to do."[3]

You don't have to be famous to invest in what matters for eternity. In fact, every single follower of Jesus is called to build their lives in ways that make a difference. Sadly, some followers of Jesus will fail to do so. Using Paul's illustration above, their houses will be entirely burned up, which means they will have nothing to offer Jesus on that day—no reward and nothing of eternal value.

Such people will still be Christians, of course. They won't be stripped of their salvation. But they will enter heaven "only as one escaping through the flames" (1 Corinthians 3:15 NIV).

May that never be true of us!

CHAPTER 17

FIVE CROWNS

"There's a mistake."

Those three words capped off what may have been the most awkward moment in the history of the Academy Awards. In 2017, presenters Warren Beatty and Faye Dunaway announced that *La La Land* had won the Oscar for Best Picture. There was an explosion of joy as the cast and crew clambered up to the stage, several of them even giving their prepared speeches as they hugged and congratulated one another.

All the while, officials in the background could be seen huddled together, talking and pointing at various envelopes. The strange scene continued for several minutes until producer Jordan Horowitz—who had already given his speech—grabbed the microphone and announced the gaffe to the stunned crowd.

"Sorry, no. . . . There's a mistake," he said. "*Moonlight*, you guys won best picture." After another moment of confusion, Horowitz had to convince the crowd they weren't experiencing a joke by holding up the envelope for the winning film, which clearly said "*Moonlight*." Turns out the confusion came about because Beatty and Dunaway were handed the wrong envelope before they came onstage.[1]

I know I'll never win an Oscar, and I don't care. But there are awards I don't want to miss, and neither do you. These aren't letters of commendation from the governor, trophies for your bookshelf, or gold watches to honor your service. Those and all the other honors, awards, and trophies of this world are fleeting.

What really counts are the eternal rewards given out in heaven.

THE REWARDED

As we saw in the previous chapter, there will come a moment after the rapture when every follower of Jesus is gathered together in a glorious assembly. Christ Himself will be there, exalted to the highest seat—the judgment seat, or *bema*. That is the moment when our King will review our lives, burning away the dross of earthly efforts and highlighting every investment we made in His heavenly kingdom.

Throughout Scripture, God has promised to reward our sincere and humble efforts for Him. Psalm 58:11 says, "Surely there is a reward for the righteous." God told Jeremiah, "Refrain your voice from weeping . . . for your work shall be rewarded" (Jeremiah 31:16). Jesus said, "Blessed are you when they revile and persecute you, and say all kinds of evil against you falsely for My sake. Rejoice and be exceedingly glad, for great is your reward in heaven" (Matthew 5:11–12).

Jesus also said, "For the Son of Man will come in the glory of His Father with His angels, and then He will reward each according to his works" (Matthew 16:27). The apostle Paul warned, "Let no one cheat you of your reward" (Colossians 2:18). And one of the last promises in the Bible is Revelation 22:12: "And behold, I am coming quickly, and My reward is with Me, to give to everyone according to his work."

At the judgment seat of Christ, we believers in Him will become *the rewarded ones*, receiving recognition for our faithful service. Oh, how I look forward to that day!

As a reminder, the *Bema* Judgment is *not* the Great White Throne

Judgment, which is described in Revelation 20. That judgment will be a pronouncement of doom on unbelievers. Those who know Jesus Christ as Lord and Savior are totally and eternally exempted from that awful moment of judgment. Romans 8:1 says, "There is therefore now no condemnation to those who are in Christ Jesus."

The judgment seat isn't about whether we will get into heaven. We will be there already. It's about how we lived our Christian lives on earth. What kind of stewardship did we exercise with our time, gifts, resources, and testimonies? Each one of us will have our moment before the Lord to give an account of ourselves—and hopefully to hear Him say, "Well done, good and faithful servant. . . . Enter into the joy of your lord" (Matthew 25:23).

THE REWARDS

What will these rewards be like? Does the Bible give us any clues? Yes, it does. At least five rewards are listed for us. The New Testament uses the word *crowns* to describe them.

First, there is the *Victor's Crown*, described in 1 Corinthians 9:25–27: "And everyone who competes for the prize is temperate in all things. Now they do it to obtain a perishable crown, but we for an imperishable crown. Therefore I run thus: not with uncertainty. Thus I fight: not as one who beats the air. But I discipline my body and bring it into subjection, lest, when I have preached to others, I myself should become disqualified."

Paul wrote this to Christians in Corinth, where the Isthmian Games took place. Contestants had to endure rigorous training. The race was always a major attraction at the games, and that is the analogy Paul used to illustrate the faithful Christian life.

If ancient athletes disciplined themselves to win relatively insignificant prizes, how much more should we be well-disciplined to win an incorruptible and imperishable prize? Walking with God demands sacrifice and self-control. We need discipline even in things that are not necessarily evil, but which can dilute our devotion to God. We must say "no" to some things so we can say "yes" to other things more pleasing to God.

Sometimes we have to turn off our screens so we can study our Bibles. We have to get up in the mornings to have our devotions. We need self-control in what comes into our minds. We can't subject our bodies to drug or alcohol abuse or allow immorality to creep into our relationships. We've got to keep our tempers under the Spirit's control and watch our attitudes and tongues. It's important to be financially self-controlled, to be generous, to be wise in our expenditures. The Bible tells us to gather with other Christians for worship. We also need—dare I mention it?—discipline in our eating habits.

It's important to remember that self-control depends on Spirit-control. Our own determination needs buttressing by grace, and we have to depend on God to strengthen us in our resolution to live disciplined lives. The Lord will help us, but we must do our part too.

Second, we read about the *Crown of Rejoicing* in 1 Thessalonians 2:19: "For what is our hope, or joy, or crown of rejoicing? Is it not even you in the presence of our Lord Jesus Christ at His coming?"

This crown involves leading others to Christ. When Paul went to the city of Thessalonica, people were saved. The gospel spread to their hearts, and through them to others. A church was born in that city. Writing to them in 1 Thessalonians 2, Paul said they would be his "crown of rejoicing" when Christ returned.

This crown involves a team effort. Whenever I have the opportunity of leading others to receive Jesus, I always find that someone else has already planted the seed of the gospel in their hearts. Paul wrote, "I planted, Apollos watered, but God gave the increase" (1 Corinthians 3:6).

Watch for opportunities to share Christ, to invite someone to church or to an outreach event. Contribute to your church and to Christian ministries. Share your testimony with your children and grandchildren. Speak up for Jesus on every occasion, and sow the Word far and wide. Whenever you do so, the Lord Himself is fitting you for the Crown of Rejoicing.

Third, the *Crown of Righteousness* is described in 2 Timothy 4:8: "Finally, there is laid up for me the crown of righteousness, which the Lord, the righteous Judge, will give to me on that Day, and not to me only but also to all who have loved His appearing."

Paul wrote this shortly before his martyrdom. Rather than dreading death, Paul was looking forward to the Second Coming. He was ready to meet Christ. The Crown of Righteousness is reserved for those who have a longing for the Lord Jesus and who watch for Him to come back.

Anticipation is a powerful emotion. In the dead of winter, we look forward to spring. Couples separated by military deployment can't wait for their reunion. Students anticipate the end of the semester. Workers look forward to their vacations. Brides and grooms are eager for their wedding day.

Can you imagine a world without anticipation? How would we feel with nothing to look forward to? Without Christ, there's no ultimate anticipation. There may be momentary prospects and incremental excitement, but lasting expectancy is missing. Everything is different for Jesus followers! Our best days are ahead, and we can anticipate all the glories of eternity. In researching and writing about heaven, I've been reminded of all the joys that await us when Jesus returns. I hope this book and the biblical truths behind it will increase your anticipation for heaven and give you a renewed sense of longing for His swift return.

Fourth, two different verses describe the *Crown of Life*.

- "Blessed is the man who endures temptation; for when he has been approved, he will receive the crown of life which the Lord has promised to those who love Him" (James 1:12).
- "Do not fear any of those things which you are about to suffer. Indeed, the devil is about to throw some of you into prison,

that you may be tested, and you will have tribulation ten days. Be faithful until death, and I will give you the crown of life" (Revelation 2:10).

The Crown of Life is given in recognition of enduring and triumphing over temptations and trials, especially persecution and martyrdom. The early Christians lived in days of intense persecution. The apostles counseled them to persevere so they could inherit the Crown of Life. In much of the Western world today, the church is facing discrimination and the erosion of religious liberty. But elsewhere around the globe, Christians face the burning of their churches, the confiscation of their goods, ostracism, and often prison, torture, and death.

The Bible says, "All who desire to live godly in Christ Jesus will suffer persecution" (2 Timothy 3:12). Satan will batter us with temptations of all kinds, and we'll face trials and persecution. But what a wonderful opportunity to lay claim to the Crown of Life!

The fifth reward is the *Crown of Glory*. Peter wrote, "The elders who are among you I exhort. . . . Shepherd the flock of God which is among you, serving as overseers, not by compulsion but willingly, not for dishonest gain but eagerly; nor as being lords over those entrusted to you, but being examples to the flock; and when the Chief Shepherd appears, you will receive the crown of glory that does not fade away" (1 Peter 5:1–4).

This crown seems especially designed for Christian leaders and for those who are faithful shepherds of God's people. I don't believe it's reserved just for church staff members. You might be the shepherd of a small group. Your flock might be your family and children. It might be your Sunday school class or small group. The Lord often gives us responsibility for the spiritual well-being of others, and what an opportunity to serve Him!

All these rewards are available to all of us, however obscure and unknown we may be on earth. It's often said, "This one life will soon be past; only what's done for Christ will last."

THE REWARDER

These may not be all the awards at the judgment seat. Thousands of other categories may be revealed on that day. But one overriding thought has lodged in my mind while pondering these things: As wonderful as our rewards are, they cannot compare with our ultimate joy—our great Rewarder, Jesus Christ.

None of these crowns—not the Victor's Crown, the Crown of Rejoicing, the Crown of Righteousness, the Crown of Life, nor the Glory Crown—can compare to our best, highest, and greatest reward of all: Him! Remember what the Lord told Abraham in Genesis 15:1: "Do not be afraid, Abram. I am your shield, your exceedingly great reward."

That brings up the best question I can ask about rewards: What are we going to do with them? Let's say you get to heaven, stand before the judgment seat of Christ, and receive three different crowns for faithful service on earth. What will become of them? The answer is found in Revelation 4:10–11, where the twenty-four elders fall down before Him who sits on the throne and cast their crowns before Him, saying: "You are worthy, O Lord, to receive glory and honor and power; for You created all things, and by Your will they exist and were created."

Think of it! We're going to take the only thing we have in heaven, which is the crown He gave us, and worshipfully give it back to Him, saying, "Thank You, Lord, for letting me be here. Thank You, Lord, for being my Redeemer. Thank You for using me a little bit on earth. Thank You for letting me be Your servant."

I don't want to be left out of that, do you? I don't want to be standing in the background watching everybody else bringing their crowns and giving them to the Lord Jesus, but, because I was a lazy Christian, I have nothing to offer.

When he was Prince of Wales, King Charles II set up a special program at the Royal College of Nursing in central London. Recently, the king showed up to give a special award to a young man named

THE PROMISE OF HEAVEN

Harrison Rigby, the one thousandth cadet to pass the program. Harrison has a lovely picture of himself with the king and the award.

But here's the ironic thing: Harrison's twin brother, Jefferson, was the nine hundred and ninety-ninth person to finish the cadet course, and he totally missed out on the reward! He joked with the king, saying, "I drew the short straw."[2]

Well, there are no short straws when it comes to being rewarded by the King of kings. Christ knows our efforts, sees our burdens, uses our gifts, blesses our work, and gives us Himself as our exceeding great Reward.

CHAPTER 18

THE MARRIAGE SUPPER OF THE LAMB

Some wedding ceremonies *seem* like they go on for days. But what about a wedding that stretches seven months from start to finish? That's what happened between two of India's most prominent citizens, Anant Ambani and Radhika Merchant.

Mr. Ambani is the son of Asia's richest man. Ms. Merchant is the heiress of a massive pharmaceutical company. The parents of the bride and groom wanted to make sure this particular nuptial ceremony was an event to be remembered—and they pulled out all the stops to make the entire world take notice.

It all started in January 2024 with an extravagant engagement party that included some of the most famous actors and singers on the Bollywood scene. In March, the couple hosted a pre-wedding party for over twelve hundred guests that featured five hundred separate dishes made by one hundred separate chefs. In May, they embarked on a four-day European cruise that included a private yacht, tours of famous castles and mansions, and musical performances by the Backstreet Boys, Katy Perry, and Italian tenor Andrea Bocelli.

Then, in July, the real party began! The families hosted a mass wedding in the rural town of Palghar. Fifty underprivileged couples were treated to their own luxurious ceremonies and given generous gifts, including groceries for an entire year. That event ended with a traditional night of song and dance during which Justin Bieber performed.

Friday, July 12, was the main event. The actual wedding ceremony was hosted at the Jio World Convention Centre in Mumbai. There, Mr. Ambani and Ms. Merchant were officially joined as husband and wife in front of thousands of guests—not to mention hundreds of A-list celebrities, plus reporters from the BBC, *The New York Times*, and more. There were sixty floral statues as part of the decorations at the convention center, with each statue constructed of more than one hundred thousand flowers. The entire celebration concluded on Sunday with a reception hosting more than fourteen thousand guests.

Whew! The ceremony is estimated to have cost the Ambani family close to a billion dollars. Taken all together, it may have been the most lavish wedding celebration in human history.[1]

And yet, let me assure you that God, the Creator of the universe, has a spectacular wedding in store for His church that will make the Ambani wedding look like a Happy Meal from McDonald's by comparison. It's called the Marriage Supper of the Lamb, and it's part of our eternal future in heaven.

The first ten verses in Revelation 19 describe that glorious marriage as two incredible events: a celebration and a ceremony. If you belong to Jesus, you'll be there for both of them with a prime seat.

Ready to learn more?

A SPLENDID CELEBRATION

"Alleluia!"

That's not a word we hear every day in our modern world, but it was a common term during the early spread of Christianity. "Alleluia" is the Greek translation of the Hebrew word *Hallelujah*, which is very common in the Old Testament. In the New Testament, however, *Alleluia* occurs only four times—and all four of them take place in Revelation 19:1–6, which describes an energetic celebration erupting throughout the heavenly realms.

To understand why the hosts of heaven are celebrating at the beginning of Revelation 19, we need to take a step back to chapter 18, which describes the fall of "Babylon"—the great and terrible world-wide combination of commerce and religion that will be finalized during the Tribulation. This financial and religious system will be run by the Antichrist and the False Prophet, and it will be used to actively control all people and to viciously persecute all who convert to Christ during that terrible time.

In writing about Babylon's fall, John recorded these verses:

The sound of harpists, musicians, flutists, and trumpeters shall not be heard in you anymore. No craftsman of any craft shall be found in you anymore, and the sound of a millstone shall not be heard in you anymore. The light of a lamp shall not shine in you anymore, and the voice of bridegroom and bride shall not be heard in you anymore. For your merchants were the great men of the earth, for by your sorcery all the nations were deceived. And in her was found the blood of prophets and saints, and of all who were slain on the earth. (Revelation 18:22–24)

Near the end of the Tribulation, John specifically emphasized that Babylon's fall will snuff out any last vestiges of joy and goodness—

including weddings. "The voice of bridegroom and bride shall not be heard in you anymore."

Then, by contrast, chapter 19 emphasizes an ebullient shout of joy and praise as the heavenly hosts prepare for the Marriage Supper of the Lamb:

> After these things I heard a loud voice of a great multitude in heaven, saying, "Alleluia! Salvation and glory and honor and power belong to the Lord our God! For true and righteous are His judgments, because He has judged the great harlot who corrupted the earth with her fornication; and He has avenged on her the blood of His servants shed by her." Again they said, "Alleluia! Her smoke rises up forever and ever!" And the twenty-four elders and the four living creatures fell down and worshiped God who sat on the throne, saying, "Amen! Alleluia!" Then a voice came from the throne, saying, "Praise our God, all you His servants and those who fear Him, both small and great!"
>
> And I heard, as it were, the voice of a great multitude, as the sound of many waters and as the sound of mighty thunderings, saying, "Alleluia! For the Lord God Omnipotent reigns!" (verses 1–6)

I love the description of this celebration as "the sound of many waters" and "the sound of mighty thunderings." As someone who lives near the Pacific Coast, I know there's no sound quite so powerful or majestic as the crashing of waves. The only thing close might be the resonant rumble of thunder in the middle of a huge storm. Yet even both those sounds mingled together do not approach the reverberating roar that will break out in heaven as the kingdom of the Antichrist begins to crumble and the King of the universe prepares to wed His bride.

It's no wonder George Frideric Handel used this passage of Scripture as the inspiration for his celebrated "Hallelujah Chorus."

Notice the reasons why God is celebrated by the host of heaven:

He is filled with glory and power (19:1), He judges with righteousness and truth (verse 2), and He reigns with sovereignty over all things (verse 6).

A STUNNING CEREMONY

After the celebration in heaven will come a ceremony unlike anything ever experienced in our universe. Revelation 19:7–9 describes the invitation:

> "Let us be glad and rejoice and give Him glory, for the marriage of the Lamb has come, and His wife has made herself ready." And to her it was granted to be arrayed in fine linen, clean and bright, for the fine linen is the righteous acts of the saints.
>
> Then he said to me, "Write: 'Blessed are those who are called to the marriage supper of the Lamb!'" And he said to me, "These are the true sayings of God."

We can gain a better understanding of these verses by exploring the rituals of a Jewish wedding ceremony during the time of the early church. There were three major steps or stages for such an occasion in ancient Jewish culture.

Step one was the legal offer of marriage, which we might call the betrothal. This was often originated and arranged by the parents of the bride and bridegroom. The payment of a dowry was typically required to solidify a legal marriage. Interestingly, these steps were often accomplished solely by the parents without the bride and groom having met one another.

Step two was the initiation of the wedding ceremony. At some point after the legal betrothal, the groom would begin to prepare a home for his bride. Typically, he would construct an additional room onto his father's property. Then, when everything had been made ready, the groom (along with his friends) would go to the house of the bride and "claim" the bride for himself, taking her back to his own house.

Step three, the final stage of the wedding, included a bridal procession followed by a marriage feast. That feast, which typically included a large number of guests, often lasted for several days.

These three stages have clear parallels with our connection to—and eventual union with—Christ.

It's also important to understand the relative importance of the groom to the bride. In modern weddings, all attention is focused on the bride, but in the Jewish weddings of John's day, the opposite was true. The groom was the central figure. That's why Revelation 19 describes the Marriage Supper of the Lamb, not the marriage supper of the bride or even the couple. The Lamb of God is the central figure. Let's look more closely at each of the three components of a wedding as they relate to Jesus followers.

OUR BETROTHAL

You were betrothed to Jesus at the moment of your conversion. As soon as you accepted God's free offer of salvation through faith in the resurrection of Christ, you were bound to Jesus in a legal sense. He took your sins upon Himself, and He draped you in His righteousness like a garment without blemish.

There is also a sense in which God "arranged" the union between His Son and the church at the beginning of history. Scripture tells us, "He chose us in Him before the foundation of the world, that we should be holy and without blame before Him in love" (Ephesians 1:4).

In that global sense, the bride of Christ is now waiting for her Groom to return and claim her as His own. Of course, while we wait, we also spread the good news of the gospel so that—when the time does come—Christ may receive His bride in full.

OUR RECEPTION

The church at present is engaged to Christ, waiting on the day when He returns to claim us as His own. Paul echoed that reality in his words to the believers in Corinth: "I have betrothed you to one husband, that I may present you as a chaste virgin to Christ" (2 Corinthians 11:2).

So, at what moment will Jesus come and "claim" His bride? The rapture.

Scripture tells us, "For the Lord Himself will descend from heaven with a shout, with the voice of an archangel, and with the trumpet of God. And the dead in Christ will rise first. Then we who are alive and remain shall be caught up together with them in the clouds to meet the Lord in the air. And thus we shall always be with the Lord" (1 Thessalonians 4:16–17).

Jesus promised this moment of reunion to His disciples, and in context to the church as a whole, before His death: "In My Father's house are many mansions; if it were not so, I would have told you. I go to prepare a place for you. And if I go and prepare a place for you, I will come again and receive you to Myself; that where I am, there you may be also" (John 14:2–3).

OUR UNION

As we look ahead to God's eschatological calendar, there are four events that will occur in a relatively short amount of time—at least in the sense of time passing here on earth. Those events are the rapture, the judgment seat of Christ (the *Bema* Judgment), the Marriage Supper of the Lamb, and the Second Coming of Jesus. All four of those events will take place while people on earth are mired in the chaos of the Tribulation.

How do we know the Marriage Supper of the Lamb will occur after the judgment seat of Christ? The answer is in Revelation 19: "'Let us be glad and rejoice and give Him glory, for the marriage of the Lamb has come, and His wife has made herself ready.' And to her it was granted to be arrayed in *fine linen, clean and bright, for the fine linen is the righteous acts of the saints*" (verses 7–8).

As you remember from the chapter on the judgment seat of Christ, as each believer is called before the *bema*, their life will be tested (or evaluated) by the fire of His omniscient gaze. Whatever is impure will be burned away. Only what is righteous will remain. Therefore, after that moment, the bride of Christ will truly be prepared and purified for her Husband.

There's one more important item to clarify about the Marriage Supper of the Lamb. While the actual wedding ceremony takes place in heaven, the post-ceremony celebration—what we might call the reception—seems to occur back on earth.

Look again at Revelation 19:

> Now I saw heaven opened, and behold, a white horse. And He who sat on him was called Faithful and True, and in righteousness He judges and makes war. His eyes were like a flame of fire, and on His head were many crowns. He had a name written that no one knew except Himself. He was clothed with a robe dipped in blood, and His name is called The Word of God. And the armies in heaven, *clothed in fine linen, white and clean*, followed Him on white horses. (verses 11–14)

After the wedding ceremony, Christ will return to earth—no longer as the Lamb, but now the conquering King. And we, His bride, will return with Him. The Antichrist and all the forces of evil will be defeated, and Satan himself will be cast into the Abyss (Revelation 20:1–6).

At that point, our wedding celebration will begin. Remember, in ancient Jewish weddings the post-ceremony feast often lasted for several days. The length of that feast typically revealed the wealth and prestige of the groom's father—the more wealthy and powerful, the more days of feasting to celebrate his son.

Our feast will last for a thousand years. That's right, the Millennium will be our heavenly reception. We as the church will spend ten centuries celebrating our union and our intimate connection with Christ.

I recently read a story about a woman from Ireland named Betty. At seventeen, she fell in love with a young man, and the two eventually got engaged. But then Betty's father refused to endorse the marriage. "Get out of it," he told her suitor. "You're too old and she's too young."

Betty moved out of her father's house and kept her engagement to the young man. They stayed together for years. Even decades. And then, thirty-five years later, they decided to officially tie the knot.

"It was always the plan [to get married]," says Betty. "We'll do it this time, we'll do it that time, but something always came up." At the age of fifty-two, however, she is certain it's her time to be a bride. "The food is booked, the music is booked, we're going to have a lovely day."[2]

As the church—as the bride of Christ—we have waited nearly two thousand years for the day when our Groom will come to claim us as His own. I have a feeling our time is coming soon, although Scripture is clear that no person knows the day nor the hour of Christ's return.

What I do know is that every aspect of that future day—the day of our union with Jesus—will be worth the wait.

CHAPTER 19

THE MARTYRS

Oh, the suffering inflicted on Christians in our world today!

While writing this book, I saw a story in the news about Jackson and Doreen Wampula, a Christian couple living in the town of Nabiganda, Uganda. Doreen was six months pregnant, and the couple was excited about the birth of their child. Wanting to share their faith, they made friends with a graduating high school senior named Kapisa, who was preparing for college. She heard the gospel and attended church with them.

This act of evangelism angered Kapisa's staunchly Islamic mother, Hanifa, who became determined to retaliate.

During Ramadan, it's customary to send food to neighbors, so Hanifa prepared a meal for Jackson and Doreen. Horrifically, she poisoned their food, then asked her daughter Kapisa to deliver the supper. When Kapisa arrived, Jackson and Doreen invited her to stay and enjoy the meal with them. She did so, then returned home without realizing she had been poisoned. That evening, Kapisa, Jackson, and Doreen all became violently ill. The pregnant Doreen died first. Jackson and Kapisa passed away soon afterward at the hospital.

"I never intended to kill my daughter," said Hanifa, "but my plan was to kill the neighbors because of taking my daughter to church."[1]

The Bible tells us that martyrs such as Jackson, Doreen, and Kapisa will receive special attention in heaven—and perhaps even a special status and reward.

THE HATED OF EARTH

What took place that evening in Uganda was an unspeakable tragedy, yet this sort of thing happens around the world every day. Christians are the hated of the earth. Some attacks against Christians are personal, such as Hanifa's plan. Many are organized. And more than we know involve torture, violence, and mass murder.

According to the watchdog agency Open Doors, 380 million Christians are currently suffering high levels of persecution and discrimination for their faith. That's more than the entire population of the United States! Thousands are murdered each year. Christians are the most persecuted group in the world.[2]

This isn't new. In the Old Testament, the Lord's people were regularly slain, from the godly Abel to the prophet Zechariah, who was murdered between the altar and the sanctuary of the temple (Luke 11:51). The psalmist said, "For Your sake we are killed all day long; we are accounted as sheep for the slaughter" (Psalm 44:22).

In the New Testament, Stephen was stoned to death in Acts 7, becoming the first in a long line of Christian martyrs—one that continues to this day. The history of the Christian church is written in blood.

It's hard to understand why advocates of a system of faith that offers good news, hope, love, and compassion to the world could be so hated, vilified, beaten, whipped, imprisoned, tortured, and murdered. Yet the devil despises the followers of Jesus, and the world detests us. Our Lord—who Himself was murdered by the torture of crucifixion—said, "If the world hates you, keep in mind that it hated me first. If you belonged to the world, it would love you as its own. As it is, you do not belong to the world, but I have chosen you out of the world. That is why the world hates you" (John 15:18–19 NIV).

The levels of persecution we see now will only grow worse after the rapture of the church. As the seven years of Tribulation begin, many people will flee to Christ for refuge and be redeemed by His blood. The spiritual awakening occurring during the opening months and years of the Tribulation will be the greatest in history. But that awakening will come at a great cost. The world and the machinery of the Antichrist will seek to destroy each new believer, and will unleash the most intense persecution in the chronicles of the world.

Jesus described this period in Matthew 24, saying, "Then they will deliver you up to tribulation and kill you, and you will be hated by all nations for My name's sake. And then many will be offended, will betray one another, and will hate one another. . . . But he who endures to the end shall be saved" (verses 9–10, 13).

The Lord reiterated this promise in the message He gave to the church in Smyrna. Jesus told them, "Do not fear any of those things which you are about to suffer. Indeed, the devil is about to throw some of you into prison, that you may be tested, and you will have tribulation ten days. Be faithful until death, and I will give you the crown of life" (Revelation 2:10).

I've already talked about rewards and crowns; but I believe every martyr in history, every person who has given their life for the Lord, will receive a special award to enjoy throughout eternity—the crown of life mentioned in that verse.

THE HEROES OF HEAVEN

The hated of earth will become the heroes of heaven. We have a vivid picture of the Tribulation martyrs in Revelation 6:9–11:

When He opened the fifth seal, I saw under the altar the souls of those who had been slain for the word of God and for the testimony which they held. And they cried with a loud voice, saying, "How long, O Lord, holy and true, until You judge and avenge our blood on those who dwell on the earth?" Then a white robe was given to each of them; and it was said to them that they should rest a little while longer, until both the number of their fellow servants and their brethren, who would be killed as they were, was completed.

Who are these martyrs? John placed them in the future, after the church has already been raptured and the dead in Christ have been resurrected. So, these martyrs are not from the church age we're living in now.

Also, since the martyrs ask for judgment on their oppressors on the earth, their murderers are obviously still living. This suggests these martyrs are faithful saints who are killed during the Tribulation period.

These men and women will recall the horrible deaths they suffered on earth and the moment when they sacrificed their lives for the sake of God's kingdom. They will form a special league in heaven, eager for God to make things right and to avenge their deaths. Each one will be given a distinctive white robe and told to remain patient—to rest for just a bit. More martyrs will be coming, more saints are being killed. But when the full measure of Christian blood has been shed, God will avenge their deaths and satisfy their longings.

We see this same group in the next chapter, in Revelation 7:13–17. John was viewing the events of the Tribulation as they unfolded, both on earth and in heaven.

He saw a great number of people in dazzling robes. The one guiding him asked him, "Who are these arrayed in white robes, and where did they come from?"

John told him, "Sir, you know."

The heavenly guide told him, "These are the ones who come

out of the great tribulation, and washed their robes and made them white in the blood of the Lamb. Therefore they are before the throne of God, and serve Him day and night in His temple. And He who sits on the throne will dwell among them. They shall neither hunger anymore nor thirst anymore; the sun shall not strike them, nor any heat; for the Lamb who is in the midst of the throne will shepherd them and lead them to living fountains of waters. And God will wipe away every tear from their eyes."

In one sense, all these things are true of every believer in heaven. But it seems there is something special about this group. The Lord will give them special honor, special attention, and perhaps a special status. According to these passages, the Lord will give five special comforts to these martyred souls.

A REFUGE
The vision of these faithful servants under the altar is meant to convey their redemption and protection.

Donald Grey Barnhouse explained, "We are not to think that John had a vision of an altar with souls peeping out from underneath. The whole teaching of the Old Testament is that the altar was the place of the sacrifice of blood. To be under the altar is to be covered in the sight of God by the merit which Jesus Christ provided and dying on the cross ... These martyred witnesses are covered by the work of the Lord Jesus Christ."[3]

A ROBE
God, in His gracious love and mercy, rewards each martyr with a white robe. This gift raises an interesting issue. Are these literal robes, and does that suggest the martyrs are given temporary bodies until their own earthly bodies are raised at the resurrection?

The Bible Knowledge Commentary thinks so, saying, "Spirits without any substance could not wear robes. The fact that they will be given robes supports the concept that when believers die they are given temporary bodies in heaven which are later replaced by resurrection bodies at the time of the resurrection."[4]

A REST

When the martyrs ask how long it will be until their deaths are avenged, they are told to "rest a little while." The word *rest* implies their situation is now secure, free from danger or distress, one that provides a good place for the exercise of patience. Again, there's a sense in which this is true for all the believers who are in heaven awaiting the moment when Christ returns to earth to establish His kingdom. But this seems to have a special significance for those who have suffered for their faith, and especially for those who will do so during the Tribulation.

The One who sits on the throne will live among them, and they will not lack for any need. "For the Lamb who is in the midst of the throne will shepherd them and lead them to living fountains of waters. And God will wipe away every tear from their eyes."

A RETRIBUTION

From the same altar in heaven where the martyrs cry out will come an angel with a sharp sickle (Revelation 14:18). This is the angel of judgment, sent to avenge them. He will "thrust his sickle into the earth and [gather] the vine of the earth" (verse 19), which represents the wicked deeds of humanity. Then he will throw the clusters of grapes into the great winepress of the wrath of God (verse 19).

The prayers of the martyrs will be answered as God tramples the wicked, causing their blood to flow like the juice from grapes crushed by a winepress.

A REWARD

The martyred saints will be honored in heaven forever; but even before that, they will be honored on earth during the Millennium.

Revelation 20:4 says, "I saw thrones, and they sat on them, and judgment was committed to them. Then I saw the souls of those who had been beheaded for their witness to Jesus and for the word of God, who had not worshiped the beast or his image, and had not received his mark on their foreheads or on their hands. And they lived and reigned with Christ for a thousand years."

During the Millennium, these slain saints will experience the justice and peace that eluded them during their lifetimes. Having been resurrected on the other side of their martyrdom, they will rule alongside Christ and hold places of great dignity and leadership in His righteous, holy, and joyful kingdom. Perhaps this also implies they will occupy great places of authority on the new earth. Jesus said, "Blessed are those who are persecuted for righteousness' sake, for theirs is the kingdom of heaven" (Matthew 5:10).

THE HOPE OF ETERNITY

That hated of earth will become the heroes of heaven and will share with all of us the hope of eternity. Most of the Western world has been spared violent persecution in recent years. But we can all recognize the increasing pressure from society and from Western governments against the expression of our faith and of our biblical worldview. Our culture is seeking to intimidate the voices of believers.

I'm often asked if the church will go through the Tribulation. There are two ways to answer that. My first answer is, "No, I believe the church will be raptured before the Tribulation." But the second answer is, "In many parts of the world, the church is facing great tribulation *right now*! Even in the West there is growing infringement on the civil rights of Christians."

Jesus said, "In the world you will have tribulation" (John 16:33).

He also said, "Blessed are you when men hate you, and when they exclude you, and revile you, and cast out your name as evil, for the

Son of Man's sake. Rejoice in that day and leap for joy! For indeed your reward is great in heaven, for in like manner their fathers did to the prophets" (Luke 6:22–23). Notice that the Lord's "great reward" is for those who are hated, excluded, reviled, and cast out as evil for the Lord's sake.

The writer of Hebrews reminded his readers they should rejoice when they are persecuted and when the authorities plunder their property for the sake of Christ. They have "an enduring possession . . . in heaven" and a "great reward" (10:34–35).

At the moment of his martyrdom, Stephen "gazed into heaven and saw the glory of God, and Jesus standing at the right hand of God." He shouted, "Look! I see the heavens opened and the Son of Man standing at the right hand of God!" (Acts 7:55–56). We typically read about Jesus sitting at the right hand of God, but as Stephen was being slain, Jesus stood to observe and to welcome him into heaven. That tells us something of our Lord's concern and appreciation for those whose faith demands their blood.

That also points toward our great and certain hope: eternity!

How we need it! The suffering on earth has never ceased. Truly outrageous things are done to believers, now as much as ever. For example—and this is hard to write—in North Korea in May 2023, the regime sentenced a two-year-old child to life imprisonment after his parents were arrested for owning a Bible.[5] Such evil is impossible to comprehend.

Even so, I know in my heart and from my Bible that almighty God will inflict His just retribution on those who abuse His people. He will bless His suffering saints in ways we cannot even imagine. The hated on earth will be the heroes of heaven. In New Jerusalem, perhaps we'll all be among the cheering crowds thrilled at the procession of champions who, led by the Lamb of God, proceed down the golden streets in a ticker tape parade.

And surely among them will be that two-year-old child, forever glorified, smiling, waving, and marching hand in hand with our Jesus!

PART 4

THE ANSWERS
ABOUT HEAVEN

But someone will say, "How are the dead raised
up? And with what body do they come?" Foolish
one, what you sow is not made alive unless it
dies. And what you sow, you do not sow that body
that shall be, but mere grain—perhaps wheat
or some other grain. But God gives it a body as
He pleases, and to each seed its own body. . . .

So also is the resurrection of the dead. The body
is sown in corruption, it is raised in incorruption.
It is sown in dishonor, it is raised in glory. It is
sown in weakness, it is raised in power. It is sown a
natural body, it is raised a spiritual body. There is a
natural body, and there is a spiritual body. And so
it is written, "The first man Adam became a living
being." The last Adam became a life-giving spirit.

1 CORINTHIANS 15:35–38, 42–45

CHAPTER 20

WON'T HEAVEN BE BORING?

There is a funny old poem about a tired housewife that has been shared for years in books and cards. No one knows who wrote it, but it goes like this:

> Here lies a poor woman who was always tired,
> She lived in a house where help wasn't hired.
> Her last words on earth were: "Dear friends, I am going
> To where there's no cooking, or washing, or sewing,
> For everything there is exact to my wishes,
> For where they don't eat, there's no washing of dishes.
> I'll be where loud anthems will always be ringing,
> But having no voice I'll be spared of the singing.
> Don't mourn for me now, don't mourn for me never,
> I am going to do nothing for ever and ever.

"Boring!"—usually pronounced "BOOORing!"—is the ultimate put-down in today's society.

Michael Crichton was one of our most brilliant writers and

producers. In his bestseller *Timeline*, he had something interesting to say about the subject of boredom. One of his characters, Robert Doniger, is the CEO of a powerful and highly secretive technology company. Near the end of the book, Doniger stands before an audience in his company's auditorium and says this: "In other centuries, human beings wanted to be saved, or improved, or freed, or educated. But in our century, they want to be entertained. The great fear is not of disease or death, but of boredom. A sense of time on our hands, a sense of nothing to do. A sense that we are not amused. But where will this mania for entertainment end?"[1]

Let's be honest: Nobody likes being bored. Not at work. Not at home. Not when we go out for a date or to do some shopping or just to spend time in nature. In our go-go-go culture, it seems like there's never a good time to be bored.

What about heaven, then? We might think, *If I feel bored down here on earth, what will it be like up there for all eternity?*

That's a common question, and it's one John Eldredge addressed in his book *The Journey of Desire:*

> Nearly every Christian I have spoken with has some idea that eternity is an unending church service. . . . . We have settled on an image of the never-ending sing-along in the sky, one great hymn after another, forever and ever, amen. And our heart sinks. "Forever and ever? That's it? That's the good news?" And then we sigh and feel guilty that we are not more "spiritual." We lose heart, and we turn once more to the present to find what life we can.[2]

If those ideas have crossed your mind, you're not alone. Many Christians believe heaven will be boring—that all we'll be doing forever and ever is strumming harps, floating on clouds, and polishing streets of gold.

Thankfully, that's not true. Not at all! In this chapter, I want to offer five reasons why heaven will not, and could not, be boring.

BECAUSE GOD IS NOT BORING

Here's a word from King David on the subject of enjoying the presence of God: "You will show me the path of life; in your presence is fullness of joy; at your right hand are pleasures forevermore" (Psalm 16:11).

What exists in God's presence? Fullness of joy! Pleasures forevermore! When we're with God, we are on the scene of endless explosions of absolute pleasure and joy. That's what heaven will be like. That's what heaven will always be.

Our God is the most exciting, adventuresome, creative person you can imagine, multiplied a billion times over. And heaven will reflect His exuberance. We can't begin to comprehend the excitement that belongs to the triune God with whom we're going to spend eternity. He spoke the universe into existence. He made the elephant, the eagle, and the earthworm. He created a donkey that could speak, a fish that could swallow a man, and a flock of ravens that could feed a prophet.

God sweeps His hand across the sky, turning it into a crimson blaze of glory. He's the One who can ignite volcanoes, send meteors hurtling through space, and zap the blackened skies with lightning bolts and thunderclaps.

He turned the Nile into blood and well water into wine. He flung fire from heaven in response to Elijah's prayers, answered Job out of the whirlwind, delivered Daniel from the lions' den, and caused the sun and moon to stand still for Joshua.

Does any of that sound boring?

Randy Alcorn sums it up well:

Our belief that Heaven will be boring betrays a heresy—that God is boring. There's no greater nonsense. Our desire for pleasure and the experience of joy come directly from God's hand. He made our taste buds, adrenaline, sex drives, and the nerve endings that convey pleasure to our brains. Likewise, our imaginations and our capacity for joy and exhilaration were made by the very God we accuse of being boring. Are we so arrogant as to imagine that human beings came up with the idea of having fun?[3]

God is not boring. Neither is our Savior.

BECAUSE JESUS IS NOT BORING

Another reason we won't be bored in heaven is because we'll be physically and visually close to Christ. Think of what an exciting life the disciples experienced in the Gospels. They heard the Sermon on the Mount with their own ears, watched their nets strain with fish at His bidding, stood in awe as dead people returned to life, participated in inexplicable miracles like the taming of vicious storms, and experienced the greatest surprise of their lives when Jesus suddenly appeared to them on the day of His resurrection.

Peter walked on water. Mary Magdalene was rid of her demons. Peter, James, and John met Moses and Elijah. Zacchaeus looked downward and saw Jesus looking up at him through the branches of a sycamore tree. And Stephen looked upward and saw Jesus standing at the throne.

Can you imagine a boring day with the Stranger of Galilee who raised the dead, healed the lepers, overturned the tables at the temple, walked across the sea, fed thousands of people with a few fish and loaves, rose from the grave, and ascended into the heavens?

All of us who have sought to walk with Christ through the years know that the Christian life is one of joy, comfort, excitement, and sometimes uncertainty as we wait to see what our Lord will do next. He is with us when the weather patterns of our lives change. He gives daily strength for daily needs. He provides promises and answers prayer.

Yet right now we don't even see Him face-to-face! Peter said, "whom having not seen you love. Though now you do not see Him, yet believing, you rejoice with joy inexpressible and full of glory" (1 Peter 1:8).

Imagine how much more majestic, awe-inspiring, precious, and joyful our lives will be when we see Jesus as He is!

BECAUSE YOU WILL NOT BE BORING

Are you a boring person? It's possible. Sometimes we get so caught up in our own interests and our own story that it becomes wearisome for other people to spend time with us. It happens.

But even if you're boring now, you won't be boring in heaven. Not even close. Paul explained why in 1 Corinthians 15: "Behold, I tell you a mystery: We shall not all sleep, but we shall all be changed—in a moment, in the twinkling of an eye, at the last trumpet. For the trumpet will sound, and the dead will be raised incorruptible, and we shall be changed" (verses 51–52).

Paul added this in his epistle to the Philippians: "For our citizenship is in heaven, from which we also eagerly wait for the Savior, the Lord Jesus Christ, who will transform our lowly body that it may be conformed to His glorious body" (3:20–21).

Not only will our "selves" be changed—meaning our personalities—but also our physical bodies will be transformed. As we saw in an earlier chapter, our new, heavenly bodies will be anything but boring! They won't malfunction or grow sick or weak. We'll have all the energy and drive and ambition imaginable, and our bodies will never weaken or suffer fatigue.

BECAUSE YOUR FRIENDSHIPS WILL NOT BE BORING

Elie Wiesel said, "Friendship marks a life even more deeply than love. Love risks degenerating into obsession; friendship is never anything but sharing."[4]

Friendship won't end at heaven's gates. Instead, it will flourish like never before in our eternal home. Scripture hints that our relationships won't be erased in heaven but instead redeemed, deepened, and made eternal. Jesus spoke of sitting down with Abraham, Isaac, and Jacob in the kingdom (Matthew 8:11), and Paul encouraged believers with the hope that we will be reunited "together" forever (1 Thessalonians 4:17). In Luke 16:9, Jesus even spoke of eternal dwellings where friends welcome each other.

So, we will retain our relationships in heaven—which is good news. But even better is that none of those relationships will be tainted by the corruption of sin.

Jonathan Edwards, one of the most insightful theologians of early America, wrote this:

> No inhabitants of that blessed world will ever be grieved with the thought that they are slighted by those that they love, or that their love is not fully and fondly returned . . . there shall be no such thing as flattery or insincerity in heaven, but there, perfect sincerity shall reign through all and in all. Everyone will be just what he seems to be, and will really have all the love that he seems to have.[5]

In heaven, everyone will be kind and honest. No one will pretend. If someone says they love you, they will really mean it—and you will feel it. Everyone will treat each other with real love, all the time.

For those reasons and more, our friends will be anything but boring in heaven. Gone will be the shallow conversations, the pretenses, and the pain of one-sided love. Instead, we'll experience friendships transformed by God's promise to make all things new (Revelation 21:5). We'll know each other fully, with no hidden agendas or misunderstandings, just as Paul wrote: "Now I know in part, but then I shall know just as I also am known" (1 Corinthians 13:12).

Imagine strolling through the golden streets of the New Jerusalem with a friend, marveling at the breathtaking beauty of God's creation.

We'll walk together by the crystal-clear river of life, watching the trees bear fruit in every season, and join the multitudes in worshiping the Lamb who was slain. Every moment will be filled with pure joy, deep love, and wonder. No jealousy, no insecurity, no weariness—just the love of Christ!

BECAUSE YOUR WORK WILL NOT BE BORING

Perhaps the main reason people think heaven will be boring is that they believe they will have nothing "constructive" to do—no meaningful work. But that's not the case. Heaven is not a place of endless idleness. It is a place of joyful activity and meaningful service.

One of the most consistent themes running through the book of Revelation is that of serving God. From beginning to end, heaven is described as a realm where God's people continue to serve Him:

- "Therefore they are before the throne of God, and serve Him day and night in His temple. And He who sits on the throne will dwell among them" (7:15).
- "Then a voice came from the throne, saying, 'Praise our God, all you His servants and those who fear Him, both small and great!'" (19:5).
- "And there shall be no more curse, but the throne of God and of the Lamb shall be in it, and His servants shall serve Him" (22:3).

When we enter heaven, we won't be put on some kind of divine Social Security list. No, listen to this welcoming speech (and promise) from the Lord Himself: "Well done, good and faithful servant; you have been faithful over a few things, I will make you ruler over many things. Enter into the joy of your lord" (Matthew 25:23).

That verse surely doesn't sound to me like we're going to be sitting around doing nothing forever and ever in heaven. It doesn't sound like retirement but a promotion! In other words, eternal life is not a break from work; it is a breakthrough to better work. It is purpose without pressure, service without fatigue, and joy without end.

There are two things against which we all revolt. One is work that is tedious and meaningless or encumbered by a difficult working environment. The other is idleness and the lack of occupation. But the work that awaits us in heaven will be a delight to the soul.

Heaven itself will be a delight to the soul. It will be filled with excitement—which is a subject Miles Daisher knows quite a lot about.

As an extreme sportsman, stuntman, and BASE jumping specialist, Miles has created a career out of seeking thrills. For more than twenty-five years, he's been leaping from buildings, antennae, and cliffs—the higher the better. He's even been a consultant for Tom Cruise as part of the *Mission: Impossible* movie franchise.

According to Miles, there's nothing quite so satisfying as taking an extreme risk. "I just love it so much. There's no feeling in the world like it. You're standing on an object, you jump off it, you're weightless. You have zero gravity.

"My favorite part, though," he continued, "is when you are on the object and you lean over to the point of commitment, when you can't stop and turn back. I'm just nuts for that feeling—that feeling of pushing off and totally going for it. I don't know, to me it's like a feeling of being alive."[6]

That's what it's like to follow Christ! There comes a moment when you lean into Him—past the point of no return. You push off from the old life and totally go for it. That's when real life begins—and that life continues in heaven.

Make no mistake, our eternal home will be the most thrilling, joy-filled, adventure-packed reality you've ever known, multiplied beyond anything you can imagine.

CHAPTER 21

WHERE ARE THEY NOW?

Journalist Linsey Davis was enjoying an ordinary flight with her young son, Ayden. She'd given her little boy the window seat, and he spent several minutes staring out the window once the airliner hit cruising altitude. He was gazing intently, his nose almost pressed against the glass.

When Ayden turned back to look at his mom, however, his face was confused. Even a little distraught.

"I don't see her," he said.

Linsey wasn't following. "You don't see who?"

"Well." The boy gazed out the window once more, then turned back to his mother. "I looked out the window looking for Grandma P in heaven."

That's when Davis connected the dots. Two months before the flight, Ayden had come home from school asking why his classmates had two sets of grandparents, but he only had one. Mom explained that her own mother, Grandma P, had passed away and was now in heaven. On the flight, her son was hoping to catch a glimpse of his grandma in the clouds.

After the conversation on the plane, Linsey was inspired to write a children's book called *How High Is Heaven?* In that story, a young boy misses his grandmother and makes several attempts to get to heaven so he can spend time with her—building a staircase with Legos, making wings out of cardboard, riding in a hot-air balloon, and so on.[1]

We may not press our noses to an airplane window, but we've all looked up, wondering about those who've gone before us. Over the years, I've stood at a lot of deathbeds, conducted a lot of funerals, said goodbye to a lot of my friends and family, and counseled more people in grief than I can remember. Two types of questions come up again and again among those standing by the graveside of a loved one:

- Where is my daddy right now? Where is my loved one? Is my little girl alive right now somewhere?
- How is it going with them? What are they doing right now on the other side of the grave? How are they?

Those aren't new questions. They've been discussed throughout history—including among those who lived in New Testament times. Paul wrote to the Thessalonian Christians so they would not be ignorant "concerning those who have fallen asleep" (1 Thessalonians 4:13). Falling asleep was, of course, a metaphor for death—the same one Jesus used to describe Lazarus (John 11:11). Dr. Luke described Stephen's death as him falling asleep (Acts 7:60), and Paul described the death of David in the Old Testament the same way (Acts 13:36).

When people ask, "Where is my loved one now?" following his or her death, they obviously are not asking about the body. They're asking about the person's soul. The material body is laid in the grave, but what happens to the immaterial person? The Bible has the answer, and it is illustrated clearly in a story told by Jesus about two individuals who went to two different places when they died.

A STORY OF TWO PEOPLE

You've likely heard the story Jesus told about the rich man and Lazarus (Luke 16:19–31). Let's pause here because this story offers something we don't see anywhere else in the Bible: a unique glimpse into the afterlife from the lips of the Lord Jesus Christ. This happens in no other place throughout Scripture, so we should certainly pay attention!

Also, notice I refer to these verses as a story, not a parable. That's important. Our Lord employed a lot of parables throughout His public ministry, but there was never a time when He used someone's given name in a parable. The characters in parables always had generic labels—"A certain man," "a judge," "an older brother." But in this passage, Jesus told us of a man named Lazarus. This was a specific man with a specific name. Why? Jesus was telling a real story.

Because this is a real story, it gives us real insight into what Lazarus and the rich man experienced after death—which means it also gives us real and meaningful insight into what our loved ones experience after they die. This is a story with real answers for each of us.

TWO MEN CONTRASTED IN LIFE

Jesus didn't name the rich man, but many over the centuries have referred to him as Dives (pronounced Dye-vees) because *dives* is the Latin term for "rich man." This particular wealthy man showed his riches by dressing in purple garments and fine linen, and by eating sumptuous foods of the finest quality for every meal. He was outwardly wealthy, displaying his assets for all to see.

The second man, Lazarus, wasn't the brother of Mary and Martha whom Jesus raised from the dead. This Lazarus was a poor beggar. Instead of fancy clothes, his body was covered in sores. Instead of dining on fancy foods, he spent much of each day lying outside the gates of Dives's house, hoping someone would provide him a few crumbs from the rich man's table. Lazarus was in such bad shape that "the dogs came and licked his sores" (Luke 16:21).

TWO MEN CONTRASTED IN DEATH

After introducing these two men, the story takes a turn by jumping to the moment of their deaths:

> "So it was that the beggar died, and was carried by the angels to Abraham's bosom. The rich man also died and was buried. And being in torments in Hades, he lifted up his eyes and saw Abraham afar off, and Lazarus in his bosom.
>
> "Then he cried and said, 'Father Abraham, have mercy on me, and send Lazarus that he may dip the tip of his finger in water and cool my tongue; for I am tormented in this flame.' But Abraham said, 'Son, remember that in your lifetime you received your good things, and likewise Lazarus evil things; but now he is comforted and you are tormented. And besides all this, between us and you there is a great gulf fixed, so that those who want to pass from here to you cannot, nor can those from there pass to us.'" (verses 22–26)

To understand where these two men went when they died, we have to understand the Old Testament's teaching about the afterlife. Before Jesus' resurrection and ascension, the Bible teaches there was an intermediate place where souls went after death. This place of the dead had two divisions separated by "a great gulf fixed" (Luke 16:26).

On one side was Paradise, also known as Abraham's bosom. This was a temporary "heaven" where the righteous dead went. It was a place of comfort, love, and companionship. On the other was a temporary "hell" called hades. This was a place of torment for the unrighteous dead. And between these two places was a great, uncrossable gulf.

THE PLACE OF THE DEAD		
Paradise (Abraham's bosom)	The Great Gulf Fixed	Hades
A temporary heaven		A temporary hell
A place for the righteous dead		A place for the unrighteous dead
A place of comfort, love, and companionship		A place of torment

Now let's take a closer look at what happened to these two men in the story Jesus told.

Jesus said that when Lazarus died, he was carried by the angels to "Abraham's bosom" (verse 22). As we have seen, the term *Abraham's bosom* is another name for Paradise, or the place where the spirit of Old Testament believers went when they died.

Please note: Jesus did *not* say, "Lazarus was carried by the angels to heaven." I will explain why in a moment.

But Dives went to hades where he was "in torments" (verse 23). In verses 23–31, Jesus went on to describe hades as a place of misery, memory, and mourning.

In many respects, the rich man and Lazarus changed places. The proud man of time became the beggar in eternity. The one who in life denied the poor man a crumb from his table was now begging the poor man to give him a drop of water on his finger. The one who in life fared sumptuously every day would now be happy with just one drop of water to cool his tongue.

A STORY OF TWO PLACES

Now let's directly and definitively answer the question: What happens today to people when they die? The Bible says they go to one of two places.

THE UNSAVED GO TO HADES

When a person dies today without knowing Christ, that person's body goes in the grave, and his soul and spirit go to hades, the intermediate "hell," until a particular point in time in the future. This is where the rich man in Jesus' story remains today.

But here's what we need to understand. Revelation 20:13–14 says that after the judgment at the Great White Throne, death and hades will give up those who are in them, and they will all be cast into the lake of fire forever. There will be a moment of final judgment that is still to come.

THE SAVED GO TO HEAVEN

As we have seen, when Old Testament believers died they went to the temporary "heaven" called Paradise or Abraham's bosom. This was a place of peace, but it wasn't yet heaven. Then something incredible happened on the Saturday between Good Friday and Easter Sunday that changed everything. Jesus, though His body rested in the grave, descended in spirit to the place of the dead—the realm we have been talking about. And He didn't go there to suffer. He went to declare victory! He stepped into the unseen world and announced the triumph of the cross.

We know this because of what Jesus said to the repentant thief: "Assuredly, I say to you, today you will be with Me in Paradise" (Luke 23:43). Remember, at that time Paradise was the temporary place where the souls of the righteous dead were gathered.

Jesus went there and 1 Peter 3 tells us He "proclaimed to the spirits in prison" (verse 19 ESV). Ephesians 4 says He "descended into the lower parts of the earth" and "led captivity captive" (verses 8–9). And in Revelation 1:18, Jesus declared, "I have the keys of Hades and of Death!"

What did Jesus do in the place of the dead? He preached victory to the fallen angels, the unrighteous dead, and to the Old Testament saints who had long waited for the Messiah. And then, in triumph, He led the righteous out of that waiting place and into the very presence of God.[2]

In other words, Jesus took the Old Testament believers from Paradise into heaven. Since then, believers no longer pass through an intermediate heaven at death. The soul and spirit of every believer now go directly to heaven because Paradise is now in the presence of God (2 Corinthians 12:2–4).

So here is the answer to the question, "Where are they now?" If your loved ones were followers of Christ, I can tell you for sure where they are. Their bodies are in the grave, waiting for the day of resurrection at the rapture; their souls and spirits are in heaven! And in 2 Corinthians 5:1–5, Paul hinted at the fact that they have some kind of intermediate body as they await their full resurrection at the rapture (1 Thessalonians 4:16–17).

A STORY WITH ONE PRINCIPLE

As we conclude this chapter, I want to focus on one eternally significant principle.

Think back to what Abraham told the rich man in Jesus' story from Luke 16: "And besides all this, between us and you there is a great gulf fixed, so that those who want to pass from here to you cannot, nor can those from there pass to us" (verse 26). Scripture also says, "And as it is appointed for men to die once, but after this the judgment" (Hebrews 9:27).

The Bible does not tell us we'll have a second chance to secure the redemption of our souls after death. Rather, it says, "Behold, now is the accepted time; behold, now is the day of salvation" (2 Corinthians 6:2).

The rich man in Luke 16 could have heard and heeded the truth of the gospel, but he let the days slip away until there was no time left. I urge you not to make the same mistake.

Many years ago, Donna and I were in Tuscaloosa, Alabama, where I spoke at the West Alabama Prayer Breakfast at the Bryant Conference Center on the University of Alabama campus. As I entered the venue, one of the organizers told me someone was waiting to see me. "I think you'll want to meet this man," he said.

I was introduced to a middle-aged man they called "Red." He had long, red hair pulled back in a ponytail and looked like he had lived a hard life.

When we met, Red grabbed my hand and began to tell me his story. His life had spiraled downward for years, and recently he'd lost all hope. He decided to take his life by speeding his car into a large tree he often passed on a local road. His plan was simple: get up to eighty or ninety miles an hour, miss the curve, and end it all.

As he prepared for that final ride, he blasted his favorite rock station—but the signal kept cutting in and out. Angry, he punched the radio, and suddenly, the rock music was gone. In its place was a preacher's voice—my voice—broadcasting a message about God's love and salvation through Turning Point.

Startled, Red pulled over and listened. That day, God reached his heart, and he was gloriously saved. He told me how his life had changed since then, hugged me, and thanked me for being there at that pivotal moment.

Red was just moments away from eternity. God, in His mercy, intervened. But Red's story is rare. Most people don't get a last-minute chance to change their trajectory. They quietly slip into eternity, holding on to whatever they trusted in life.

I hope you're not gambling with your future. If you are, the decision you make today will determine where you spend eternity.

CHAPTER 22

ARE THEY WATCHING US?

During a CNN presidential town hall in 2023, former New Jersey governor Chris Christie was asked about his Italian background. He replied, "As far as being the first Italian American president, let me guarantee this. The food in the White House will be better. Guaranteed. The food will be better, for sure." That drew some applause.

Then Christie added, "And secondly, I have to say this because I know my mother is watching from heaven and she was a Sicilian American. She would make sure that I corrected the Italian American thing. Sicilians are very sensitive about that. And I'll tell you the greatest two lessons my mother taught me. First, she said, you can be anything you want to be if you're willing to work hard enough. She drilled that into my head every day, and I wouldn't be standing on the stage if I didn't believe that. And second, she said to me, Christopher, be yourself, because then tomorrow you don't have to try to remember who you pretended to be yesterday."[1]

Again the humor was nice, but the part of the exchange that drew my interest was Christie's assumption his mother was watching the debate from heaven. Do our loved ones who go to heaven watch from the grandstands, as it were, as we go about our lives? Do they see all or part of our successes and failures? Perhaps the telecommunications lines are turned on at certain times so they can see poignant moments in our lives, like graduations or weddings or additions to our families. What do you think?

Hank Hanegraaff says this is one of the most frequent questions he gets on his *Bible Answer Man* broadcast. "People seem desperate to know whether or not loved ones in paradise know what is happening on earth at the present."[2]

Some people would say, "Yes, at least to some extent." Those who think this way typically reference the martyrs in heaven who cry out to God, asking how long until those who persecuted them are judged (Revelation 6). If those martyrs were aware that their tormentors were still prospering—the thinking goes—then people in heaven must be aware of what's happening on earth.

In my opinion, though, there is some trouble with that line of thinking. After all, Revelation 6 takes place during the Tribulation period, after the rapture of the church, and it simply tells us the martyrs who were killed in the Tribulation are eager for God's judgment to dispense with evil and evildoers on the earth. There is not a definitive indication that the martyrs (or any other person in heaven) have specific knowledge of what happens on earth.

To be honest, I cannot find any passage in the Bible that clearly teaches that those in heaven are watching us or keeping track of what's unfolding in our daily lives.

And beware! There is not a single passage of Scripture that tells us we can or should try to contact someone who has passed away. Even if they can see us (which I doubt), we cannot see them or interact with them. Attempting to do so takes us into the dark world of the occult, somewhere we don't want to be.

With those caveats firmly established, let's see what Scripture teaches about this emotionally weighty question.

THE VIEW FROM HEBREWS

Some of the confusion on this issue arises from a misinterpretation of Hebrews 12:1–2. Those verses say, "Therefore we also, since we are surrounded by so great a cloud of witnesses, let us lay aside every weight, and the sin which so easily ensnares us, and let us run with endurance the race that is set before us, looking unto Jesus."

"There," say some. "We have a great cloud of people in the heavens watching like spectators in the bleachers while we run our earthly race."

But wait! Notice the first word of the passage—*Therefore*. That points back to the Old Testament heroes of the faith, which the writer lists as examples for us to follow. In the previous chapter, he wrote about Abel, Enoch, Noah, Abraham, Isaac, Jacob, Joseph, Moses, and others, who had successfully lived by faith. Then he said, "Therefore, since we have so many witnesses—so many examples to inspire us—let us run the race."

The word *witness* could refer to someone who is seeing, witnessing, and watching in real time. But in this case I believe it refers to those who are speaking to us through the testimony of their lives, whose examples inspire us. There are *seeing* witnesses and *speaking* witnesses. The *seeing* witnesses observe things in real time ("we are witnessing an earthquake right now"). The *speaking* witnesses tell us of things they have experienced ("he is bearing witness about the moment Christ saved him").

John MacArthur said this about the passage in Hebrews and the biblical heroes listed: "They are active witnesses who speak to us by their example; not passive witnesses who watch us with their eyes."[3]

David Allen, in his commentary on Hebrews, wrote,

189

The identification of these heroes of faith as "witnesses" has been interpreted in two ways. Perhaps besides these heroes being faithful witnesses in the past, now they are witnessing from heaven the lives of present believers. The overall context, however, favors the meaning to be that their lives have borne witness to their faith. The author's focus is on the importance of current believers learning from those who have gone before, not on those who have gone before watching current believers. As Moffatt puts it, "It is what we see in them, not what they see in us, that is the writer's main point."[4]

Another commentator put it similarly: "We are watching them for encouragement rather than them watching us in examination."[5]

My own view is that when we get to heaven, we'll have so much to learn, to discover, and to think about that we'll not want to be distracted by the stresses and heartbreaks of earth. I don't really want my father and mother watching everything I do on earth. It's not because I'm doing things that are wrong. It's just that life on earth is hard. I know they'd be distressed at some the of things I've had to endure, including illnesses and attacks. I prefer to think of them simply enjoying their reunion with each other and with the Lord. I'll have plenty of time to catch them up on my life when I'm with them throughout eternity.

THE VIEW FROM HADES

Another passage that's sometimes used to suggest people in heaven can see what's happening on earth is the story of Lazarus and the rich man in Luke 16. As we discussed in the previous chapter, both men died and Lazarus, the beggar, was carried to heaven and comforted by Abraham, while the rich man went to hades. Luke 16:23 says, "In Hades, where he was in torment, he looked up and saw Abraham far away, with Lazarus by his side" (NIV). The man called to Abraham, begging him to send Lazarus with a drop of water on his finger to "cool my tongue, because I am in agony in this fire" (verse 24 NIV).

Abraham said, "Son, remember that in your lifetime you received your good things, while Lazarus received bad things, but now he is comforted here and you are in agony. And besides all this, between us and you a great chasm has been set in place, so that those who want to go from here to you cannot, nor can anyone cross over from there to us" (verses 25–26 NIV).

Then the rich man begged Abraham to send Lazarus back to earth as a resurrected man to witness to his five brothers so they might avoid hades. But Abraham said, "If they do not listen to Moses and the Prophets, they will not be convinced even if someone rises from the dead" (verse 31 NIV).

Some people suggest the rich man was aware of what was happening on earth, for he was concerned about his brothers. But the rich man's plea wasn't based on immediate knowledge of his brothers at that moment; it was based on how he had last seen them. In heaven and in hades, we will have awareness of our past earthly life. Abraham said, "Son, remember that in your lifetime . . ." There is nothing in that passage to suggest that either the rich man or Lazarus had current knowledge of specific events regarding people on earth.

Those are the views from Hebrews and from hades. Now, let's talk about the view from heaven.

THE VIEW FROM HEAVEN

There *are* eyes watching you from heaven. But I don't think they belong to our loved ones. The Bible teaches that angels are aware of what's happening on earth. Those supernatural beings watch over us, and we are glad for it!

But most of all, the eyes of the Lord are on you and me. The Bible says, "For the eyes of the LORD run to and fro throughout the whole earth, to show Himself strong on behalf of those whose heart is loyal to Him" (2 Chronicles 16:9). Proverbs 15:3 says, "The eyes of the LORD are in every place, keeping watch on the evil and the good." Peter wrote, "For the eyes of the LORD are on the righteous, and His ears are open to their prayers" (1 Peter 3:12). Hebrews 4:13 says, "And there is no creature hidden from His sight, but all things are naked and open to the eyes of Him to whom we must give account."

This is worth pondering. If God is constantly watching you and watching over you, don't you think it should affect where you go, what you do, and how you live? What comfort that should give us! The Lord sees our every tear and trial, and He stoops down to help us.

When Hagar languished in the desert, fearful for her son and herself, the Lord came to her aid. In response, she gave a special name to the Lord: "You are the God who sees me." She exclaimed, "I have now seen the One who sees me" (Genesis 16:13 NIV). Hagar gave the Lord a name we cherish to this day: El-Roi, the God Who Sees.

When Violet Liddle was a little girl growing up in Cambridge, England, she would come down the stairs every morning and see that Scripture verse hanging on the wall. It was the quotation from Hagar from the King James Version: "Thou God Seest Me."

She later wrote, "For the first years of my life, my understanding of God was that he watched me continually, and knew as soon as I did anything wrong. . . . Still, I don't really regret this introduction to God because it did instill in me an understanding that God is always around us, and I'm glad that over the years I've come to recognise that the verse is a promise of God's loving care."[6]

Violet became a housemaid who brought her witness of Jesus Christ into the homes of her clients—like George Bernard Shaw and Winston Churchill, whom she served at 10 Downing Street. She excelled in all she did because she was conscious of God's constant watchfulness.

Do you ever sense eyes watching you from above?

Perhaps our modern technology has made this a little easier for us to comprehend. *The New York Times* recently carried an article under the headline, "When Eyes in the Sky Start Looking at You." The writer described the surveillance satellites circling the earth, and he wrote, "Soon satellites will be able to watch you everywhere all the time."[7]

Much of the information about the newest satellites is classified, but Christopher Scolese, director of the U.S. National Reconnaissance Office, said, "You can't hide because you're constantly being looked at."[8] *The New Atlantis* also ran an article about this, saying, "Anytime you walk outside, satellites may be watching you from space."[9]

When you look upward, especially into the night sky, you can be sure some of those twinkling lights are satellites with their cameras trained on you. But if that thought bothers you, remember that far above the starry skies the gracious eyes of God are watching over you, aware of your problems, answering your prayers, and guiding your footsteps.

So, do our loved ones watch us from heaven? I can't find a verse in the Bible that teaches they can. This doesn't mean they are totally ignorant of what's happening here. Every day the population of heaven increases as more and more Christians leave this world behind and arrive in Glory. Perhaps these arriving souls bring good news about us to our loved ones. And perhaps sometimes the Lord Jesus Himself passes along some information—"Did you just hear the angels singing over there? That's because your son has led another person to faith in Christ."

I cannot be dogmatic about these things, but let me end this chapter with something my friend Erwin Lutzer said when asked the same question addressed here. His response was, "There is no evidence that those in heaven can actually see us on earth, though that might be possible. It is more likely that they can ask for regular updates on how we are doing. I cannot imagine that such a request would be denied."[10]

The Bible doesn't answer every question about heaven. Rather than speculate about its glorious mysteries, let's rejoice in what God *does* say to us.

For He is the God who sees us!

CHAPTER 23

WILL WE REMEMBER?

Harrison Ford should stick to cars, don't you think? He gained his pilot's license when he was fifty-three, but crashed in his helicopter in 1999, overshot a runway in 2000, and landed in the wrong place at John Wayne Airport in 2017, nearly colliding with an American Airlines jet. In 2020, he had another near miss at another Los Angeles airport when he mistakenly crossed an active runway.

Ford's most serious crash occurred in 2015. He took off from Santa Monica airport in a vintage World War II–era fighter aircraft. Just as he gained altitude, the engine sputtered and died. The actor crashed onto a golf course, suffering broken bones and a head injury that left him with retrograde amnesia. He later said he remembered the engine stalling and his call to the control tower. After that he has no memory of anything that happened. Five full days are blanked out of his mind.

Ironically, Ford once played an amnesia victim in the movie *Regarding Henry*. When reminded of that, Ford dryly said about his accident, "This was not a movie."[1]

Some people wonder whether we'll experience some kind of

retrograde amnesia when we get to heaven. Will we remember who we were and what we did on earth? Will we remember the sins we committed, the harms we inflicted, and the embarrassments we endured? Will we remember our loved ones? What about those who are absent from the joys of heaven?

These are excellent questions. We've already touched on the question of whether we will recognize one another in heaven—with the answer being yes. In a similar way, I also believe we'll remember our lives on earth even after we begin our new lives in heaven.

Some people use Isaiah 65:17 to suggest our memories will be wiped clean in heaven. That verse says, "For behold, I create new heavens and a new earth; and the former shall not be remembered or come to mind." At first glance, that seems to say that we'll enjoy the new heavens and earth without any recollection of the old earth. We'll have a sort of amnesia about our past lives.

But Isaiah is talking here about the coming Golden Age—the thousand-year reign of Christ, which is the doorway, as it were, into the new heavens and new earth. He links the Millennium to the eternal state. Look at the extended passage from the New International Version:

> "See, I will create
> new heavens and a new earth.
> The former things will not be remembered,
> nor will they come to mind. . . .
> I will rejoice over Jerusalem
> and take delight in my people;
> the sound of weeping and of crying
> will be heard in it no more.
> Never again will there be in it
> an infant who lives but a few days,
> or an old man who does not live out his years;
> the one who dies at a hundred

will be thought a mere child;

the one who fails to reach a hundred

will be considered accursed." (verses 17, 19–20)

During the time Isaiah describes, death will still occur. Lifespans during the Millennium will be much longer, as I wrote about in my book *The Coming Golden Age*. Isaiah spoke of those who die at age one hundred as having an early death, a tragedy, because most people during this era will live much longer.

Isaiah uses the phrase "new heavens and a new earth" in verse 17 because the Millennium is the period that transitions us from earth into eternity. It anticipates heaven. But what he is specifically describing is the thousand-year reign of Christ.

Now, let's go a step further. Regardless of the time period Isaiah has in mind, he is using hyperbole. He is overstating for the sake of emphasis. The apostle Paul did the same thing when he wrote, "Brethren, I do not count myself to have apprehended; but one thing I do, forgetting those things which are behind and reaching forward to those things which are ahead, I press toward the goal for the prize of the upward call of God in Christ Jesus" (Philippians 3:13–14). Paul didn't literally forget his past; he simply discounted its impact on his future. He was looking ahead, not behind.

Even today you'll hear similar phrases. Have you ever tried to repay a favor to someone, but they replied, "Forget about it!"? Have you ever told someone who had a bad dream to "put it out of your mind"? Or has anyone ever said to you, "Forget I mentioned it"?

That's the way Isaiah was talking. In the future, we'll not literally forget the past, but our new state of mind—the amazing awareness and insight we gain upon entering the gates of New Jerusalem—will put everything into its proper perspective.

I believe we'll have better minds, better memories, and better maturity in heaven than we do now. We'll lose none of our faculties, but our new and increased knowledge will make sense of everything.

WE WILL HAVE BETTER MINDS

Erwin Lutzer wrote, "One minute after we die, our minds will be clearer than ever before. . . . Death does not change what we know; our personalities will just go on with the same information we have stored in our minds today."[2]

I would go even further. When our bodies are glorified at the resurrection, our brains are included in the glorification process. The things that cloud our thoughts and hinder our minds will be gone.

In the world today, we're prescribed life-saving drugs, but some of those can alter important brain functions. Some can lead to addictions that harm the brain. We'll be free from those in heaven.

Some people have cognitive difficulties because of accidents or illnesses. I live in a military city, and I have active servicemen and women in my church. I've talked with many of them about TBIs—traumatic brain injuries—sustained in the line of duty. Athletes can suffer similar injuries. Those will be gone in heaven!

Fatigue and chronic stress can cloud our brains, but in heaven we'll never grow weary or stressed. Strokes and infections can harm our cognitive processes, and so can degenerative diseases, such as Alzheimer's and Parkinson's. But not in heaven—because there our bodies and our minds will be completely renewed.

Some people are born with intellectual challenges, but in heaven they'll be whole.

Sin can also taint our minds, and Satan can tempt us with his lies. But he will never be seen in the new heavens, the new earth, or the city of New Jerusalem.

Jesus told us to love the Lord with all our minds (Luke 10:27). We'll be able to do that better in heaven than now on earth. God is very concerned about our minds. It's a frequent subject in Paul's epistles. He told us to have the mind of Christ; to be spiritually minded; to be renewed in the spirit of our mind; and to set our minds on things above (Philippians 2:5; Romans 8:6; Ephesians 4:23; Colossians 3:2).

We'll be able to do all that more completely and more fully when we really *are* above!

WE WILL HAVE RICHER MEMORIES

Having a glorified brain in a glorified body also means we'll have better memories. I once heard of a man who said, "I have a photographic memory; I just forgot to load the film." How often we all feel that way!

Most of us have forgotten a lot of our life experiences. How many of us could name all our schoolteachers and classmates or recall what we were doing thirty years ago? We remember events that deeply inscribe themselves on our brains, but our minds aren't designed to recall all the specifics of daily life.

A few individuals can. They have HSAM—highly superior autobiographical memory. They can remember what happened on practically every day of their lives since childhood. There are reportedly less than one hundred people currently alive with this condition. I can't speculate as to whether we'll all have enhanced memories like that in heaven, but if our minds are glorified, our memory capacities will be heightened. I think we'll find it much easier to memorize long passages of Scripture, for example, not to mention be much better at matching names with faces.

But what about memories of our former lives on earth? Perhaps we'll have total recall of everything that happened to us, but I'm not concerned about it. I do believe we'll remember those important occasions that shaped our lives.

Returning to the story of the rich man and Lazarus in Luke 16, Abraham told the rich man who was suffering in hades, "Son, remember that in your lifetime you received your good things, and likewise Lazarus evil things" (verse 25). This indicates people in hell can remember their lives on earth. It's sensible to believe those in heaven can do the same. The martyrs in Revelation 6:10 remembered they had been murdered for their faith on earth, and they were eagerly waiting for God to avenge them.

Revelation 15:3 talks about the heavenly population singing the song of Moses and of the Lamb. That seems to imply we'll remember the songs Moses wrote on earth, such as Psalm 90.

As we saw in an earlier chapter, Jesus will reward His followers at the *Bema* Judgment for faithful service on earth. It would be strange if we didn't remember what we're being rewarded for.

One writer said, "Memory is a basic element of personality. If we are truly ourselves in Heaven, there must be continuity of memory from Earth to Heaven. We will not be different people, but the same people marvelously relocated and transformed. Heaven cleanses us but does not revise or extinguish our origins or history. Undoubtedly we will remember God's works of grace in our lives that have comforted, assured, sustained, and empowered us to live for him."[3]

WE WILL HAVE GREATER MATURITY

All of that brings us to the crux of the matter. If we can remember what happened on earth, including the tragedies and heartaches, won't that diminish our joy? An even more poignant question is this: How can we be happy in heaven if we remember loved ones who aren't there—who are in hell?

Revelation 21:4 says of our entrance into heaven, "And God will wipe away every tear from their eyes; there shall be no more death, nor sorrow, nor crying. There shall be no more pain, for the former things have passed away." How can we be happy when some whom we loved are not with us?

Perhaps that's the greatest mystery we'll consider in this entire book. I do not know exactly how God will give us unbroken joy under these conditions. He is a God of infinite grace, and He does all things well (Mark 7:37). The Bible says that now "we see in a mirror, dimly" (1 Corinthians 13:12). The Lord has told us, "For My thoughts are not your thoughts, nor are your ways My ways. . . . For as the heavens are higher than the earth, so are My ways higher than your ways, and My thoughts than your thoughts" (Isaiah 55:8–9).

Jesus said, "What I am doing you do not understand now, but you will know after this" (John 13:7). Our Christian experience is based on faith, which includes a choice to trust God's integrity when we don't have all the answers.

Somehow God will give us a maturity beyond anything we can imagine. Though we will not be all-knowing like our almighty Lord, we will have enhanced minds, improved memories, and unparalleled maturity. We'll understand better. Until then, we walk by faith, and we trust God with unanswered questions.

We also need to do all we can to win the lost to Christ. The issue of heaven or hell is one of the zeal-producers for our witness and Christian work. You never know when the Lord will use you to change someone's eternal destination.

That was what motivated ninety-two-year-old Pauline Jacobi. She had finished her grocery shopping at a Walmart in Dyersburg, Tennessee, and had just gotten into her vehicle to drive home. Just then a man opened the passenger's side door, jumped in, and told her he had a gun. He said he would shoot her if she didn't give him money.

"I'm not going to give you my money," Pauline told him. In fact, she told him *no* three times, and then she said, "If you kill me I'll end up in Heaven and you'll end up in Hell. Jesus is in this car and He goes with me everywhere I go."

The man looked away from her and tears formed in his eyes. Pauline spent ten minutes explaining the gospel to him, and she led him in prayer asking for forgiveness. He received Jesus into his life. Then Pauline voluntarily gave him ten dollars and said, "Now, don't you go spending it on anything wicked!" He agreed, kissed her on the cheek, and left the car.[4]

We need to be equally bold, don't we?

Somehow I think Pauline Jacobi and her would-be robber will recall that moment when they're both in heaven and praise God for His infinite grace! In heaven, their minds will be clear, their memories full, and their hearts mature in ways we can't yet imagine. That's what we know. And we can fully trust our Lord with all the rest.

CHAPTER 24

WHAT ABOUT THE CHILDREN?

On the morning of November 10, 2013, a youth pastor named Cameron Cole stumbled into what he later called "the most magical conversation of my life." A lost LEGO propelled Cameron and his three-year-old son Cam into a discussion that changed both of their lives forever.

During that conversation, little Cam—a bright-eyed, curly-haired boy—told his father to "get in the car" so they could go see Jesus. His father explained they wouldn't see Jesus until they were in heaven. Naturally, the little guy started asking questions about heaven. The conversation ended with Cam professing his faith in Christ with childlike simplicity.

That night, Cam mysteriously died. No medical reason was apparent for his death. The doctors listed it as Sudden Unexplained Death in Childhood (SUDC). For Cam's parents, Cameron and Lauren, this was the start of a journey into their worst nightmare—their "descent into a dark, sad valley."

Cameron later wrote in his book *Heavenward,* "Amidst the sorrow and grief of my child's death, something radically new happened in my daily mindset. Heaven became an almost present part of my perspective. This transformation made sense: this is where my firstborn child now lived.

"As the sorrow of grief subsided," he continued, "*heavenwardness* provided richer fellowship with Jesus. I had more perspective and hope. I had more comfort and more patience. . . . Though I was suffering deeply from the loss of my son, God was blessing my inner life in a unique way."[1]

One of the most frequent questions I receive about heaven is also one of the hardest: What happens to children who pass away? It's not a new issue. Both the nation of Israel in the Old Testament and the Gospels in the New Testament open on that particular note. The story of the exodus begins when Pharaoh orders the deaths of all the baby boys among the Hebrew slaves in Egypt. The Gospel of Matthew begins with King Herod sending his soldiers to kill the baby boys in Bethlehem in an attempt to destroy the little one whom the Magi called the King of the Jews.

The death of children has been one of the world's greatest sorrows throughout history, both biblical and secular, and in the personal histories of millions—including many reading these words. Some have lost children through illnesses or tragic accidents. Others have grieved miscarriages or stillbirths. Untold millions of preborn children have been lost through abortion. Some children have been slain in wars or horrendous acts of violence.

As a lifelong pastor, I've stood beside small caskets trying to comfort others when my own heart was broken over the scene before me. But I praise the Lord because, through the tears, there's a sunbeam of hope. Scripture gives us reasons to trust that infants and young children are not lost forever. Instead, they are given the gift of bypassing the sorrows of this world and are instantly transported to heaven where we'll meet them and enjoy their fellowship throughout eternity.

So what exactly does Scripture say about this incredible hope? Here are several biblical truths that assure us young children who die are welcomed into heaven.

THE COMPASSION OF JESUS

Let me begin with this clear reality: The Lord loves children, and He loves babies. He loves the preborn, and He loves the newborn. He loves the infant, and He loves the toddler. The words *child* and *children* occur ninety times in the Gospels, highlighting God's love for them. Even in the womb, God knows and loves the unborn baby.

In Psalm 139, David wrote, "For You formed my inward parts; you covered me in my mother's womb. I will praise You, for I am fearfully and wonderfully made. . . . Your eyes saw my substance, being yet unformed. And in Your book they all were written, the days fashioned for me, when as yet there were none of them. How precious also are Your thoughts toward me, O God! How great is the sum of them!" (verses 13–14, 16–17).

In Matthew 19, parents brought their children to Jesus so that He could pray for them and lay hands on them. When the disciples tried to turn them away, Jesus said, "Let the little children come to Me, and do not forbid them; for of such is the kingdom of heaven" (verse 14). Jesus made it clear: Children belong to Him.

Jesus was the kind of person children loved to be around and parents trusted. He was gentle, approachable, and full of love. If Jesus welcomed children so eagerly on earth, why would He not welcome them into heaven as well?

Theologian Robert Lightner wrote, "Throughout His earthly ministry, Jesus gave an extra measure of tender attention to children. He claimed for them a place in His kingdom. He even chose children to illustrate the fundamental character of those who would enter the kingdom of God."[2]

THE CHARACTER OF THE FATHER

Second, God isn't willing for children to be lost.

When Jesus told His parable of the lost sheep, He said: "If a man has a hundred sheep, and one of them goes astray, does he not leave the ninety-nine and go to the mountains to seek the one that is straying? And if he should find it, assuredly, I say to you, he rejoices more over that sheep than over the ninety-nine that did not go astray. Even so it is not the will of your Father who is in heaven that one of these little ones should perish" (Matthew 18:12–14).

In these verses Jesus revealed the Father's heart for children. He is like a shepherd who refuses to let even one be lost. His will is that no child should be forgotten or perish.

The character of God radiates committed love for children. The Bible has a lot to say about hell and the tragedy of being separated from God eternally for those who reject Christ's offer of salvation. But there is no passage in Scripture that indicates in the slightest that children will be there.

Lightner wrote, "In all of the Bible references to infants and young children, not once is there so much as a hint that they will ever be eternally lost and separated from God if they die before they have had an opportunity to respond to the gospel."[3]

Bible scholars often refer to an "age of accountability" at which young people become mature enough to rightly consider the gospel (Deuteronomy 1:39; Isaiah 7:16). After they become capable of making their own moral decisions, these young people carry the same responsibility to receive God's free gift of salvation as everyone else. But prior to the age of accountability—an age that varies depending on how quickly a child matures—young children are not condemned for their sin because they are unable to fully understand the reality of their sinfulness.

Mark Hitchcock put it this way,

At some point, every person who grows to maturity, except those with serious mental challenges, reaches a point of personal, moral accountability before God to either accept or reject the gospel of Jesus Christ. . . . If a child dies before reaching this age of accountability, or if due to mental challenges a person never reaches this point, the Lord applies the saving benefits of Christ's redeeming work to that person at the moment of death and brings that soul immediately into His presence in heaven. . . . This saving grace of God would also embrace pre-born children—those whose lives are terminated by miscarriage or abortion.[4]

THE CONDITION OF DEATH

There's another observation we can make based on the story of a twelve-year-old child mentioned in the Gospels—the daughter of Jairus. The girl had died and her family and friends were inconsolable. Jesus visited the home and heard mourners wailing loudly. He told them, "Do not weep; she is not dead, but sleeping" (Luke 8:52).

They jeered Him, but He took the parents to the room where the girl's body was residing, took her hand, and said, "Little girl, arise." Her spirit returned, she arose at once, and Jesus told them to give her something to eat (8:49–56).

Those words of Jesus—"She is not dead, but sleeping"—were not just spoken to Jairus. They are for every mom or dad or grandparent who has ever lost a little one. The miscarried child, the stillborn baby, the aborted infant, the child who died of SIDS or perished in a car accident or in a natural disaster—they are not dead but sleeping.

This is biblical terminology. When we die in Christ, our spirits go at once to be with the Lord, and our bodies fall asleep until awakened and glorified at the rapture. The daughter of Jairus is a prototype of every child who dies, who falls asleep in Jesus, and whom the Lord will raise up with resurrection glory.

Pastor Richard Hipps and his wife, Patricia, faced the serious illness and death of their little girl, Alex. Their dear friend John H. Hewett walked through this sorrow with them, and he later applied the words of Jesus a bit differently, but meaningfully: "I live in the confidence that, shortly after 5:00 that winter morning, Alex heard the Jesus she had already spied in her hospital room say . . . 'Little girl, arise.' . . . What a welcome that must have been, heavenly host flocking to greet a new saint of God with a white robe and great laughter."[5]

THE CONFIDENCE OF DAVID

There's one final scripture that strongly bears on what happens to little children when they die. In the Old Testament, King David had an illicit affair with a beautiful woman named Bathsheba and even arranged her husband's death. Bathsheba gave birth to a son—David's child—but the baby was terribly sick. David pleaded in prayer for the boy's life, fasting and weeping. For an entire week, David couldn't function, so great was his anxiety for the child. But when the boy passed away, David washed and changed his clothes and ate the food his servants prepared for him.

"We don't understand you," said his advisers. "While the child was still living, you wept and refused to eat. But now that the child is dead, you have stopped your mourning and are eating again."

David responded, "I fasted and wept while the child was alive, for I said, 'Perhaps the LORD will be gracious to me and let the child live.' But why should I fast when he is dead? Can I bring him back again? I will go to him one day, but he cannot return to me" (2 Samuel 12:21–23 NLT).

David knew his separation from his child was temporary. Though the boy wasn't going to return to this temporal life on earth, David was certain of seeing him again and being with him forever. After all, this is the same man who wrote in Psalm 23, "Surely goodness and mercy shall follow me all the days of my life; and I will dwell in the house of the LORD forever" (verse 6).

Our few moments on earth are nothing compared to our eternal fellowship with those we love on the new earth. Our lifespan is like the pop of a flashbulb compared to eternity. David clearly found his hope, comfort, and cheer in the assurance that his baby had gone to heaven and that they would soon be reunited.

Cameron Cole, whom we met at the beginning of the chapter, said this regarding his son's passing: "I have often thought that Cam and I are both hugging the same massive oak tree. He stands on one side and I the other. The girth of the tree is so immense that we cannot see each other. Nevertheless, we grip the oak tree with the same joy, affection, and pleasure. In reality, the oak tree is Jesus.

"As I miss him and yearn to be with him, my heart and mind naturally turn upward. My son's life in glory put my heart and mind on a heavenly swivel."[6]

If you've lost a little one, let your heart and mind turn upward. Put your head on a heavenly swivel and let the soon-approaching joys of your coming reunion lift your mind to Jesus, who never saw a child He didn't love enough to die for.

They are all safe and happy in His heavenly home. Hallelujah!

CHAPTER 25

IS THERE HOPE
AFTER SUICIDE?

It was an off-duty moment for Officer Christian Campoverde of the New York Police Department. But when he saw an opportunity to save a life, he took it without hesitation.

Campoverde was doing a little Christmas shopping at the Queens Center Mall when he observed a fellow patron who seemed to be having a mental-health episode. The man was mumbling to himself and acting erratically. Stepping closer, Officer Campoverde realized the man was talking about killing himself.

When the man abruptly left the area, the officer followed him to a balcony high up in the mall complex. A dangerous height, and an even more dangerous drop. The man had one leg over the balcony before Officer Campoverde walked up and engaged him in conversation. Having recently completed the NYPD's Crisis Intervention training, he knew this was a serious situation.

What saved the day? Filled with compassion, the officer asked the man, "Is it OK if I give you a hug?"

Thankfully, wonderfully, the man said yes. Then, after accepting the embrace, he allowed Officer Campoverde to take him away from the balcony and stay with him until more official help arrived.

For his part, the officer was glad to be in a position to make a difference, saying, "I just saw somebody who needed help."[1]

I'm sure you've noticed there are many people today who find themselves in a similar situation—dealing with thoughts of suicide and needing help. According to 2023 statistics, more than 12.8 million Americans contemplated suicide during the previous year; that's more than 5 percent of the adult population. Alarmingly, the numbers are even higher for those between the ages of eighteen to twenty-five. More than 12 percent of young adults have seriously considered ending their lives.[2]

Maybe you recognize your own struggle within these numbers. If so, I want you to know that help is available. The good news of heaven isn't limited to some future moment out in eternity. Heaven is a reality for today. It offers hope and healing for today. So, if you are in any way dealing with suicidal thoughts, please find someone to talk with—today. Talk about your hopes for heaven and what you would like to be different here on earth.

But there's another element of this topic that is worth talking about. Actually, it's a question I receive often through the various channels of our ministry: Does committing suicide disqualify a person from going to heaven?

We can answer that question by looking to God's Word.

AN AFFIRMATION OF ETERNAL SECURITY

There are two things we can say for certain when it comes to suicide and eternal security for believers in Jesus. First, suicide is a sin. It is rebellion against God and an active rejection of His stated will. Meaning, it is morally wrong. Second, suicide does not disqualify a

Christian from entering heaven. It is not a "mortal sin," to use the vocabulary of the Catholic church.

Those two truths provide all the guiderails we need to discuss this difficult but important topic.

How do we know that suicide is a sin? Because of God's Word. Consider:

- "You shall not murder" (Exodus 20:13).
- "For the commandments, 'You shall not commit adultery,' 'You shall not murder,' 'You shall not steal,' 'You shall not bear false witness,' 'You shall not covet,' and if there is any other commandment, are all summed up in this saying, namely, 'You shall love your neighbor as yourself'" (Romans 13:9).
- "For this is the message that you heard from the beginning, that we should love one another, not as Cain who was of the wicked one and murdered his brother. And why did he murder him? Because his works were evil and his brother's righteous" (1 John 3:11–12).

Other than the limited exceptions of capital punishment and self-defense (including just war and soldiers in combat), the Bible consistently teaches that ending a human life is wrong. That includes your own life, which means suicide is a sinful action. Ending our own lives is wrong because it fails to recognize both the gift and responsibility given to each of us—a gift that is wrapped up in the preciousness of life.

Even so, Scripture is also clear that Jesus' death on the cross paid the penalty for all our sins. His blood washes us whiter than snow (Psalm 51:7). Therefore, anyone who has received God's grace through faith need not fear that a moral failure will disqualify them from eternal life. We are eternally secure.

As Jesus told us, "My sheep hear My voice, and I know them, and they follow Me. And I give them eternal life, and they shall never perish; neither shall anyone snatch them out of My hand" (John 10:27–28).

I want to pause here to make something clear, because I believe it to be important—especially given the statistics I mentioned earlier. While the act of suicide is undoubtedly sinful and does produce undesirable consequences (more on that to follow), the same is not true for suicidal thoughts. Or the desire to escape the difficulties of life. Or seasons of anxiety, depression, sadness, or grief.

For many, many people in the world today, life is filled with struggles. There are hardships and burdens. Sicknesses and betrayals. Losses and deprivations. As Jesus famously promised, "In this world you will have trouble" (John 16:33 NIV)—and trouble always takes its toll.

My point is this: There's nothing wrong with you if you don't feel happy all the time. You're not a bad person or an ineffective believer if each day of your life isn't brimming with sunshine and roses.

In fact, you're in good company. Consider David, who spent much of his life hunted by a king who wanted him dead. And then, even when he became king, David was forced to publicly confront the darkness inside his own heart. As a result, David often cried out to God with vivid descriptions that sound very much like depression.

For example:

> Have mercy on me, O LORD, for I am in trouble;
> My eye wastes away with grief,
> Yes, my soul and my body!
> For my life is spent with grief,
> And my years with sighing;
> My strength fails because of my iniquity,
> And my bones waste away. (Psalm 31:9–10)

Consider Jeremiah, who was forced to watch the destruction of

Jerusalem and the temple, and who then wrote this about God, among many other lamentations:

> He has hedged me in so that I cannot get out;
> He has made my chain heavy.
> Even when I cry and shout,
> He shuts out my prayer.
> He has blocked my ways with hewn stone;
> He has made my paths crooked. (Lamentations 3:7–9)

Consider Jesus, who was so overcome with grief at the thought of being separated from the Father that His sweat "became like great drops of blood falling down to the ground" (Luke 22:44).

So no, you don't have to repent for dealing with anguish, sorrow, fear, pain, or even doubt. All of that is part of life on this side of the grave—all of that and more. But that's the wonderful news of this book: There is more life on the other side of that grave than anything we could imagine! Heaven is real, and we will spend eternity there with Jesus.

AN ABANDONMENT OF EXPECTED STEWARDSHIP

Speaking of Jesus, let's go back to the question at the heart of this chapter: What happens to a Christian if they take their own life? From a doctrinal perspective, suicide is a sin; thankfully, there is no sin that can nullify the blood of Christ once it has been applied to our hearts.

But what about a personal perspective? What about that moment when we come face-to-face with our Lord and Savior, Jesus Christ? Matthew 25 records the words we yearn to hear in that moment: "Well done, good and faithful servant; you were faithful over a few things, I will make you ruler over many things. Enter into the joy of your lord" (verse 21).

I think about those words every day. I have no greater desire in my life right now than to hear those words spoken over me when I finally stand before my Lord and my King. I want to see Jesus look upon me with pride—and smile. I want to feel Him clasp my shoulders and clap me on the back. I want to hear Him declare, with gladness in His voice, "David, well done."

The question is, Will Jesus speak those words to one of His servants who intentionally steps away from that service by ending their life prematurely? When a person's last act here on earth is to reject their Master's calling to "Go, make disciples of all nations," can that person reasonably expect their Master to greet them in heaven with appreciation?

I don't know the answer to those questions. At the same time, I sure don't want to find out.

What's at stake here is stewardship. Every resource you and I possess has been given to us by God for us to invest in His kingdom—and to produce a return. We are called to sow our gifts, talents, and treasures in this life so that we can help reap a harvest for eternity. That's true of our financial resources, of course, but also much more.

You and I are called to be stewards of our physical bodies, for example. Paul told us, "Or do you not know that your body is the temple of the Holy Spirit who is in you, whom you have from God, and you are not your own? For you were bought at a price; therefore glorify God in your body and in your spirit, which are God's" (1 Corinthians 6:19–20).

We are called to be stewards of our time. Scripture says, "So teach us to number our days, that we may gain a heart of wisdom" (Psalm 90:12). And, "Walk in wisdom toward outsiders, making the best use of the time" (Colossians 4:5 ESV). And, "See then that you walk circumspectly, not as fools but as wise, redeeming the time, because the days are evil" (Ephesians 5:15–16).

Suicide is a loss of the time and life God has given us. God wants us to use each day wisely and trust Him, even when life feels overwhelming.

Beyond that, suicide is a rejection of our God-given purpose. Remember, the Creator of the universe handcrafted every single human being. He designed each person with a specific purpose in mind, and He did so long before humanity even came on the scene: "He chose us in Him before the foundation of the world, that we should be holy and without blame before Him in love, having predestined us to adoption as sons by Jesus Christ to Himself, according to the good pleasure of His will" (Ephesians 1:4–5).

That means each of us has been created for a special purpose. Each of us is created to fill a special role in God's grand narrative of life: "For we are His workmanship, created in Christ Jesus for good works, which God prepared beforehand that we should walk in them" (Ephesians 2:10).

In my mind, it would be a great dishonor for someone to enter the very throne room of that same Creator knowing they had spurned His purpose and scorned that work.

Pastor and theologian Erwin Lutzer sums up this discussion well:

> Believers are "sealed with the promised Holy Spirit, who is the guarantee of our inheritance until we acquire possession of it, to the praise of his glory" (Ephesians 1:13–14). A believer who commits suicide enters heaven on the coattails of failure and might deserve few rewards, for he/she has neglected the presence of the Spirit, the words of Christ, and the aid of the church which God has mercifully provided to every believer. However, all who have been justified by faith in Christ belong to Him, and He will take them to be with Him forever.[3]

In writing this chapter, it's not my goal to make anyone feel sorrowful about the choices of others, nor to make anyone feel shame over their own struggles. Instead, my goal is to teach what the Word of God says. Just as importantly, my goal in this chapter and throughout every chapter of this book is to encourage all believers to keep pressing forward toward the promise of heaven. Because truly, there is no greater reward possible for our faithful service to the King!

Jasmin Paris understands what it means to keep pressing forward. As an ultra-marathoner, she made it her goal to become the first woman in history to complete an infamous race known as the Barkley Marathons. (Yes, "marathons," plural.) Held in the ominously named Frozen Head State Park in Tennessee, the Barkley Marathons is a grueling combination of distance, elevation, and environmental obstacles. Competitors must run through the woods for more than one hundred miles covering sixty-five thousand feet of elevation—which is twice the height of Mount Everest. The race is divided into five laps, all of which must be completed within sixty total hours.

Since the race's inception in 1986, only twenty people have finished it.

Jasmin entered the race in 2022, but she wasn't able to finish the fourth lap, let alone start the fifth. The same thing happened in 2023. And it *seemed* like the same thing would happen in 2024. "That final kilometer was the first point, I think, where I actually started to doubt that I was going to make it," said Jasmin. "I did believe in myself until that point and then suddenly I was like, 'it's going to be really down to the wire.'"

And yet, despite being awake for more than two full days, despite being scratched by briars and bitten by bugs, despite reaching a level of physical and mental exhaustion inconceivable to most people—she pressed on. She kept going. And she finished the race with ninety-nine seconds to spare.[4]

That's my encouragement for anyone who feels overwhelmed and under-resourced for the race we call life: Don't give up. Never give up! If you need help, that's okay. Help is available, both professionally and spiritually. But keep going.

Remember the words and the example of Paul: "I have fought the good fight, I have finished the race, I have kept the faith. Finally, there is laid up for me the crown of righteousness, which the Lord, the righteous Judge, will give to me on that Day, and not to me only but also to all who have loved His appearing" (2 Timothy 4:7–8).

CHAPTER 26

CREMATION
OR BURIAL?

A friend of mine was traveling through Japan, encouraging missionaries and speaking to Christian groups. In one church, the pastor wanted to take him on a tour of their modest building, but because of the language barrier much of the tour involved pointing and gesturing. After a while, they came to a room with a panel in the ceiling that lowered to form a ladder. My friend carefully climbed into the attic. As his eyes adjusted to the dim light, he saw several shelves containing small boxes. The pastor waved toward them with a meaningful look on his face.

The understanding came to my friend at once: This was the church's cemetery. Each box contained the ashes of a member who had passed away. Because Japan has a large population on limited land, virtually everyone who dies is cremated.

It's common to drive through Europe and America and see old churches surrounded by gravestones. But did you ever visualize a church with the graveyard in the attic?

That brings up a subject that's increasingly discussed in America: cremation. But don't say that word in Disneyland! One of the most vexing problems at all the Disney parks involves large numbers of people sneaking a loved one through the main gates in the form of ashes. Lots of people want their ashes spread on the grounds of "The Happiest Place on Earth." When this happens, it triggers what park employees informally call "Code Grandma," which involves cleanup by HazMat teams and often results in shutting down rides or areas of the park for a period of time.[1]

In recent years, the discussion about burial or cremation has entered our Christian conversations. With the rising cost of funeral procedures, more people are choosing cremation, usually the less expensive option. I know this is on the minds of many because it is one of the most frequent questions that comes in the mail at Turning Point. This end-of-life issue is emotional, and it can create divisions in a family. In this chapter, I want to investigate these things and share in simple terms what the Bible says about burial, cremation, and resurrection.

BURIAL

The consistent pattern in both the Old and New Testaments is burial for those who pass away. Abraham went to lengths to purchase land containing a cave to serve as his family tomb (Genesis 23), and his loved ones were buried there. Joseph asked that his embalmed body be carried from Egypt to his homeland of Israel for burial (Genesis 49:29–33). Hebrews 11:22 says, "By faith Joseph, when he was dying . . . gave instructions concerning his bones."

A few more references: Moses died and God "buried him in a valley in the land of Moab" (Deuteronomy 34:6). Ruth told Naomi, "Where you die, I will die, and there will I be buried" (Ruth 1:17).

Death by burning is occasionally mentioned in the Old Testament as a punishment for sin. For example, Leviticus 20:14 says, "If a man marries a woman and her mother, it is wickedness. They shall be burned with fire, both he and they, that there may be no wickedness among you." In Leviticus 10, Aaron's sons violated the holy procedures of tabernacle worship. "So fire went out from the LORD and devoured them" (verse 2). Achan and his family were stoned to death for their sins and their bodies were cremated (Joshua 7:24–26).

But under ordinary circumstances burial was the way the Old Testament saints dealt with the remains of their loved ones. The historian Tacitus noted that one of the distinguishing characteristics of the Jews as compared to the Romans was that Jews "prefer to bury and not burn their dead."[2]

In the New Testament, too, bodies were buried with dignity. The greatest example involved the crucified remains of Jesus of Nazareth. Joseph of Arimathea boldly asked Pontius Pilate for the Lord's body; "he wrapped it in a clean linen cloth, and laid it in his new tomb which he had hewn out of the rock" (Matthew 27:58–60). As soon as the Sabbath ended, Mary Madgalene and some other women "bought spices, that they might come and anoint Him" (Mark 16:1).

When Stephen became the first Christian martyr by being stoned to death in Jerusalem, "devout men carried Stephen to his burial, and made great lamentation over him" (Acts 8:2).

When Dorcas died, her weeping friends "washed her, [and] they laid her in an upper room," preparing to bury her (Acts 9:37). In other words, the early Christians retained the Jewish respect for the dignity of the body as having been created by God, wishing the deceased person to be buried properly and with honor.

Influenced by these Old and New Testament customs, the first Christians after the apostolic era rejected the widespread practice of Roman cremation. This was sometimes a major affront to the Romans and sometimes even resulted in Christians being persecuted.[3]

We can see for ourselves in the catacombs of Rome that the followers of Christ practiced burying their dead. Early Christian preachers like Irenaeus and Tertullian rejected cremation.[4] Another early Christian leader, Minucius Felix, wrote, "We do not fear loss from cremation even though we adopt the ancient and better custom of burial."[5]

This may be why the Romans often burned Christians to death. Norman Geisler and Douglas Potter wrote, "The intense persecutions that many Christians faced involved the burning of bodies as a direct mocking of the Christian belief in the resurrection. This is because the Romans held the belief that burning human remains would make it impossible to be resurrected in the future."[6]

Albert Mohler leans into the fact that "virtually every Christian church of every tradition, whether in the east or in the west, whether Roman Catholic, Eastern Orthodox or Protestant, virtually all of those theological traditions insisted upon some form of burial and opposed cremation until very recently."[7]

CREMATION

What I've told you so far seems like a strong case for burial as opposed to cremation, yet something is missing from all those biblical and historical references. There is not a single Scripture verse that commands burial or condemns cremation. Every sin known to man is condemned in some way at some place in the Bible, and those warnings are vital for our morality and behavior. But nowhere does Scripture command us to practice burial or prohibit us from practicing cremation.

Notice the way the Word of God puts it in John 19:40: "Then they took the body of Jesus, and bound it in strips of linen with spices, as the custom of the Jews is to bury."

John called burial "the custom of the Jews," not "the law of the Lord."

The Bible says that "the LORD God formed man of the dust of the ground" (Genesis 2:7), and after Adam and Eve sinned, He told them, "For dust you are, and to dust you shall return" (Genesis 3:19). Psalm 103:14 says, "For He knows our frame; He remembers that we are dust." Ecclesiastes 3:20 says, "All go to one place: all are from the dust, and all return to dust." Given enough time, our physical bodies all disintegrate. Whether buried or cremated, we end up in the same state of dust and ashes.

Of course, not everyone is buried or sent to a crematorium. Please bear with me here. As awful as it is to contemplate, some people are devoured by sharks or lions; some are blown to pieces in an explosion; some die of exposure in a desert and gradually decompose in the blistering sunshine; some are incinerated in fires; and some drown and slowly decompose in the depths of the sea.

Maybe that's why God seems to have given us flexibility on this issue. Some cultures and settings, such as Japan, which I mentioned earlier, have a long history of cremation. In some cases, the financial cost or the wishes of the deceased or the family may influence this decision.

Some of our Christian beliefs are essential and we cannot compromise them—the existence of God, the resurrection of Christ, and so forth. In other areas, Christians can prayerfully follow the path of wisdom. Some people may have one custom, and some another.

The apostle Paul discussed this in Romans 14 when some of the believers disagreed about matters involving diet and holidays. His advice: "Let each be fully convinced in his own mind" (verse 5). He warned against arguing about things in which the Bible seems to allow various options. He told them, "Therefore let us stop passing judgment on one another. Instead, make up your mind not to put any stumbling block or obstacle in the way of a brother or sister. . . . . So whatever you believe about these things keep between yourself and God" (Romans 14:13, 22 NIV).

John MacArthur wrote, "Obviously any buried body will eventually decompose (Ecclesiastes 12:7). So cremation isn't a strange or wrong practice—it merely accelerates the natural process of oxidation.

The believer will one day receive a new body . . . thus the state of what remains of the old body is unimportant. . . . What we need to focus on as Christians is not how to dispose of our earthly bodies, but that one day new bodies will be fashioned for us like the Lord's glorious resurrection body. . . . That transformation will be eternal!"[8]

RESURRECTION

That brings us to the truly critical question: Can God track down and restore our DNA from the dust? Does He have sufficient power and authority to reclaim and reassemble our molecules at the resurrection? Can He keep track of us even when we're particles scattered by the wind, washed away by the water, and absorbed into nature?

Of that, I have no doubt! If He could create the universe *ex nihilo*— out of nothing—He can certainly recreate our bodies. The Bible says, "For in Him all things were created . . . and in Him all things hold together" (Colossians 1:16–17 NIV).

We have a sort of preview of this in Ezekiel's valley of dry bones. This vision actually concerns the rebirth of the nation of Israel, but it's told using a graphic analogy of the resurrection of the human body. Ezekiel saw a valley filled with lots of dry bones, and they were very dry (Ezekiel 37:2). Suddenly Ezekiel heard a rattling sound and the bones came together, bone to bone, each to the body with which it belonged. Then tendons and flesh appeared, and then skin covered them. Next, breath entered into them and they came to life and stood on their feet like a vast army (verses 1–10).

The Lord knows how to do that! He can reverse the processes of death and resurrect us into a very great army. Here is the way the apostle Paul put it:

For all creation is waiting eagerly for that future day when God will reveal who his children really are. . . . And we believers also groan, even though we have the Holy Spirit within us as a foretaste of future glory, for we long for our bodies to be released from sin and suffering. We, too, wait with eager hope for the day when God will give us our full rights as his adopted children, including the new bodies he has promised us. (Romans 8:19, 23 NLT)

Let me end this chapter by telling you about a man who was both buried *and* cremated! He was born sometime in the 1320s in a small town in England. His parents named him John Wycliffe. God gave him a good mind, and he excelled at Oxford University. When he felt God calling him to the priesthood, he eagerly embraced his profession. But John was disturbed by the state of the church. Nearly two hundred years before Martin Luther, he began preaching the gospel of grace.

Wycliffe faced continual pressure and persecution for his biblical views, but his courage and intellect—and the popularity of his preaching—kept him out of jail. He is among the very first to labor toward an English Bible translation. More than 250 full or partial Wycliffe Bible manuscripts are still in existence, and he paved the way for William Tyndale and others who determined, despite opposition from both clergy and government, to provide the Bible in the language of the people.

Wycliffe would likely have been martyred for his faith had he not suffered a stroke and died of natural causes. He was buried in the cemetery of Lutterworth Church. His influence and writings continued to live, however, causing the authorities to hate him more in death than they had in life. In 1428, they exhumed his remains, burned them to dust, and threw them into the little Swift River flowing through the town of Lutterworth. His enemies thought that was the end of him.

An early biographer gave us the rest of the story: "They burnt his bones to ashes and cast them into the Swift, a neighboring brook running hard by. Thus the brook hath conveyed his ashes into the Avon; Avon into Severn; Severn into the narrow seas; and they into the main ocean. And thus the ashes of Wycliffe are the emblem of his doctrine which now is dispersed the world over."[9]

We need not agonize over what happens to our bodies on this planet. Let's just ask God to use us while we *are* on earth. And when the glorious upward tug of God brings us into His presence, we'll rejoice with our new bodies—and maybe, at some point in Hallelujah Square we'll find John Wycliffe and thank him for his work in giving us a book that says in his Middle English . . .

Deth is sopun vp in victorie.
(1 Corinthians 15:54)
[Death is swallowed up in victory.]

CHAPTER 27

WILL THERE BE MARRIAGE IN HEAVEN?

During my years as a pastor, I've officiated lots of weddings. Since our church is in California, some have been outdoors. I like outdoor weddings, but weather is always a factor. *People* magazine reported on the recent nuptials of Mason and Ashley Sargent in Indian Hill, Ohio. Two hundred guests were enjoying the wedding dinner under open skies when a massive rainstorm suddenly broke over them.

"I had to make the quick decision to just embrace the rain," Ashley recalled. She impulsively kicked off her shoes and went running into the downpour like a delighted child. Her new husband quickly joined her. Then the groomsmen. Then everyone! People were dancing in puddles, lifting their faces to the raindrops, and sliding down the grassy bank like kids on a summer day.

Photographer Annie Tuckett, who captured it all with her camera, said, "They ran into the rain, shedding their shoes and their worries, choosing memories over perfection. . . . I felt the energy of pure, care-free joy all around me, and there were so many moments where I got teary just watching it all unfold. I kept thinking, 'I can't believe I get to witness this.'"

The bride later spoke of a lesson learned: "It has taught us from the beginning of our marriage that things will never be perfect, but it's how you respond to challenges and deal with hardship that makes our marriage our own version of perfect."[1]

I can't see myself sliding down a hill of rain-slickened grass at this stage in my life, but I can appreciate that spontaneous joy and exuber-ant response. And Ashley is right—on this earth things will never be perfect, so we have to respond as wisely as we can.

In heaven, it will be different!

But will there be any weddings in heaven? Will there be marriage? Jesus addressed this question when some critics tried to trap Him. They were a group of scholars from the Jewish sect of the Sadducees. These were the elite liberals of their day, scholars who did not believe in heaven, the afterlife, angels, or the immortality of the soul.

THE SADDUCEES' QUESTION

During the last week of our Lord's natural life, when He was debating different groups in the temple, the Sadducees challenged Him with a hypothetical puzzle:

Then some Sadducees, who say there is no resurrection, came to Him; and they asked Him, saying: "Teacher, Moses wrote to us that if a man's brother dies, and leaves his wife behind, and leaves no children, his brother should take his wife and raise up offspring for his brother. Now there were seven brothers. The first took a wife; and dying, he left no offspring. And the second took her, and he died; nor did he leave any offspring. And the third likewise. So the seven had her and left no offspring. Last of all the woman died also. Therefore, in the resurrection, when they rise, whose wife will she be? For all seven had her as wife." (Mark 12:18–23)

From the beginning of the passage, Mark clues us into the fact this group was asking a deceptive question, for they didn't actually believe there would ever be a moment when the dead are raised. Secure in their disbelief, they reached back into the Old Testament and found a Mosaic law regulating the maintenance of heirs in the families of Israel. In Deuteronomy 25, Moses wrote that if a young married man died without an heir, his brother was to marry the widow and produce an heir so his brother's inheritance could continue.

The Sadducees used this to craft a ridiculous question, which they didn't think the great Rabbi of Galilee could answer. But Jesus never faced an unsolvable question, for in Him are hidden all the treasures of wisdom and knowledge (Colossians 2:3).

OUR QUESTIONS

Before looking at our Lord's answer, let's take a moment to bring ourselves into the picture. We have some questions, too, don't we? Perhaps you've been married more than once. Perhaps you're a widow or a widower, and maybe the Lord has brought someone into your life. Do you sometimes ask yourself, *If I marry again, will I end up with two husbands (or two wives) in heaven? That sounds awkward.*

Perhaps you've remarried after a divorce. Or maybe you've hesitated to become remarried because you feel it would be a kind of betrayal of the husband or wife who is already waiting for you in heaven. "Will he (or she) be disappointed if I get married again? If the Lord brings someone into my life and it seems His will to marry again, will that upset my spouse in heaven?"

These are real questions. They come to our minds, but we hesitate to share our innermost concerns with others. I want to give you some biblical reassurance, but as long as I've plunged into this subject, I might as well include the next question lurking in our minds: Will there be sexual activity in heaven? Many people consider physical intimacy with their married partner one of life's greatest pleasures. And some wouldn't be as interested in going to heaven if they thought they would be sentenced to some kind of eternal celibacy.

I have some things to say about these things, but first let's listen to how Jesus answered the Sadducees. Right out of the gate, He turned the tables on them, saying, "Are you not therefore mistaken, because you do not know the Scriptures nor the power of God?" (Mark 12:24).

In other words, these Sadducees were underestimating God. They didn't grasp the wonders of His Word or the extent of His power. In a certain sense, we're apt to do the same. Our questions about marriage and sex in heaven are normal and natural ones. But we should also remember that no matter how greatly we love God and how keenly we think of heaven, we are still underestimating Him and His future plans for us.

Everything I write about heaven in this book or will ever preach on this subject is, by necessity, an understatement. I have neither the vision nor the vocabulary to do justice to God's eternal home for us. Deuteronomy 29:29 says, "The secret things belong to the LORD our God, but those things which are revealed belong to us and to our children forever."

God has revealed much to us, yet there is so much more. We are blessed to have a faith that nurtures a sense of mystery and wonder. We walk by faith, and our faith is in a God so high and holy, so massive and majestic, that we can never fully comprehend all the vastness of His person or His plans. Our minds are limited; our vision is constrained; our knowledge is hampered by our earthly limitations.

As you'll see, that's the thought that undergirds this chapter. Keep that in mind as we hear what Jesus said next: "For when they rise from the dead, they neither marry nor are given in marriage, but are like angels in heaven" (Mark 12:25).

Did Jesus really just say that?

Oh no! No marriage? I'm going to be single in heaven? No mention of sex? That's pretty disappointing . . .

Now you're doing what the Sadducees were doing—underestimating the Lord. We will be like the angels in that we will never die, the eternal population of eternity will be established, and procreation—one of the purposes of sex—will be unneeded. But don't assume you'll feel like an everlasting celibate, a single soul without love or pleasure. And don't undervalue God's ability to abundantly fulfill the promise of Psalm 16:11: "At Your right hand are pleasures forevermore."

Jesus was not telling us we will have poorer relationships and less pleasure in heaven—but more! Our lives will advance to a new stage. In Revelation 21:4–5 the Lord said, "The old order of things has passed away. . . . I am making everything new!" (NIV).

There will be a higher, holier, and happier order to the way life happens.

Commentator John Nolland wrote this about Jesus' words: "The core thought is that resurrection involves progress into a new mode of being that transcends present limitations."[2] Another scholar, Craig Blomberg, wrote, "In the life to come, all interpersonal relationships will no doubt far surpass the most intimate and pleasurable of human intercourse as we now know it."[3]

God has some wonderful surprises for us in heaven. You may not like surprises as a rule, but you'll like these! Our relationships will be deeper, our enjoyments richer, our recreation happier. If things are different in heaven, they will simply be raised to a new level of excellence.

Of all the comments I've read about this, C. S. Lewis, as usual, says it best:

I think our present outlook might be like that of a small boy who, on being told that the sexual act was the highest bodily pleasure should immediately ask whether you ate chocolates at the same time. On receiving the answer "No," he might regard absence of chocolates as the chief characteristic of sexuality. In vain would you tell him that the reason why lovers in their carnal raptures don't bother about chocolates is that they have something better to think of. The boy knows chocolate: he does not know the positive thing that excludes it. We are in the same position. We know the sexual life; we do not know, except in glimpses, the other thing which, in Heaven, will leave no room for it.[4]

Again, there is a lot of mystery to this. Jesus was a man during His earthly lifetime. In other words, He was of the male gender. Was He still a male after His resurrection? Certainly. So we can assume we will still retain our gender in heaven. When Jesus said we'd be like the angels, He did not mean we would be genderless. He simply meant we wouldn't need to be creating new people. There will be a different, but better, order to things.

Let's not create artificial disappointments in our mind by under-estimating the power of God and His Word and His eternal plan! There may be some mysteries I can't explain right now, but I can tell you God's ultimate explanations will be marvelous!

CHRIST'S QUESTION

By the way, Jesus wasn't at all finished with the Sadducees. What He said about marriage was almost an aside to the real point He wanted to make. He knew they didn't believe in the resurrection, eternal life, or heaven. So having dispensed with their hypothetical riddle, He turned the tables on them with a question of His own.

"Now about the dead rising—have you not read in the Book of

Moses, in the account of the burning bush, how God said to him, 'I am the God of Abraham, the God of Isaac, and the God of Jacob'? He is not the God of the dead, but of the living. You are badly mistaken!" (Mark 12:26–27 NIV).

The Sadducees rejected all the Old Testament books except the first five—the Torah: Genesis, Exodus, Leviticus, Numbers, and Deuteronomy. They claimed Moses said nothing in those books about resurrection or eternal life. So Jesus went right to the epicenter of Moses' life—the story of the burning bush—to confound them. You can read about this in Exodus 4. While herding sheep in the desert, Moses saw a bush aflame, but it kept burning on and on without being consumed. He drew closer, and the Lord spoke to him from the flames: "I am the God of your father, the God of Abraham, the God of Isaac and the God of Jacob" (Exodus 3:6 NIV).

I'm overwhelmed with the brilliance of Jesus Christ and His confidence in every syllable of the Word of God. Our Lord's entire argument here for the reality of eternal life is based on the tense of the verb used by God.

Abraham, Isaac, Jacob, and Moses' father were all dead. But the Lord did not say "I *was* the God" of those men. He said, in effect, "I *am* still, right now, the God of your father, and of Abraham, Isaac, and Jacob. They didn't cease to exist when they died. They are still alive, and I am still their God. I am not the God of the dead but of the living."

This is one of the reasons I have so much confidence in every syllable, every word, every sentence of the Bible. Jesus said, "For assuredly, I say to you, till heaven and earth pass away, one jot or one tittle will by no means pass from the law till all is fulfilled" (Matthew 5:18). Jots and tittles were small strokes of the pen associated with some of the letters of the Hebrew alphabet. You can trust God's Word, including this simple sentence: "I am the God of Abraham, Isaac, and Jacob."

At this very moment, the Lord has a living relationship with my parents, with your loved ones, and with all those who have already fallen asleep in Christ. It's not—He *was* their God. It's—He *is* their God.

If He is your God now, He will be your God the moment you slip from the shadowy slopes of earth into the glory of eternity. That's a great comfort to my wife, Donna, and me. We've been blessed with a long and happy marriage, and we've traveled the world together. We've devoted our lives to working side by side for the Lord. She is far closer to me than any other human being I've ever known, and we are seldom apart. God has blessed us with a wonderful family, and I can't imagine being without her, or her without me. I am hopeful the rapture will occur before either of us dies. But if not, a day is coming when we will be temporarily separated from the other.

That's why this chapter is so personal to me. As wonderful as our earthly union has been, what's ahead of us will be, as Paul said, "far better" (Philippians 1:23).

In heaven, I'll love Donna more perfectly and purely than I've ever been able to on earth. Our time will be more precious, and we won't have to worry about illness, hospitalizations, or misunderstandings. We'll love each other without stress or fatigue. Without worry or weariness. I will love her with a passion I never knew on earth, and by God's grace she will feel the same about me.

And together, we, along with you, will be the *bride of Christ*, loving and serving and enjoying Him, world without end!

CHAPTER 28

WILL THERE BE ANIMALS IN HEAVEN?

Like most of us, Melanie Epperson didn't enjoy the bustle and chaos of moving. A resident of New York near Buffalo, she'd arranged for her grandson to keep track of her little puppy, Snuggles, while she carried boxes and organized her new space. The dog was a light-brown Yorkshire terrier mix who was playful and cuddly and cute. A perfect companion for a new home.

Taking a moment to rest, Melanie looked over to make sure her grandson was settled—but she didn't see Snuggles. There was a moment of confusion, followed by a burst of panicked searching, followed by a sad-but-inescapable conclusion: Snuggles had run off. He was lost.

Melanie did everything she could to find her little puppy. She kept up hope for a long time. Eventually, though, certainty settled over her like a shroud, and she accepted the truth that Snuggles was gone.

At least, she *thought* that was the truth!

Eleven years later—yes, eleven whole years after that moment of loss—Melanie received a call from her daughter telling her a dog had been dropped off at the City of Buffalo Animal Shelter. A microchip scan confirmed it wasn't just any dog. It was Snuggles!

"When I got that call, at first, I thought my daughter was joking," said Melanie. "I thought she was playing around."

Nobody knew where the pooch had been for more than a decade, but that didn't matter. The dog had been well cared for, and Melanie was soon reunited with her long-lost pet.

"I just never thought I would ever see him again," she said, adding that she intends to make good use of the time they have left together. In her words, "I have another 4 to 5 good years to snuggle Snuggles."[1]

Personally, I hope Melanie Epperson gets eleven more years to snuggle Snuggles, just to make up for lost time. Eventually, though, there will be another separation between the two of them. A deeper and more fundamental moment of loss. What happens after that?

As you might imagine, I receive a lot of questions about heaven through my work as a pastor and through our ministry at Turning Point. What you might not know is that many of those questions are about pets rather than people. The big one is: Will I see my pet again in heaven?

I understand the emotional weight behind that question, and I will answer it in the pages that follow. But I also think it's helpful to start with a broader spectrum of what Scripture teaches about the relationship between humanity, the animal kingdom, and our eternal future. So, let's tackle the subject of animals in heaven by looking at the four stages in the story of our world: creation, fall, redemption, and restoration.

ANIMALS ABOUNDING AT CREATION

Here's something we can say with certainty right at the beginning of this conversation: God cares about animals. We know that because animals were part of His good plan for creation from the very beginning.

On day five of the creation week, God commanded the waters of the earth to abound with "an abundance of living creatures" (Genesis 1:20). He also filled the sky with birds and other flying animals. Then, on day six, He commanded the earth to bring forth cattle and "creeping" things (verse 24) and other beasts. God designed every animal that lives in the sea, in the air, and on land.

Notice what happened at the end of day six:

Then God said, "Let Us make man in Our image, according to Our likeness; let them have dominion over the fish of the sea, over the birds of the air, and over the cattle, over all the earth and over every creeping thing that creeps on the earth." So God created man in His own image; in the image of God He created him; male and female He created them. Then God blessed them, and God said to them, "Be fruitful and multiply; fill the earth and subdue it; have dominion over the fish of the sea, over the birds of the air, and over every living thing that moves on the earth." (verses 26–28)

From the very beginning of our experiences on this planet, human beings have been set apart as stewards over the natural world. That's what it means for Adam and Eve to "have dominion" over creation—and notice that God specified He intended us to be stewards over the fish and birds and cattle and creeping things and "all the earth."

Why does that matter? In the same way that our relationship with God was originally unstained, so was our relationship with the natural world—including with all animal life. Our interaction as part of the natural ecosystem was designed to be perfect, so much so that God originally intended for humanity to follow a vegan diet (Genesis 1:29–30).

Unfortunately, the perfect nature of that relationship did not endure for long.

ANIMALS ALIENATED AT THE FALL

When our earliest ancestors brought sin into the world, the bond between God and humanity was fractured. Sin separated us from our Creator, which sent shock waves through human history.

In that same moment, the bond between animals and humanity was also broken. Sin not only separated us from our Creator, but also from the rest of creation—which continues to send shock waves through the natural world and the animal kingdom.

We know Adam and Eve were removed from the garden of Eden as a consequence for their sin (Genesis 3:22–24). But did you know Scripture lists another consequence that occurred *before* Adam and Eve left the garden? Here it is: "Also for Adam and his wife the LORD God made tunics of skin, and clothed them" (Genesis 3:21).

Remember, at the end of Genesis 1, God gave plants to both humanity and the animal world as a source of food, and He declared His creation to be "very good" (verse 31). Now, at the end of Genesis 3, the connection between humanity and animals has devolved so far and so quickly that animals were killed so that their skins could partly cover the shame of human failure.

As you know, the fallout of sin has spread far beyond that garden and far beyond Adam and Eve. What was once "very good" became dysfunctional. People hunted animals for food. Animals hunted animals for food. Spiders began to bite. Wasps and scorpions began to sting. Mosquitos and ticks developed a taste for blood. All of creation descended into disarray.

Recent centuries have not been kind to our fellow residents of this planet. As the human population has exploded across the globe—and as industrialization continues to gobble up natural resources—we have disrupted animal populations, food chains, and entire ecosystems.

According to the International Union for Conservation of Nature, there are currently more than forty-seven thousand species under threat of extinction. That includes 26 percent of all mammals,

26 percent of freshwater fish, 12 percent of birds, and a whopping 38 percent of all trees.[2]

According to Scripture, things are going to get worse. Much worse. The seven years known as the Tribulation will be a horrifying period of time on earth—a time of judgment and chaos and terror. During that period, our planet will suffer cataclysmic events that will potentially end the lives of billions of people.

Those events will be equally unkind to animal life. Here's what we know from the book of Revelation:

- The third seal judgment will unleash food scarcity across our planet, which will affect animals as well as people (6:5–6).
- The first trumpet judgment will destroy a third of the trees on earth (8:7).
- The second trumpet judgment will kill a third of all life in the sea (8:8–9).
- During the second bowl judgment, "every living creature in the sea" will die (16:3).
- During the sixth bowl judgment, the great Euphrates River will dry up, which will devastate huge ecosystems across thousands of miles (16:12).

In short, human sinfulness has decimated the animal population on earth. That devastation will only increase until the return of Christ our Savior.

ANIMALS ACHING FOR REDEMPTION

One Sunday after I preached about the return of Jesus, a little girl came up to me with a big smile on her face. "I know there will be animals in heaven," she said confidently.

I smiled back and asked, "You do? Well, how do you know that?"

She didn't even pause. "Easy. You told us that when Jesus comes back at the end of the Tribulation, He'll be riding a white horse. Right?"

I nodded. "That's right."

"Well," she said, "where do you think He got the horse? From heaven, of course!"

I think she made a pretty good point!

So let's get to the elephant in the room—pun intended. Let's tackle the question I mentioned earlier: Will our pets join us in heaven?

The Bible doesn't address that question directly. We are never told that specific animals will rejoin us in eternity, nor are we told they won't. Therefore, we need to do a little digging to look for principles that can help us make an educated guess.

Let's start with a fascinating passage from the book of Romans:

> For the creation was subjected to futility, not willingly, but because of Him who subjected it in hope; because the creation itself also will be delivered from the bondage of corruption into the glorious liberty of the children of God. For we know that the whole creation groans and labors with birth pangs together until now. Not only that, but we also who have the firstfruits of the Spirit, even we ourselves groan within ourselves, eagerly waiting for the adoption, the redemption of our body. (8:20–23)

Jesus redeemed humanity through His blood shed on the cross. He purchased forgiveness for our sins, setting us free both now and in eternity. Likewise, according to Paul, "creation itself also will be delivered from the bondage of corruption." And, in the same way that you and I inwardly long and ache to escape the corruption of sin, the created world—including animals—"groans and labors with birth pangs" in longing for redemption.

That being the case, there does seem to be a distinction made in Genesis 1 between human beings and the rest of creation. Humanity was created "in the image of God." Moreover, human beings were designed to demonstrate dominion over the rest of creation. That means a person is not the same as a monkey or a spider or a whale. Or even a beloved pet. We are stewards of those animals, set above them for the purpose of managing them well here on planet Earth.

Does that mean all hope is lost for Melanie Epperson enjoying snuggles from Snuggles in God's heavenly kingdom? No—not at all, as we'll see below.

ANIMALS APLENTY AT THE RESTORATION

So far, most of what we've discussed applies to the past and the present. But what about the future? What *does* Scripture tell us about the fate of animals after our current age?

Well, for starters, we know there will be animals on earth with us during the Millennium. More than that, we know the relationship between humans and the animal kingdom will be completely repaired during that time. According to the prophet Hosea, "In that day [God] will make a covenant for them with the beasts of the field, with the birds of the air, and with the creeping things of the ground" (Hosea 2:18). God will restore our link to the animal world so that it resembles His original intention in the garden of Eden.

Prophesying about that new reality, Isaiah painted these startling pictures about what life will look like during the thousand-year reign of Christ:

> The wolf also shall dwell with the lamb,
> The leopard shall lie down with the young goat,
> The calf and the young lion and the fatling together;
> And a little child shall lead them.
> The cow and the bear shall graze;
> Their young ones shall lie down together;
> And the lion shall eat straw like the ox.

The nursing child shall play by the cobra's hole,
And the weaned child shall put his hand in the viper's den.
They shall not hurt nor destroy in all My holy mountain,
For the earth shall be full of the knowledge of the LORD
As the waters cover the sea. (Isaiah 11:6–9)

Can you imagine a toddler playing with a cobra as if it were a kitten? What a strange and wonderful time the Millennium will be!

What about after those thousand years? Will animals be with us in the eternal state? I think so, and I explained why in *The Coming Golden Age:*

If God loves animals so much that He created them with all their diverse beauty (Genesis 1:20–25), if He saved them from the flood (6:19), if He was so concerned for the cattle of Nineveh that He withheld judgment (Jonah 4:11), if He showed Job His glory by taking him on a zoological tour of the world (Job 39:1–30), if He cares for the sparrows and knows when even one of them falls to the ground (Matthew 10:29)—if He so delights in animals on earth, don't you think there will be lots of animals, not just during the Millennium but in the new heaven and new earth?

I think so too.[3]

Remember, there were animals in the garden of Eden before sin entered the world: "So Adam gave names to all cattle, to the birds of the air, and to every beast of the field" (Genesis 2:20). As we've seen in these pages, the new heavens and new earth will be more than a replica of God's original vision for creation—they will be a glorious expansion of that vision.

So, is it possible that God's expanded creation in the new heavens and new earth could include specific, unique animals such as Snuggles? Such as your own beloved pet? Yes, the Bible suggests that such an outcome could happen! Of course, I'm not guaranteeing that

Snuggles or your specific pet will be waiting for us in the eternal state. I simply believe God recognizes genuine love in many forms, and that "with God all things are possible" (Matthew 19:26).

Speaking of possible and impossible, a young woman named Marjorie Courtenay-Latimer made an unlikely scientific discovery back in 1938. She was a museum curator in South Africa, and one of her duties was to visit the local fish markets and inspect any specimens thought to be unusual. On a particular day in December, she found something unusual indeed. In her own words, "I picked away at a layer of slime to reveal the most beautiful fish I had ever seen. It was pale mauvy blue, with faint flecks of whitish spots; it had an iridescent silver-blue-green sheen all over. It was covered in hard scales, and it had four limb-like fins and a strange puppy-dog tail."

Latimer didn't know it yet, but she'd found a coelacanth—a type of bony fish believed to have gone extinct. So, this was almost like discovering a dinosaur in the middle of a local market.

Latimer was determined to identify her specimen, so she convinced a taxi driver to load the 127-pound beast in the back of his cab, then attempted to store it at the local morgue. She was denied, but she pressed forward by having the fish preserved through taxidermy. Then she began the arduous process of gaining the attention of a renowned ichthyologist named J.L.B. Smith.

It took some perseverance on Latimer's part, but when Smith finally came to see the specimen, he was overwhelmed: "That first sight [of the fish] hit me like a white-hot blast and made me feel shaky and queer, my body tingled. I stood as if stricken to stone. Yes, there was not a shadow of doubt, scale by scale, bone by bone, fin by fin, it was a true Coelacanth."[4]

Marjorie Courtenay-Latimer was a good steward of her responsibilities as a museum curator and as someone who loved nature. Humanity as a whole will receive another opportunity to fulfill our role as stewards over creation when we reach our final home in heaven. And this time we will fulfill that role to the glory of God.

PART 5

THE APPLICATION
OF HEAVEN

*If then you were raised with Christ, seek those
things which are above, where Christ is, sitting
at the right hand of God. Set your mind on
things above, not on things on the earth. For
you died, and your life is hidden with Christ in
God. When Christ who is our life appears, then
you also will appear with Him in glory. . . .*

*Therefore, as the elect of God, holy and beloved, put
on tender mercies, kindness, humility, meekness,
longsuffering; bearing with one another, and forgiving
one another, if anyone has a complaint against another;
even as Christ forgave you, so you also must do. But
above all these things put on love, which is the bond
of perfection. And let the peace of God rule in your
hearts, to which also you were called in one body; and
be thankful. Let the word of Christ dwell in you richly
in all wisdom, teaching and admonishing one another
in psalms and hymns and spiritual songs, singing with
grace in your hearts to the Lord. And whatever you
do in word or deed, do all in the name of the Lord
Jesus, giving thanks to God the Father through Him.*

COLOSSIANS 3:1–4, 12–17

CHAPTER 29

HOW TO BE HEAVENLY MINDED

For twenty-five-year-old Chris Allen, everything seemed to be happening in slow motion.

He was walking along the sidewalk in downtown Cincinnati when he noticed a woman getting ready to cross the street in front of him. She was wearing a large pair of headphones and looking down at the phone in her hands. Both thumbs were pecking furiously, which meant she was probably texting. Her entire focus was down at the screen.

That was bad news because she was walking directly into the road—and a car was driving straight for the place she was about to step.

Without stopping to think, Chris shot forward and gently grabbed the woman by her shoulders, half spinning and half pulling her back away from the road. At the same moment, the car drove by without even slowing down.

"I was trying to wave to her," Chris said. "She couldn't hear me obviously, so I ran out and just kind of pulled her back. After all that happened, she was kind of in shock."[1]

I'm sure you've noticed that many people have started living their lives with their heads down. They're looking down at screens while they walk. They're looking down at screens in the classroom or in the office. They're even looking down at screens while they're sitting at restaurants or around the dinner table with other people!

I call this a "heads down" perspective, and it's dangerous. Just ask the woman who almost got struck by a car in Cincinnati! More broadly, constantly keeping our focus "down" in the demands of everyday life can keep us from noticing the ways God is working around us and steadily bringing blessings into our lives. It can also prevent us from seeing spiritual hazards on track to take us down.

As citizens of heaven, we are created to live with a "heads up" perspective. We've been called to say no to the concerns of the world and say yes to the concerns of God. Oftentimes that means we need to pay less attention to the things of "now" and more attention to the things that are ahead.

The apostle Paul revealed the importance of perspective for all followers of Jesus in this well-loved passage from Colossians 3:

> If then you were raised with Christ, seek those things which are above, where Christ is, sitting at the right hand of God. Set your mind on things above, not on things on the earth. For you died, and your life is hidden with Christ in God. When Christ who is our life appears, then you also will appear with Him in glory. (verses 1–4)

It's impossible to miss the core teachings of this passage. First, "seek those things which are above, where Christ is." Second, "Set your mind on things above, not on things on the earth."

Paul was describing a heavenly perspective—a way of looking at the world that focuses on heavenly realities more than earthly realities. Now, does that mean Christians are called to ignore earthly things?

Not at all. Scripture reminds us many times to make wise financial decisions, to be loving spouses and caring parents, to be upstanding citizens of our nations, and to work productively in our jobs. Those all require us to pay attention to "earthly" concerns.

Having a heavenly perspective means tuning in to eternity as our *primary* focus. Our main concern. Heaven is to be the factor that motivates us, changes us, and energizes us. Our eternal home (more than our present reality) should make our eyes shine, put a spring in our step, and synthesize our divided attention toward a single, laser-like goal.

Why should we make an effort to gain this type of heavenly mindset? Because heaven is our true home and the place of our eternal allegiance. As Paul wrote to the Christians in Philippi, "Our citizenship is in heaven, from which we also eagerly wait for the Savior, the Lord Jesus Christ" (Philippians 3:20).

That raises an important question: How do we develop a heavenly mindset? How do we pry our focus away from all the worldly concerns that tug at our minds and hearts every day, and instead intentionally shift that focus toward heaven? Toward eternity?

The answer is not by thinking about a time or a place. It's about focusing on a person. Four times in Colossians 3:1-4, Paul mentioned Christ. To set our hearts on heaven is to set our hearts on Jesus. So here, from Paul's written words to the Colossians, are four steps you can take to become so heavenly minded that you are also of earthly good.

FOCUS ON CHRIST'S CONNECTION TO YOU

As a follower of Jesus, one of the most true things that can ever be said about you is that you are connected with Christ. That connection is what will point you to heaven, even when you are surrounded and sometimes overwhelmed by the pressures of this world.

Three times in this chapter's key passage, Paul used the phrase "with Christ" to highlight our union with Jesus:

- "You were raised *with Christ*" (3:1).
- "Your life is hidden *with Christ* in God" (3:3).
- "You also will appear *with Him* in glory" (3:4).

No matter what else you may be experiencing today—no matter what kinds of distractions are pulling your focus downward—the truth remains that you are already "with Christ." You have been joined to Him through a lifeline that can never be severed. Therefore, the more you consciously shift your focus to consider that connection, the more you will see the world from a heavenly perspective.

Paul noted another way we are "with Christ" in Romans 6: "For if we have been united together in the likeness of His death, certainly we also shall be in the likeness of His resurrection, *knowing this, that our old man was crucified with Him*, that the body of sin might be done away with, that we should no longer be slaves of sin. For he who has died has been freed from sin" (verses 5–7).

The great Chinese Christian preacher and writer Watchman Nee grasped the importance of that "with." In 1927, he had been struggling with issues of temptation and his sinful nature. One morning he was sitting upstairs reading the book of Romans, and he came to those words, "Knowing this, that our old man was crucified with Him" (6:6). For Nee, it was as if the words had come to life on the page. He leapt from his chair, ran downstairs, and grabbed a kitchen worker by the hands. "Brother," he shouted. "Do you know that I have died?"

The worker only stared in puzzlement. Nee blurted out, "Do you not know that Christ has died? Do you not know that I died with Him? Do you not know that my death is no less truly a fact than His?"[2]

Why was Watchman Nee so excited about dying with Christ?

Because he realized the parts of him that were so attached to earthly things had perished. The parts of him that were so pulled by temptation had perished. Which meant he was free to chase after heavenly pursuits.

The same is true of you and me. We died with Christ; therefore, we can live each day from a heavenly perspective.

FOCUS ON CHRIST'S CONTROL OVER YOU

Focusing on Jesus is the key to developing a heavenly mindset. So it's worth asking the question: When you think about Jesus, what do you see? Do you picture a gentle Jesus, meek and mild? A nice, kind, reasonable Teacher? Or do you picture the risen and ascended Lord of all things? The sovereign King of all creation?

Paul pictured the latter. He wrote of "those things which are above, where Christ is, *sitting at the right hand of God*" (Colossians 3:1).

To describe Jesus as "sitting at the right hand of God" is to emphasize His control over the universe. God's throne room is the hub of all existence—the place where God's presence is concentrated and His will is proclaimed. Jesus sits on that throne, exhibiting unlimited power, authority, grandeur, and might.

When we focus on the reality of Christ's control, not just over the universe but also over our own lives, we find the problems that seemed so huge just a moment ago becoming smaller. More manageable. Even insignificant. Because Christ is on the throne.

Here's an exercise I think can be helpful in shifting our focus from earthly problems to a more heavenly perspective. To start, close your eyes and allow your mind to dwell on the major issues or problems you are facing right now. Those items that have brought stress to your day, week, month, or year. The fires that need to be put out.

Do you have your list? Now, read the following Scripture passage out loud:

I also pray that you will understand the incredible greatness of God's power for us who believe him. This is the same mighty power that raised Christ from the dead and seated him in the place of honor at God's right hand in the heavenly realms. Now he is far above any ruler or authority or power or leader or anything else—not only in this world but also in the world to come. God has put all things under the authority of Christ and has made him head over all things for the benefit of the church. And the church is his body; it is made full and complete by Christ, who fills all things everywhere with himself. (Ephesians 1:19–23 NLT)

Do you see the way temporary issues give way to eternal reality? Even when the world seems to spin out of control, be calm; this is only how it *seems*. In reality, almighty God is still on His throne. In the words of that old spiritual, "He's got the whole world in His hands."

FOCUS ON CHRIST'S CARE FOR YOU

Let's explore another "with" Paul described in Colossians 3: "For you died, and your life is hidden with Christ in God" (verse 3).

Can you think of a more secure place to be than "with Christ in God"? I can't. Just as your hand might gently enfold a rose petal, God's hand gently enfolds you—and Christ alongside you. You are wrapped up in Christ's care and concern and protection.

This is true of you right now. Notice that Paul didn't instruct us to "hide ourselves in Christ." No, we are "hidden." Meaning, it's already finished. It's an accomplished fact. If you are a Christ-follower, then you are with Christ, in God, and you are ultimately free and safe—both now and for eternity.

Jesus Himself referred to this reality when He said, "I give them eternal life, and they shall never perish; neither shall anyone snatch them out of My hand. My Father, who has given them to Me, is greater than all; and no one is able to snatch them out of My Father's hand" (John 10:28–29).

For believers, nothing that happens in the present can affect our eternal future. Talk about a heavenly perspective!

FOCUS ON CHRIST'S COMMITMENT TO YOU

How can you become heavenly minded in the midst of the trials and sufferings and worries of your world? By choosing to focus on your connection with Christ, on His control over all things (including your problems), on His unending care for you—and finally, by focusing on Christ's commitment to you.

Paul declared in Colossians 3:4, "When Christ who is our life appears, then you also will appear with Him in glory."

Part of being "with" Christ is becoming more like Him. Each day that you serve Jesus here on earth, you are being transformed to something just a bit closer to His image; this is the process of sanctification. But when Christ returns in glory, you will experience a change that will be both sudden and dramatic. He will come in His glorious resurrection body, and then you will have a perfect resurrection body as well.

As Paul described in a different epistle: "For our citizenship is in heaven, from which we also eagerly wait for the Savior, the Lord Jesus Christ, who will transform our lowly body that it may be conformed to His glorious body, according to the working by which He is able even to subdue all things to Himself" (Philippians 3:20–21).

I know there are many distractions in a given day that pull your focus downward—including many disturbances in your own body. You've been afflicted with sickness, sadness, weariness, and pain. But Christ's promise to you is one of eternal renewal. Eternal perfection! That includes your spirit, your mind, and your body.

Keeping your focus on that future blessing will help you maintain a heavenly mindset no matter what obstacles stand in front of you today.

Speaking of focus, I recently read about a young woman named Melissa King from Cornwall, England, who participated in a ground-breaking study conducted by the University of Plymouth. When she first joined the study, Melissa described herself as a "non-runner." She was interested in being healthy, but she didn't run or jog or anything like that. The goal of the study was to determine if specific motivational techniques could help non-runners train for and successfully complete an ultramarathon—a race typically quite a bit longer than the standard marathon distance of 26.2 miles.

Melissa was part of a group that used Functional Imagery Training (FIT) in their preparation. The goal of FIT is to imagine and focus on highly detailed pictures that represent your goals. Someone like Melissa King, for example, might picture in her mind the moment of crossing the finish line at the end of the ultramarathon—the roar of the crowd, the feelings of joy and accomplishment, and more. But she might also create a picture of the moment when she describes the race to her coworkers, imagining their amazement and pride in her achievement.

According to the study from Plymouth University, Melissa and the other participants who used Functional Imagery Training were five times more likely to finish the race than those who focused on more conventional training.[3]

Here on earth, picturing our goals can help us find success. But our ultimate strategy for developing a heavenly mindset is to focus on our picture of Jesus—and to allow His presence to pull our gaze upward for all eternity.

CHAPTER 30

MOTIVATED
BY HEAVEN

In June 2024, Amber Finucan was walking to work when she realized she'd been transported to a completely new city—although one that was strangely familiar.

Normally Amber works as a retail manager at Rising Star Coffee Roasters on Superior Avenue in downtown Cleveland. But seemingly overnight, Superior Avenue was gone—changed instead to Concord Street. More surprising, Cleveland itself had disappeared. As she walked, Amber noticed trash cans labeled with "Metropolis Waste Management" and old-style cop cars with "Metropolis Police" emblazoned on the side panels. Most jarring of all, the famed Leader building had been replaced by offices for a newspaper called *The Daily Planet*.

If you're a comic book fan or movie buff, you already understand what happened to downtown Cleveland. It had been transformed into the fictional city of Metropolis to facilitate the filming of a new *Superman*.

What did the residents think of that transformation? Amber Finucan, at least, was pretty happy. "It's like being in Neverland," she said. "It's like being a tourist at work—it's wild!" Safe to say others were less enthusiastic, especially since the movie production shut down several busy streets during rush hour. After all, the "transformation" óf the city wouldn't offer any long-term benefits for Clevelanders during the filmmakers' time there.[1]

Did you know many people feel the same way about heaven? Even many Christians? They see the idea of a future in heaven as impractical for the present, and they think of people like me as being "too heavenly minded to do any earthly good." In fact, one man told me the church should be more worried about the potholes in Chicago than the streets of gold in heaven.

Could they be right? Could making a big deal about heaven (as we are doing in this book) actually distract us from making a real influence here on earth? I don't think so. The reason I say that is because God Himself made a big deal about heaven.

Why do you suppose God gave us so much information about the future? Why does the Bible end with vivid descriptions of the new heaven and the new earth?

Because nothing is more relevant to how we live today than what we believe about tomorrow. God didn't fill the Bible with details about the future just to satisfy our curiosity or to spark theological debates. He gave us these promises to strengthen our lives today.

The truth is that heaven is transformational. Yes, we will be transformed when we enter our eternal home, but I'm talking about today! Heaven transforms us now. It works in our hearts and minds. It gives us perspective. It makes us hopeful, steady, forward-looking. It infuses us with strength, comfort, confidence, and a sense of purpose. The Bible's teaching about heaven is like a rocket booster, pulling us forward toward the most meaningful life possible.

Peter had a lot to say about this present-tense understanding of heaven. In 2 Peter 3, he listed four ways heaven should impact us here and now. Read the following verses and see if you can spot the implications Peter had in mind as he wrote these words:

> Therefore, beloved, looking forward to these things, *be diligent*
> to be found by Him in peace, without spot and blameless. . . .

Consider that the longsuffering of our Lord is salvation . . .
Beware lest you also fall from your own steadfastness . . . *Grow*
in the grace and knowledge of our Lord and Savior Jesus Christ.
(verses 14–18)

In light of everything God has told us about our tomorrow in
heaven, how should we live today?

BE GRITTY

Angela Duckworth wrote an influential book called *Grit* that became
an instant success in the business world and beyond. According to
Duckworth, "grit is about having what some researchers call an 'ultimate concern'—a goal you care about so much that it organizes and
gives meaning to almost everything you do. And grit is holding steadfast to that goal. Even when you fall down. Even when you screw up.
Even when progress toward that goal is halting or slow."[2]

Peter had grit. The biblical word he used was *diligence*, but the
idea is the same: an unwavering, determined pursuit of what matters
most. For Peter, that meant serving Christ with all his heart, no matter the setbacks. And he called us to live the same way. "Therefore,
beloved, looking forward to these things, be diligent to be found by
Him in peace, without spot and blameless" (2 Peter 3:14).

This kind of diligence—this spiritual grit—is essential for the
Christian life. That is why Peter used the word *diligent* two other
times in this short letter:

- "But also for this very reason, giving all diligence, add to your
  faith virtue, to virtue knowledge" (2 Peter 1:5).
- "Therefore, brethren, be even more diligent to make your call
  and election sure, for if you do these things you will never
  stumble" (verse 10).

This isn't the language of comfort or convenience. It's the vocabulary of determination. Peter calls us to put our heads down, press forward, and refuse to coast through life.

In verse 14, he said this starts by making "peace" with God. If there's something you need to confess, confess it. If there's someone you need to forgive, forgive them. Let go of bitterness, worry, and fear. That's how you live in peace.

Then, Peter told us to "be found by Him . . . without spot." Stay away from things you know are wrong. If there's a habit, a website, or a friendship pulling you away from God, be strong enough to walk away. That takes grit—but God gives strength to those who ask.

Finally, aim to be "blameless." That means living with integrity when no one's watching. It means owning up when you mess up, and doing what's right even when it's hard.

BE GRATEFUL

Peter went on to say, "And consider that the longsuffering of our Lord is salvation" (2 Peter 3:15).

We can feel frustrated when we look at the world and see so much confusion and chaos. It makes us long for heaven, even while we might wonder why Jesus hasn't come back yet. But Peter reminded us that God has a purpose in waiting. He is giving one more opportunity for someone to come to Christ. Maybe it is a family member, a friend, or a neighbor. It could even be you.

Heaven is real, and it will arrive soon! While we wait for our eternal home, we should live with grateful hearts. Let's thank God for saving us—and also thank Him for the time He gives others to come to Him. Every day we're here is a reminder of His longsuffering.

So instead of asking, "Why is God waiting?" it is better to say, "Thank You, Lord, for waiting. Thank You for being patient with me. And thank You for giving others more time to know You."

BE ON GUARD

Next, Peter said the promise of heaven should lead us to be on guard. He wrote, "You therefore, beloved, since you know this beforehand, beware lest you also fall from your own steadfastness, being led away with the error of the wicked" (2 Peter 3:17).

I don't believe Peter was suggesting we can fall from our salvation in Christ. Instead, he was exhorting us to be strong in our profession of faith. We must know what we believe, and we must let nothing sway us from it.

We have too many superficial Christians nowadays, and too many churches have roots that don't sink deeply enough into Scripture. But you and I are responsible before God to stay rooted and grounded in faith, to rightly divide the Word of God, and to maintain the integrity of our beliefs and behaviors.

A lot of false teachers circulated through the world in the days of the apostles. Peter, Paul, James, and Jude confronted them and earnestly contended for the integrity of the message of the gospel. Things haven't changed much. The devil still has his agents who ask, "Did God really say . . . ?" (Genesis 3:1 NIV).

The more we study the Bible, the more we will be convinced of its truthfulness and trustworthiness. We must be on guard about what we believe or else we might be led astray by evil teachers.

BE GROWING

Finally, Peter said, "Grow in the grace and knowledge of our Lord and Savior Jesus Christ. To Him be the glory both now and forever. Amen" (2 Peter 3:18).

These are the final recorded words of the apostle Peter. With this verse, his remarkable ministry came to a close. His last message was simple: Keep growing; keep moving forward. Do not stop now.

Why? Because heaven is ahead. The certainty of heaven motivates us to keep growing in the faith.

The Rocky Mountain bristlecone pine is one of the oldest trees on earth. It never stops growing, even after thousands of years. That is a picture of the Christian life. As long as we are here, we are called to grow. We grow in grace, in knowledge, in love, in endurance, in joy, in wisdom, in compassion. We are never done.

Every time I open the Bible, I learn something new. I may have studied a passage a hundred times before, but God still teaches me through each encounter. Every page offers something fresh for those who are willing to learn. The longer I live, the more I realize I have barely scratched the surface. But I keep growing, and so do you. That is why Peter's final challenge is for us to grow in grace and in the knowledge of our Lord and Savior.

When we remember that heaven is our future, it lifts our eyes and stirs our hearts. It makes us want to grow. I do not want to enter heaven prayerless and distracted. I want to enter with an open Bible, a willing heart, and a life that is bearing fruit.

Spiritual growth is God's will for every believer. It is not optional! Even the apostle Paul said he hadn't arrived, but he kept pressing forward (Philippians 3:12–14).

So how do we keep growing as we look forward to heaven? It starts with prayer.

GROWTH THROUGH PRAYER

Peter told us, "The end of all things is at hand; therefore be serious and watchful in your prayers" (1 Peter 4:7). The closer we come to Christ's return, the more we need prayer. It's not always easy, but praying consistently creates a climate for spiritual growth. Praying Christians are growing Christians.

GROWTH THROUGH THE WORD

We also grow by drinking from Scripture. Peter said, "As newborn babes, desire the pure milk of the word, that you may grow thereby"

(1 Peter 2:2). And Revelation 22:7 says, "Blessed is he who keeps the words of the prophecy of this book."

Psalm 19 is a great passage about the power of the Bible for those who follow its instruction. Here, from that chapter, is a short list of how the Bible will change you when you read it and obey it. The Bible will:

- Restore your soul (verse 7).
- Renew your mind (verse 7).
- Rejoice your heart (verse 8).
- Refocus your vision (verse 8).
- Reinforce your life (verse 9).
- Reorder your values (verse 10).
- Redirect your path (verse 11).
- Reward your obedience (verse 11).

GROWTH THROUGH THE CHURCH

One final way we grow is by staying engaged with our church family. Hebrews 10:24–25 urges us to encourage one another, "and so much the more as you see the Day approaching." The closer we are to heaven, the more we need each other.

So keep learning about your future and your inheritance and the glory to come. Let these truths shape your perspective and make you an optimist—even in grief, hardship, or loss. Growth begins with God's will, is nurtured through prayer and the Word, and flourishes in the fellowship of the church.

One man who embodied all of this was Dr. Charles McCoy. Dr. McCoy never married but devoted his life to pastoring a church in Oyster Bay, New York, and earning seven college degrees. At seventy-two, he retired, uncertain about the future. "I just lay on my bed thinking my life's over," he wrote. "What have I done for Christ?"

Then he met a missionary who invited him to India. Though

hesitant at first, he agreed. When warned of the risks, Dr. McCoy simply said, "It's just as close to heaven from there as it is from here."

Soon after arriving in Bombay, he was robbed, lost his passport, and discovered the missionary he'd planned to meet was gone. At a loss, he decided to visit the mayor's office. Dr. McCoy handed his business card to the receptionist and was told to return that afternoon. When he did, he was surprised to find a reception in his honor, attended by prominent officials of Bombay. His commanding presence, white hair, and long list of degrees made him appear like a U.S. dignitary.

Dr. McCoy spoke for thirty minutes, giving his testimony about Jesus. Afterward, a military officer invited him to speak at India's equivalent of West Point, and more invitations followed. Soon he became a sought-after preacher across India and Asia, and for the next sixteen years he proclaimed Christ with power and purpose. Finally, at age eighty-eight, he arrived in what was then Calcutta, stopped at the front desk for his room key, stepped onto the elevator, and was whisked up—to heaven.[3]

That's another reason why heaven is transformational—because it's never far away. Indeed, for the child of God, it's only a breath away. Wherever life takes us, our eternal home is secure—a city built by God, prepared by Jesus. May we live with joyful anticipation as we await that final journey, and may we take as many with us as we can.

CHAPTER 31

ONE WAY

It was Easter week 2025 in Washington, D.C., when pastor Greg Laurie showed up at 1600 Pennsylvania Avenue with his Bible and sermon notes, ready to preach a message to White House staffers in the ornate Eisenhower Executive Office Building. His agenda also included dinner in the Blue Room with the President of the United States.

But when he reached the gate, something unexpected happened. The Secret Service blocked his way. For some reason, Laurie's name wasn't on the official list of approved visitors, and he wasn't allowed through the gate.

Thankfully, this opposition turned out to be only a temporary delay. After some clerical confirmations, the problem was solved, and Laurie did get onto the grounds. But the incident provided a poignant lesson.

Laurie said, "It reminded me of something far more serious— what Jesus said will tragically happen to some people one day when they step into eternity. They'll expect to be welcomed into Heaven, but their name won't be in the Book of Life."[1]

THE WARNINGS OF CHRIST

Not everyone is going to heaven. Jesus warned us on many occasions to make sure we have a relationship with God through faith in Him. He said, "I am the way, the truth, and the life. No one comes to the Father except through Me" (John 14:6). We don't get to heaven by trying to live nobly or righteously, for all of us fall short of the perfection of God. We don't get to heaven by placing our faith in a philosophical or religious system. Salvation happens when we are granted a relationship with God through faith in Jesus Christ—that is the only way.

People accuse Christians of being narrow-minded when we say this, but Jesus Himself said it first. And that's not all He said.

In His Sermon on the Mount, Jesus declared, "Enter by the narrow gate; for wide is the gate and broad is the way that leads to destruction, and there are many who go in by it. Because narrow is the gate and difficult is the way which leads to life, and there are few who find it. . . . Not everyone who says to me, 'Lord, Lord,' shall enter the kingdom of heaven, but he who does the will of My Father in heaven" (Matthew 7:13–14, 21).

What is the Father's will? Jesus told us in John 6:40: "And this is the will of Him who sent Me, that everyone who sees the Son and believes in Him may have everlasting life."

Jesus warned His critics, "If you do not believe that I am He, you will die in your sins" (John 8:24).

John 3:36 says, "He who believes in the Son has everlasting life; and he who does not believe the Son shall not see life, but the wrath of God abides on him."

How could this be clearer? And yet so many people don't want to believe what Jesus Himself had to say. John MacArthur wrote,

It is ironic that so many who are downplaying the exclusivity of Christ are doing it because they believe it is a barrier to "relevance." Actually, Christianity is not relevant at all if it is merely one of many possible paths to God. The relevance of the gospel has always been its absolute exclusivity, summed up in the truth that Christ alone has atoned for sin and therefore Christ alone can provide reconciliation with God for those who believe only in Him.[2]

We can't talk of heaven without warning about hell. Jesus cautioned us about a place of "outer darkness" where there will be "gnashing of teeth" (Matthew 8:12). He told us, "And do not fear those who kill the body but cannot kill the soul. But rather fear Him who is able to destroy both soul and body in hell" (Matthew 10:28).

He had this to say about His return: "The Son of Man will send out His angels, and they will gather out of His kingdom all things that offend, and those who practice lawlessness, and will cast them into the furnace of fire. There will be wailing and gnashing of teeth" (Matthew 13:41–42).

These are somber warnings we should take with utmost gravity.

D. B. Hatfield, one of the descendants of the Hatfield-McCoy feud, became aware of these truths at the age of fifteen. He described himself as a lonely adolescent living in Chattaroy, West Virginia. One Sunday night he walked into town to see what was going on, and he saw a church lit up and a lot of people gathering. He ambled in and took a seat. The singing and preaching were good, and something moved in his heart. Going home, he went straight to his room and fell asleep. During the night, he had a dream in which he saw the fiery gates of hell, and he was just outside, headed for them.

"I woke myself up with a loud, frightful scream and sat directly up in bed, and there I pondered what I had seen in my sleep. Right there I made up my mind that I didn't want to go to hell, and from that moment I began to make amends and to rectify some things in my lifestyle. I didn't know that if I, by faith, repented of my past youthful sins, Christ would forgive me."

Hatfield spent months reading his Bible. One year later at a church revival meeting, he gave his life to Jesus and trusted Him for salvation.[3] Hatfield went on to serve the Lord for seventy-seven years as an evangelist, pastor, and missionary. His fear of hell was replaced by his love for heaven. We need a similar experience!

THE WORK OF CHRIST

The Bible isn't being cruelly restrictive in recording the pathway to salvation. Instead, Scripture is gloriously welcoming in giving us an exclusive gospel. The entire plan regarding the work of Christ is sensible and logically compelling. From the days of Adam and Eve, human beings have been imperfect in their attitudes, choices, actions, and words. The Bible says, "For all have sinned and fall short of the glory of God" (Romans 3:23).

Almighty God is pure, perfect, holy, and eternal. Nothing sinful can dwell in His presence, and since we have all fallen short of that standard, we are alienated from Him. The entire story of the Bible involves God choosing a man, Abraham, who became the father of the nation of Israel. From that nation, God raised up a Messiah—Jesus Christ—born of a virgin who had been miraculously overshadowed by the Holy Spirit (Luke 1:35).

Jesus was thereby fully human and fully God. He was unique. No one has ever possessed two natures before, and no one ever will again. Only Jesus is both God and man. He had to be God in order to save us, for no one else is powerful enough to reach into this sinful world and lift us to heaven. The Lord said in Isaiah 43:11, "I, even I, am the LORD, and besides Me there is no savior."

But only as a sinless human being could Jesus offer Himself as the perfect sacrifice and die for our sins, shedding His blood for us. Hebrews 9:26 says, "He has appeared to put away sin by the sacrifice of Himself."

That's why Peter told his audience in Jerusalem, "Nor is there salvation in any other, for there is no other name under heaven given among men by which we must be saved" (Acts 4:12).

Erwin Lutzer shared the testimony of a woman named Widia who was born into a Muslim family and grew up believing that Muhammad was a prophet of God. She prayed five times a day toward the city of Mecca. At age eighteen, she moved from Indonesia to Germany to attend fashion design school. There she met a man who gave her a Bible and encouraged her to read it.

At first Widia resisted opening the book, but she eventually began, as her friend suggested, in the Gospel of John. She was impressed, especially because Jesus often said, "I tell you the truth."

"Truth was very important to me," Widia later wrote, "and this showed He spoke with authority. Unlike Christians, we Muslims could never say for sure whether we are going to heaven when we died. We could only say, 'If God wills, I will go to heaven.' So I lived with this burden of fear that when I stood before God on the day of judgment, my bad deeds would end up outweighing my good deeds. However, the Bible said Jesus took my sins upon Himself and died for me. And that by trusting in Him, I could go to heaven."

Widia continued, "I really wanted to accept Him as Savior, but was afraid to because I knew doing so would upset my family and I could either be killed or forever banned from them."

One night Widia had a dream in which the Lord Jesus appeared to her. In her dream, He said, "Widia, I am the way, the truth, and the life. Follow Me."

"I couldn't resist the Holy Spirit anymore and decided to trust in Christ, alone in my college dorm room. It wasn't until after I became a Christian that I read John 14:6 and saw the same words that the Lord Jesus spoke to me in my dream."[4]

Jesus is the way—the pathway to heaven. He is the truth—the trustworthy man who provides certainty and surety. He is the life—the everlasting and abundant existence we need. No one else can compare to Him, replace Him, or do what He alone came to do.

One of the Bible's simplest explanations of God's plan for the human race is given in 1 Timothy 2:5: "For there is one God and one Mediator between God and men, the Man Christ Jesus." The Living Bible makes it even simpler: "God is on one side and all the people on the other side, and Christ Jesus, himself man, is between them to bring them together."

One scholar wrote, "Why is Jesus the exclusive path to God? Because He alone lived a sinless life, died a vicarious death, and rose from the dead. Jesus is the exclusive path to God because no one has ever or will ever live a life like He lived. His life was the perfect sacrifice for imperfect people who could never sacrifice enough to save themselves."[5]

That's why I urge you to exclusively place your faith in the One who expressly said, "I am the way, the truth, and the life."

THE WELCOME OF CHRIST

When you do that, you've got something wonderful ahead of you. The apostle Peter wrote, "Therefore, my brothers and sisters, make every effort to confirm your calling and election. For if you do these things, you will never stumble, and you will receive a rich welcome into the eternal kingdom of our Lord and Savior Jesus Christ" (2 Peter 1:10–11 NIV).

Notice those words *rich welcome*. When was the last time you had a rich welcome anywhere? The word *rich* in the original Greek implies something abundant, exceedingly strong, and excessively wonderful. Have you ever seen someone welcomed home like that?

Through out American history, we've had moments when we celebrated heroes who came home. When Neil Armstrong, Buzz Aldrin, and Michael Collins returned from orbiting and landing on the moon in 1969, New York City threw them a three-hour ticker tape parade. Then they flew to Chicago for another parade. Later that afternoon they flew to Los Angeles for a state dinner hosted by President Richard Nixon. At every event, tens of thousands of people cheered as the men sat on the raised seats of a custom Chrysler Imperial convertible, waving at the crowds.[6]

Talk about a rich welcome home!

Now, I confess that I don't know exactly how we'll be welcomed into heaven. Will there be a parade? A state banquet? Marching bands? I don't know. But if this sinful world can richly welcome home its heroes, how much richer will be our welcome when the Lord ushers us into heaven!

Jesus said, "Then the King will say to those on His right hand, 'Come, you blessed of My Father, inherit the kingdom prepared for you from the foundation of the world'" (Matthew 25:34). When it comes down to it, we don't need a ton of ticker tape. We just need the smile of Jesus. We need His "well done!"

We can never earn our way into His eternal kingdom. It's a gift that comes by grace through faith. The Bible says, "But now that you have been set free from sin and have become slaves of God, the benefit you reap leads to holiness, and the result is eternal life. For the wages of sin is death, but the gift of God is eternal life in Christ Jesus our Lord" (Romans 6:22–23 NIV).

I began this chapter by telling you about how Greg Laurie was barred from the White House because his name wasn't on the approved list. Let me end by telling you about one person who did get onto the White House grounds without an invitation. I don't know the youngster's name, but on April 18, 2023, a toddler squeezed through the fence on the north side of the White House while his hapless parents could do nothing to lure him back. Security alerts immediately sounded, and the Secret Service scooped up the child and returned him to his folks. One agent said, "We were going to wait until he learned to talk to question him, but in lieu of that, he got a time-out and was sent on his way with his parents."[7]

My friend, none of us will be able to slip through the fence of the New Jerusalem, and we don't need to. Through Jesus Christ and Him alone, we'll march through the gates with thanksgiving. And who knows? Maybe there will be bands playing, ticker tape falling, and crowds shouting.

But this we know for sure: Those who trust Christ alone for the safekeeping of their souls will receive a rich welcome when they enter the pearly gates. We will fall down before our Lord Jesus Christ, and we'll thank Him for all He did to give us a life that will never end and a home that will never fade away.

EPILOGUE

HOW TO KNOW
FOR SURE

There have been many memorable moments in my decades of ministry, but one of the most unforgettable was the day I spent with Dr. Billy Graham in the final years of his life.

I had just written a book called *God Loves You*, which I dedicated to Dr. Graham in honor of his lifetime of telling millions about the love of Jesus. Somehow arrangements were made for me to travel to his house on the East Coast and present him a copy of the book—an invitation I eagerly accepted.

When we got to the house, I sat down next to that legend of faith, who by that time was well over ninety years old. He had just been visiting with a group of politicians, and I could see he was physically tired. So, I read the dedication, shook his hand, and expressed my gratitude for his many years of faithful service. Then I got up to leave, feeling grateful for his hospitality.

"Wait a minute." I can still hear his deep Carolina drawl as he called out after me. "Where are you goin', young man?"

He asked me to sit back down, which I did. Then we spent the better part of an hour just talking together about life. And ministry. And his unshakable hope in the promise of heaven. I remember he told me how much he was looking forward to being with Ruth, his beloved wife—and how much he longed to see Jesus, his beloved Savior.

That confidence in heaven was a consistent theme throughout Dr. Graham's life and ministry. In fact, he declared these words during a crusade in Greenville, South Carolina, all the way back in 1966:

> I can stand here tonight and say to you on the authority of this [Bible], I *know* my sins are forgiven. I *know* I'm going to heaven. I *know* that I'm going to live as long as God lives because the moment I received Christ, I became a partaker of God's own life. Now I'm going to live a billion years and I'll only have begun. I know that. Not because of any goodness of my own. I'm not going to heaven because I've lived a good life. I'm not going to heaven because I've preached to great crowds of people. I'm going to heaven because of what Christ did on that cross.[1]

Now, let me ask you a question. In fact, this is the most important question you could ever answer: Do you *know* you are on your way to heaven? Do you *know*, with 100 percent certainty and 100 percent clarity, that your last breath here on earth will be immediately followed by your first breath in God's heavenly kingdom?

Do you know for sure?

If your answer is anything less than "Yes, I am 100 percent certain of my eternal destiny in heaven," then I implore you to pay attention to these final pages more carefully than any other document you've ever encountered. Because these words may literally save your life for eternity.

God made clear in His Word that every single human being living today has been separated from Him through the corruption of sin. Paul told us in the book of Romans, "For all have sinned and fall short of the glory of God" (3:23). That same book declares, "The wages of sin is death, but the gift of God is eternal life in Christ Jesus our Lord" (6:23). The word *death* in that passage refers not only to the end of our physical lives, but also to a spiritual separation from God that is eternal. The "death" of our spiritual selves leads to hell.

In short, God is holy but we are sinful. Therefore, we have no hope of heaven on our own.

But don't stop there! We don't have to make it on our own! No, God desires a relationship with us. God desires a relationship with *you*. For that reason, He made a way for our sins to be forgiven and our relationship with Him to be restored.

Jesus is that way. As God in human form, Jesus came to our world and lived a perfect life. In His perfection, He offered Himself as a sacrifice for all people by dying on the cross. Through His blood, He paid the penalty for our sins. "He personally carried our sins in his body on the cross," the Bible tells us, "so that we can be dead to sin and live for what is right. By his wounds you are healed" (1 Peter 2:24 NLT).

Because of Jesus, you have a free, guaranteed ticket to heaven. He has offered it to you, and all you need to do is accept that offer through faith. Scripture says, "For it is by grace you have been saved, through faith—and this is not from yourselves, it is the gift of God—not by works, so that no one can boast" (Ephesians 2:8–9 NIV).

Right now you may be thinking, *Dr. Jeremiah, I believe I accepted that gift. I think so. But how can I be sure? How can I know with the same level of confidence that Dr. Graham knew he was bound for heaven?*

The answer again comes from God's Word. Look at these two incredible promises:

- "For God so loved the world that He gave His only begotten

Son, that whoever believes in Him should not perish but have everlasting life" (John 3:16).
- "If you confess with your mouth the Lord Jesus and believe in your heart that God has raised Him from the dead, you will be saved" (Romans 10:9).

Whoever believes in Jesus *will* be saved. There is no doubt in that promise. No wiggle room. And, even more practically, we can be confident of our salvation simply by confessing with our mouth and believing in our heart. That's all it takes. When you take those two steps, "you will be saved."

That's something you can do right now. Right this moment. If there is any doubt in your heart about your name being written in the Lamb's Book of Life, take a moment to kneel down or bow your head. Speak to Jesus from your heart, and confess these words with your mouth:

> *Lord Jesus, I trust You have offered me a place in heaven. I trust You have offered me eternal life—and I accept that gift. Right now I choose to believe in my heart that You died on the cross for my sins and were raised from the dead, and I confess with my mouth that You are Lord. You are Lord of my life. I confess that I have sinned against You throughout my life, and right now I repent of every one of those sins. I accept Your forgiveness for every single sin.*
>
> *I speak this prayer in Your name, Lord Jesus. Amen.*

You may not believe this, but I have been praying for you to make that decision—to claim that promise as your own. The fact that you've made it this far into this book means you've learned a lot about heaven. You've learned a lot about eternity and eternal life.

But please hear me: I didn't write this book so you would be smarter about heaven. I wrote this book so you would *go* to heaven—so you would be sure of your eternal salvation. That way we can meet up one day along the streets of gold within New Jerusalem and talk together about all the wonders we've experienced and all the wonders that still await us in that perfect place. That eternal home.

I look forward to seeing you there!

INDEX

SCRIPTURE INDEX

ACKNOWLEDGMENTS

A page full of "thank you's":

To Donna—my life's partner, my inspiration, and my encourager for more than sixty-two years. Your love fuels the fire in my life.

Thanks to the team at Thomas Nelson, especially Damon Reiss, for your continued support and encouragement with these annual projects. We've completed at least one book a year for more than fifteen years working together as a team.

To Sealy Yates, my literary agent: Who would have thought, when we began working together so many years ago, that God would allow us to have such favor in the publishing world? Thank you, Sealy, for all you do.

And then to Beau Sager, Sam O'Neal, and Rob Morgan: Without your involvement in the creative process, none of this would be possible. You are great friends and great partners, and I love each one of you.

To my oldest son David Michael, who serves as the president of Turning Point—one of the greatest book delivery systems in existence. You lead it with diligence and determination. I am proud of you and thank you for all you do to make sure these books reach as many people as possible.

To Paul Joiner: Your brilliant ideas are all over this campaign, as they always are.

To Beth Anne Hewett, administrative assistant par excellence: You keep everything organized and on track, no matter what the day brings. And Cheryl Storm: thank you for watching over all things "church" on my behalf!

Yes, it takes all these people, and others I don't even know about, to write a book about heaven.

And above all, to God Almighty, the original occupant of the third heaven. This book is about Him.

NOTES

INTRODUCTION

1. Talia Wise, "Dolly Parton Holds to the Hope of Heaven After Husband's Death: 'I'm Going to See Him Again Someday,'" The Christian Broadcast Network, June 4, 2025, https://cbn.com/news/entertainment/dolly-parton -holds-hope-heaven-after-husbands-death-im-going-see-him-again.

CHAPTER 1

1. Daniel Shorn, "Transcript: Tom Brady, Part 3," CBS News, November 4, 2005, https://www.cbsnews.com/news/transcript-tom-brady-part-3/.
2. Peter Toon, *Heaven and Hell: A Biblical and Theological Overview* (Nelson, 1986), 204.
3. Mark Buchanan, *Things Unseen* (Multnomah Publishers, 2002), 51.
4. Mark R. McMinn, *Why Sin Matters: The Surprising Relationship Between Our Sin and God's Grace* (Tyndale House Publishers, 2004), 53.
5. *The Wizard of Oz*, directed by Victor Fleming, produced by Mervyn LeRoy, released August 15, 1939, MGM.
6. Jacob Uitti, "Who Wrote 'The Wizard of Oz' Classic 'Over the Rainbow?'" *American Songwriter*, February 6, 2023, https://americansongwriter.com /who-wrote-the-wizard-of-oz-classic-over-the-rainbow/.

CHAPTER 2

1. Rebecca McPhee, "The Man Who Bought a Tropical Island and What He Did With It," Explorers Web, April 19, 2022, https://explorersweb.com /man-who-bought-tropical-island/.
2. C. S. Lewis, *The Problem of Pain* (Macmillan, 1978), 145–47.

3. George Kennan, *E. H. Harriman: Volume II* (Houghton Mifflin Company, 1922), 346.
4. John Piper, "Peace to Those with Whom He Is Pleased," *Desiring God*, accessed June 4, 2025, https://www.desiringgod.org/articles/peace-to -those-with-whom-he-is-pleased.
5. Vaneetha Rendall Risner, *Walking Through Fire* (Nelson Books, 2021), 204.
6. Risner, *Walking Through Fire*, 190.
7. William Barclay, *The Gospel of John—Volume 2* (Saint Andrews Press, 2001).

CHAPTER 3

1. Jennifer Smith, "REVEALED: Grieving Boy Who Sent Heartbreaking Message in a Balloon to His Law Professor Father 'in Heaven' Was by His Side When He Was Shot Dead in Street Mugging," *The Daily Mail*, December 8, 2016, http://www.dailymail.co.uk/news/article-4013544/Little -boy-s-heartbreaking-note-dead-father-lands-woman-s-garden-balloon -child-hoped-reach-time-Christmas.html.
2. Stephen J. Wellum, *Systematic Theology: From Cannon to Concept, Volume 1* (B&H Academic, 2024), 622.
3. Hensleigh Wedgwood, *A Dictionary of English Etymology: Vol II* (Trübner & Co., 1862), 231.
4. "International Dark Sky Places," *DarkSky*, accessed June 7, 2025, https:// darksky.org/what-we-do/international-dark-sky-places/.
5. Steven Smith, "U.S. Pilot Killed in WWII Is Accounted for 80 Years After Bomber Named 'Heaven Can Wait' Crashed into Ocean," CBS News, updated February 25, 2025, https://www.cbsnews.com/news/uss-pilot-killed -wwii-accounted-for-herbert-tennyson-bomber-heaven-can-wait/.

CHAPTER 4

1. Lilly Blomquist, "Everything to Know About Kate Middleton's Engagement Ring," *Brides*, October 31, 2024, https://www.brides.com/kate-middleton -engagement-ring-8737094.
2. Amy Judd, "After 70 years, DNA Test Reunites 3 Long-Lost Siblings Across the Pond," Global News, June 14, 2024, https://globalnews.ca/news/10568317 /long-lost-siblings-reunite-dna-test/.
3. Emmet Pierce and Kristin Kurens, "Unexpected Heirs: 9 Extraordinary Real-Life Inheritance Stories," Money Talks News, May 1, 2025, https:// www.moneytalksnews.com/slideshows/heirs-chosen-at-random -and-6-other-incredible-inheritance-tales/.
4. Giles Tremlett, "Wealthy Loner Picks Heirs from Phone Book," *The*

Guardian, January 15, 2007, https://www.theguardian.com/world/2007
/jan/16/gilestremlett.mainsection.

5. Lauren Walker, "Hidden Vincent Van Gogh Self-Portrait Discovered on Back of Famous Painting," *The Brussels Times*, July 14, 2022, https://www.brusselstimes.com/255114/hidden-vincent-van-gogh-self-portrait-discovered-on-back-of-famous-painting.

CHAPTER 5

1. Michael Odell, "He Swims in Ice and Climbs Everest. Meet Tough Guy Wim Hof," *The Times of London,* March 7, 2017, https://www.thetimes.com/life-style/health-fitness/article/wim-hof-swims-in-ice-and-climbs-everest-in-shorts-so-would-you-go-to-his-training-camp-9bkmx8glf.

2. Rachel Hosie and Eammon Jacobs, "7 Actors on the Shocking Toll Losing Weight for Roles Took on Their Bodies and Minds," *Business Insider*, September 6, 2024, https://www.businessinsider.com/how-actors-cutting-weight-for-role-downsides-2023-7#kumail-nanjiani-said-that-losing-weight-for-eternals-made-his-relationship-with-food-worse-4.

CHAPTER 6

1. "Video: Soldier Comes Home and Surprises His Kids in Maine," 6 KWQC, September 6, 2018, https://www.kwqc.com/content/news/Video-Soldier-comes-home-and-surprises-his-kids-in-Maine-492580161.html.

2. "Whitney Houston Had Premonition About Death," *TMZ*, updated May 12, 2019, https://www.tmz.com/2012/02/15/whitney-houston-premonition-death-jesus-bible/#.TzvnCXJkHEU.

3. R. T. Kendall, *Whatever Happened to the Gospel* (Charisma House, 2018), 176.

4. Robert Elmer Smith, *Modern Messages from Great Hymns* (Abingdon Press, 1916), 67.

5. Fanny Crosby, "Saved by Grace," Hymnary.org, accessed June 23, 2025, https://hymnary.org/text/some_day_the_silver_cord_will_break_cros.

CHAPTER 7

1. Mark Porter, "The Man Behind the Rebuilding of 9/11's Ground Zero," *Reuters*, September 1, 2021, https://www.reuters.com/world/us/man-behind-rebuilding-911s-ground-zero-2021-09-01/.

2. Sam Blum, "Larry Silverstein Spent Years Tussling with the City to Rebuild the World Trade Center. Now He's Ready to Talk About It," *Inc.*, September 11, 2024, https://www.inc.com/sam-blum/larry-silverstein-spent-years-tussling-wth-the-city-to-rebuild-the-world-trade-center.html.

3. Blum, "Larry Silverstein Spent Years Tussling."
4. W. A. Criswell, "The New Creation," *W. A. Criswell Sermon Library*, September 16, 1984, https://wacriswell.com/sermons/1984/the-new-creation1/.
5. Katie White, "Meet Julian Baumgartner, the Conservator Whose Hypnotic YouTube Videos of Art Restorations Have Gone Viral," ArtNet, April 7, 2022, https://news.artnet.com/art-world/conservator-julian-baumgartners-viral-youtube-videos-art-restoration-2094911.

CHAPTER 8

1. Eliot Brown and Rory Jones, "What Went Wrong at Saudi Arabia's Futuristic Metropolis in the Desert," *The Wall Street Journal*, updated March 9, 2025, https://www.wsj.com/finance/saudi-arabia-neom-sindalah-15b9f25a.
2. F. W. Boreham, *Wisps of Wildfire* (Epworth Press, 1924), 202–03.
3. Charles F. Pfeiffer and Everett F. Harrison, eds., *The Wycliffe Bible Commentary* (Moody Press, 1962), 1522.

CHAPTER 9

1. Henry M. Morris, *The Revelation Record* (Tyndale House, 1983), 452–43.
2. Steve Palace, "The Scream of Sam Kinison—Religious Preacher Turned Rock Star Comedian," *The Vintage News*, December 17, 2018, https://www.thevintagenews.com/2018/12/17/sam-kinison/.
3. Bruce Lambert, "Sam Kinison, 38, Comedian, Dies; Wife Injured in Head-On Collision," *The New York Times*, April 12, 1992, 46.

CHAPTER 10

1. Jacob Uitti, "Behind the Song: 'Won't You Be My Neighbor?'" *American Songwriter*, September 13, 2021, https://americansongwriter.com/behind-the-song-wont-you-be-my-neighbor/.
2. "Citizenship by Investment," *Global Residence Index*, accessed June 7, 2025, https://globalresidenceindex.com/citizenship-by-investment/.
3. David Allen, *The New American Commentary: Hebrews* (B&H, 2010), 591.
4. Herbert Lockyer, *All the Angels in the Bible* (Hendrickson Publishers, 1995), x.
5. Eric Lindquist, "Twist of Fate," *Leader-Telegram*, May 15, 2025, https://www.leadertelegram.com/news/front-page/twist-of-fate/article_59deba79-0889-59d8-a848-e62d59ef05f1.html.

CHAPTER 11

1. From multiple press reports, including Natalie King, "Farmer Wins Monster $32 Million Jackpot from 83 Cent Ticket and Dies Weeks Later Spending It,"

The Mirror US, December 13, 2024, https://www.themirror.com/news/world-news/farmer-who-won-32m-lottery-857235.

2. Daniel Kim, "Will We Need the Bible in Heaven?" *English Compass*, May 1, 2014, http://www.englishcompass.org/articles/will_we_need_the_bible_in_heaven.

3. *Mary Hart: Memories and Letters*, arranged by her sisters Sophie S. Harris and Elizabeth M. Gillison (Butler & Taner Frome & London, 1896), 321–22.

4. Russell E. Gehrlein, "My Testimony: How I Came to Faith in Jesus," Reflections on Theological Topics of Interest, December 6, 2020, https://regehrlein.wordpress.com/2020/12/06/my-testimony-how-i-came-to-faith-in-jesus/.

5. David Parish and Richard Higginson, "Humphrey Monmouth and the Monmouth Society," *Faith in Business Quarterly*, Volume 20.2, accessed May 9, 2025, https://fibq.org/wp-content/uploads/2020/04/FiBQ20.2_Monmouth.pdf.

6. Dana and Bill Wichterman, *Stewards Not Owners* (Simon & Schuster, 2025), foreword.

7. Bob Grahmann, *Transforming Bible Study* (IVP Connect, 2003), 21.

CHAPTER 12

1. Lee Strobel, *Seeing the Supernatural* (Zondervan, 2025), xii–xiii. See also Leonardo Blair, "Ohio Pastor Says Angel Named 'Johnny' Saved His Life After Crash," *The Christian Post*, February 24, 2016, https://www.christianpost.com/news/ohio-pastor-says-angel-named-johnny-saved-his-life-after-crash.html.

2. Randy Alcorn, *Heaven* (Tyndale House Publishers, 2004), 177–78.

3. Charles Hadden Spurgeon, "The Angelic Life," *Metropolitan Tabernacle Pulpit*, vol. 14, November 22, 1868, https://www.spurgeon.org/resource-library/sermons/the-angelic-life/#flipbook/.

4. David E. Garland, *Baker Exegetical Commentary of the New Testament: 1 Corinthians* (Baker Academic, 2003), 203.

5. Victoria Saha, "Group of Friends United After 74 Years Apart," *ABC 7 News*, April 18, 2025, https://www.kswo.com/2025/04/18/group-friends-reunite-after-74-years-apart-they-seem-like-long-lost-family/.

CHAPTER 13

1. Derek Lew, "My Club 33 Experience," MadChatters.net, April 2, 2016, https://madchatters.net/2016/04/02/my-club-33-experience/.

2. William Temple, *Nature, Man and God* (MacMillan, 1949).

3. "Largest Gospel Choir," Guinness World Records, accessed March 29, 2025, https://www.guinnessworldrecords.com/world-records/largest-gospel-choir.

CHAPTER 14

1. Jordyn Noennig, "'We Just Needed Some Extra Happiness This Year': Wisconsin Farmer Plants 2 Million Sunflowers," *Milwaukee Journal Sentinel*, September 15, 2020, https://www.jsonline.com/story/entertainment /2020/09/15/wisconsin-sunflower-farm-available-picnics-walking-and -photos/5798378002/.
2. Lauren M. Johnson, "A Farmer Planted Over 2 Million Sunflowers to Provide a Respite During This Rough Year," *CNN.com*, updated September 7, 2020, https://www.cnn.com/2020/09/06/us/sunflower-fields-in-wisconsin-trnd /index.html.
3. D. L. Moody, "Heaven: Its Certainty," *Heaven* (1908), accessed May 5, 2025, https://webfiles.acu.edu/departments/Library/HR/restmov_nov11/www .mun.ca/rels/restmov/texts/dasc/HVN04.HTM.
4. Sally Herships, "Lee Horton Reflects on Coming Home After Years in Prison," NPR, April 11, 2021, https://www.npr.org/2021/04/11/986203268 /lee-horton-reflects-on-coming-home-after-years-in-prison.

CHAPTER 15

1. Dylan Morgan, "North Korean Defector Yeonmi Park's Warning to Americans," *The Epoch Times*, December 10, 2024, https://www. theepochtimes.com/us/north-korean-defector-yeonmi-parks-warning-to -americans-5774081?welcomeuser=1.
2. "NASA Astronaut Butch Wilmore Discusses Attending Church in Space," *FoxNews.com*, March 31, 2025, https://www.foxnews.com/video /6370839942112.

CHAPTER 16

1. George Sweeting, *Who Said That?: More Than 2,500 Usable Quotes and Illustrations* (Moody Publishers, 1995), 283.
2. J. Dwight Pentecost, *Prophecy for Today: God's Purpose and Plan for Our Future* (Zondervan, 1961), 158.
3. Daniel Trainor, "Simone Biles Details Thanksgiving Dinner Plans with Husband Jonathan Owens—After the Bears Game (Exclusive)," *US Weekly*, November 27, 2024, https://www.usmagazine.com/entertainment/news /simone-biles-details-post-game-thanksgiving-plans-with-jonathan -owens-2/.

CHAPTER 17

1. Patrick Ryan, "The 12 Most Shocking Oscar Moments Ever (from Will Smith to 'La La Land')," *USA Today*, updated February 17, 2025, https://www.usatoday.com/story/entertainment/movies/2025/02/16/oscars-most-shocking-moments-ranked/78210497007/.
2. Grace Capel, "King Charles Praises Essex Boy for Being 1,000th to Pass Course," *The Clacton Gazette*, March 14, 2025, https://www.clactonandfrintongazette.co.uk/news/25005418.king-charles-praises-colchester-boy-1-000th-pass-course/.

CHAPTER 18

1. Elise Taylor, "The Best of Vogue Weddings," *Vogue*, July 14, 2024, https://www.vogue.com/slideshow/anant-ambani-radhika-merchant-wedding-exclusive.
2. Siobhan Breatnach, "Meet the Engaged Irish Woman Who's Waited 35 Years to Get Married," *The Irish Post*, August 12, 2016, https://www.irishpost.com/life-style/meet-engaged-irish-woman-whos-waited-35-years-get-married-97576?.

CHAPTER 19

1. "Woman Poisons Her Daughter and Christian Couple," *The Alabama Baptist*, April 25, 2025, https://thealabamabaptist.org/woman-poisons-her-daughter-and-expectant-christian-couple/.
2. "Watch List 2025," *Open Doors*, accessed May 30, 2025, https://www.opendoors.org/en-US/persecution/countries/.
3. Donald Grey Barnhouse, *Revelation: An Expository Commentary* (Zondervan, 1971), 133–34.
4. *The Bible Knowledge Commentary*, ed. John F. Walvoord and Roy B. Zuch (Victor, 2000), 948.
5. "Faces of the Persecuted: Illyong Ju," *Persecution.org*, May 30, 2025, https://www.persecution.org/2025/05/26/faces-of-the-persecuted-illyong-ju/.

CHAPTER 20

1. Michael Crichton, *Timeline* (Random House, 1999), 443.
2. John Eldredge, *The Journey of Desire: Searching for the Life We've Only Dreamed Of* (Nelson Books, 2000), 111.
3. Randy Alcorn, *Heaven* (Tyndale House Publishing, 2004), 394.
4. Elie Wiesel, *The Gates of the Forest* (Shocken Books, 1966), 26.
5. Jonathan Edwards, *Heaven: A World of Love* (Calvary Press, 1999), 27–29.
6. Bill Gutman, *Being Extreme* (Kennington Books, 2002), 4.

CHAPTER 21

1. Sam Gilette, "Linsey Davis Writes Kids' Book to Help Her Son Find 'Solace' After He Asks to Visit His Grandma in Heaven," *People*, February 15, 2022, https://people.com/parents/linsey-davis-writes-kids-book-to-help-her-son/.
2. Adapted from Phil Cotnoir, "He Descended to the Dead? Recovering Holy Saturday," *The Gospel Coalition*, April 19, 2025, https://ca.thegospelcoalition .org/article/he-descended-to-the-dead-recovering-holy-Saturday/. See also Matthew Y. Emerson, *"He Descended to the Dead": An Evangelical Theology of Holy Saturday* (InterVarsity Press, 2019).

CHAPTER 22

1. "CNN Republican Presidential Town Hall with Chris Christie," CNN Live Event/Special, June 12, 2023, https://transcripts.cnn.com/show/se/date/2023 -06-12/segment/07.
2. Hank Hanegraaff, *AfterLife* (Worthy Publishing, 2013), chapter 14.
3. John MacArthur, "Do Those in Heaven Know What Is Happening on Earth?" *Grace to You*, accessed May 7, 2025, https://www.gty.org/library /questions/QA108/do-those-in-heaven-know-what-is-happening-on-earth.
4. David L. Allen, *The New American Commentary: Hebrews* (B&H, 2010), 572.
5. P. H. Hacking, *Opening Up Hebrews* (Day One Publications, 2006), 82.
6. Violet Liddle and Mary Batchelor, *Serving the Good and the Great* (Zondervan, 2004), 17.
7. William J. Broad, "When Eyes in the Sky Start Looking Right at You," *The New York Times*, February 20, 2024, https://www.nytimes.com/2024/02/20 /science/satellites-albedo-privacy.html.
8. Audrey Decker, "'You Can't Hide': Spy Agency Will Have 100 New Sats on Orbit by Year's End," *Defense One*, October 2, 2024, https://www.defenseone .com/threats/2024/10/you-cant-hide-spy-agency-will-have-100-new-sats -orbit-years-end/400047/.
9. Lars Erik Schönander, "The Open Sky: How Revolutions in Space, Imaging, and AI Could Open Up Satellite Surveillance to the Masses," *The New Atlantis* (Fall 2023): 55–61, https://www.thenewatlantis.com/publications /the-open-sky.
10. Erwin Lutzer, *Heaven and the Afterlife* (Moody Publishers, 2016), 225.

CHAPTER 23

1. Dr. Omar Memon, "How Many Plane Crashes Has Harrison Ford Had?" *Simple Flying*, February 18, 2024, https://simpleflying.com/harrison-ford -plane-crashes-history/; and Jen Juneau, "Harrison Ford Says Calista Flockhart Doesn't Fly with Him in Vintage Planes After Near-Death Crash,"

People, February 8, 2023, https://people.com/movies/harrison-ford-says
-calista-flockhart-doesnt-fly-with-him-in-vintage-planes-after-near-death
-crash/.

2. Lutzer, *Heaven and the Afterlife*, 223.
3. Alcorn, *Heaven*, 68–69.
4. Fulcrum7 Staff, "92-Year Old Grandmother Rebukes Burglar With God's
Word," Fulcrum7, November 26, 2017, https://www.fulcrum7.com/news
/2017/11/26/92-year-old-grandmother-rebukes-burglar-with-gods-word.

CHAPTER 24

1. "Never Too Young: The Legacy of Cam Cole," *Mountain Brook Magazine*,
November 1, 2018, https://mountainbrookmagazine.com/cameron-cole
-book/; Cameron Cole, *Heavenward* (Crossway, 2024), 1, 3–4.
2. Robert Lightner, *Safe in the Arms of Jesus* (Kregel Publications, 2000), 19.
3. Lightner, *Safe in the Arms of Jesus*, 15.
4. Mark Hitchcock, *55 Answers to Questions About Life After Death*
(Multnomah Books, 2005), 236.
5. Richard S. Hipps, ed., *When a Child Dies* (Authors Choice Press, 2008), front
matter.
6. Cole, *Heavenward*, 9, 38.

CHAPTER 25

1. "Off-Duty Cop Helps Save Suicidal Man's Life by Asking for a Hug," Fox13
Seattle, December 29, 2015, https://www.fox13seattle.com/news/off-duty
-cop-helps-save-suicidal-mans-life-by-asking-for-a-hug.
2. "Data Collections," U.S. Substance Abuse and Mental Health Services
Administration, accessed May 16, 2025, https://www.samhsa.gov/data/.
3. Erwin Lutzer, "Suicide and Salvation," Moody Church Media, May 16, 2025,
https://www.moodymedia.org/articles/suicide-and-salvation.
4. George Ramsay, "'Being a Woman Was Never a Barrier,' Says Jasmin Paris
After Historic Barkley Marathons Finish," CNN, April 6, 2024, https://
www.cnn.com/2024/04/06/sport/jasmin-paris-barkley-marathons-spt-intl
/index.html.

CHAPTER 26

1. Julie Tremaine, "'Not a Pretty Fate': Disney Rides Shut Down Because People
Dump Cremated Ashes," SFGATE, March 24, 2024, https://www.sfgate.com
/disneyland/article/spreading-ashes-shuts-down-disney-rides-19362025.php.
2. Tacitus, *The Histories*, 5.5.

3. Norman L. Geisler and Douglas E. Potter, *What in Cremation Is Going On?* (Bastion Books, 2014), 16.
4. Geisler and Potter, *What in Cremation is Going On?*, 43.
5. Minucius Felix, *Octavius*, 34.
6. Geisler and Potter, *What in Cremation is Going On?*, 44.
7. Albert Mohler, *The Briefing*, January 7, 2022, https://albertmohler.com/2022/01/07/briefing-1-7-22/.
8. John MacArthur, "Does the Bible Prohibit Cremation?" Grace to You, accessed June 10, 2025, https://www.gty.org/library/questions/QA177/does-the-bible-prohibit-cremation.
9. *The History of the Church of Christ, Vol. IV* (The Religious Tract Society, 1840), 92.

CHAPTER 27

1. Tereza Shkurtaj, "Couple's 200-Person Wedding Ruined by Sudden Downpour. Then, Bride Does the Unexpected (Exclusive)," *People*, May 25, 2025, https://people.com/rain-threatens-200-person-wedding-couples-unexpected-response-changes-everything-exclusive-11738381.
2. John Nolland, *The Gospel of Matthew: A Commentary on the Greek Text* (W.B. Eerdmans, 2005), 905.
3. Craig L. Blomberg, *The New American Commentary*: Matthew, vol. 22 (B&H Publishers, 1992), 333.
4. C. S. Lewis, *Miracles* (Collier Books, 1960), 159–60.

CHAPTER 28

1. Althea Castro de la Mata, "'Never Thought I Would Ever See Him Again': Reunited 11 Years Later, Snuggles the Puppy Finds His Way Home," WKBW, March 22, 2025, https://www.wkbw.com/news/local-news/never-thought-i-would-ever-see-him-again-reunited-11-years-later-snuggles-the-puppy-finds-his-way-home#google_vignette.
2. "Red List," International Union for Conservation of Nature, accessed April 17, 2025, https://www.iucnredlist.org/about/background-history.
3. David Jeremiah, *The Coming Golden Age* (HarperCollins Christian Publishers, 2024), 170.
4. Kat Eschner, "In the 1930s, This Natural History Curator Discovered a Living Fossil—Well, Sort Of," *Smithsonian*, December 22, 2017, https://www.smithsonianmag.com/smart-news/1930s-curator-discovered-living-fossil-well-sort-180967616/.

CHAPTER 29

1. "Stranger Saves Texting Woman from Being Hit by Car," FaithPot, October 17, 2022, https://www.faithpot.com/man-saves-woman-from-car/.
2. Bob Laurent, *Watchman Nee: Man of Suffering* (Barbour Publishing, 1998) 67–68.
3. Jonathan Rhodes et al., "From Couch to Ultra Marathon: Using Functional Imagery Training to Enhance Motivation," *Journal of Imagery Research in Sport and Physical Activity* 16, no. 1 (2021): 20210011, https://doi.org/10.1515/jirspa-2021-0011.

CHAPTER 30

1. Kaylee Remington, "Crews Continue Building Metropolis, as 'Superman' Descends Over Downtown Cleveland," Cleveland.com, June 4, 2024, https://www.cleveland.com/entertainment/2024/06/crews-continue-building-metropolis-as-superman-set-takes-over-downtown-cleveland.html.
2. "What Is Grit?" AngelaDuckworth.com, accessed March 24, 2025, https://angeladuckworth.com/qa/.
3. Franklin Graham and Jeanette W. Lockerbie, *Bob Pierce: This One Thing I Do* (Word, 1983), 115–21.

CHAPTER 31

1. Jon Brown, "Pastor Greg Laurie Uses Snafu at White House to Spread the Gospel," *The Christian Post*, April 19, 2025, https://www.christianpost.com/news/pastor-greg-laurie-uses-snafu-at-white-house-to-spread-gospel.html.
2. John MacArthur, *Why One Way?* (Thomas Nelson, 2002), ix–x.
3. D. B. Hatfield, *Triumphant: The Gates of Hell Cannot Have Me* (self-published, 2003), 157–59.
4. Erwin Lutzer, *The Cross in the Shadow of the Crescent* (Harvest House Publishers, 2013), 223–24.
5. Derwin L. Gray in *The Popular Encyclopedia of Apologetics*, ed. Ed Hinson and Ergun Caner (Harvest House Publishers, 2008), 125.
6. "Ticker Tape Parade for Apollo 11," NASA, March 1, 2010, https://www.nasa.gov/image-article/ticker-tape-parade-apollo-11/.
7. Arlette Saenz, "Tiny Troubles: Toddler Infiltrates White House Grounds," CNN, April 18, 2023, https://www.cnn.com/2023/04/18/politics/white-house-toddler/index.html.

EPILOGUE

1. Billy Graham, "What's Wrong with the World?" Billy Graham Evangelistic Association, accessed June 11, 2025, https://billygraham.org/classics /whats-wrong-with-the-world.

ABOUT THE AUTHOR

DR. DAVID JEREMIAH is the founder of Turning Point, an international ministry committed to providing Christians with sound Bible teaching through radio and television, the internet, live events, and resource materials and books. He is the author of more than seventy books, including *Where Do We Go from Here?*, *The World of the End*, *The Great Disappearance*, and *The Coming Golden Age*.

Dr. Jeremiah serves as the senior pastor of Shadow Mountain Community Church in El Cajon, California. He and his wife, Donna, have four grown children, twelve grandchildren, and one great-grandchild.

stay connected to the teaching of

DR. DAVID JEREMIAH

· · · · · · · ·

Publishing | Radio | Television | Online

FURTHER YOUR STUDY OF THIS BOOK

. . . .

The Promise of Heaven **Resource Materials**

To enhance your study on this important topic, we recommend the correlating audio message album, study guide, and DVD messages from *The Promise of Heaven* series.

Audio Message Album

The material found in this book originated from messages presented by Dr. Jeremiah. These messages are conveniently packaged in an accessible audio album.

Study Guide

This 144-page study guide correlates with the messages from *The Promise of Heaven* series by Dr. Jeremiah. Each lesson provides an outline, an overview, and group and personal application questions.

DVD Message Presentations

Watch Dr. Jeremiah deliver *The Promise of Heaven* original messages in this special DVD collection.

To order these products, call us at 1-800-947-1993
or visit us online at www.DavidJeremiah.org.

MORE RESOURCES FROM
DR. JEREMIAH
• • • • • • • •

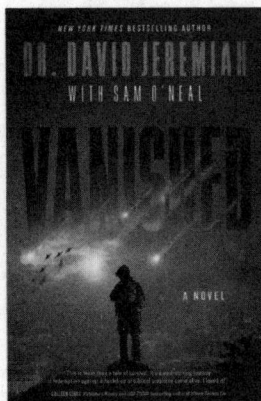

Vanished

In a world grappling with increasing natural disasters and global turmoil, many are asking about the future. Now, a powerful new pathway to understand God's end-time plan and share the hope of Christ has emerged. Discover *Vanished*, a new gripping apocalyptic thriller from Dr. David Jeremiah and celebrated story writer Sam O'Neal.

Based on Dr. Jeremiah's extensive research on Bible prophecy, this novel puts you right in the middle of the action, following military leader John "Haggs" Haggerty as he navigates a world on the brink of the Rapture. It's a thrilling, fast-paced story infused with sound biblical doctrine.

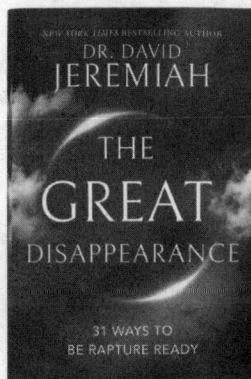

The Great Disappearance

In *The Great Disappearance: 31 Ways to be Rapture Ready*, Dr. David Jeremiah examines the next event on God's prophetic timetable, the Rapture. This is not a book of doom and gloom or a sensational read about setting dates, but one of hope and joy as we see God's plan unfold all around us. Through careful biblical reflection, Dr. Jeremiah describes in detail the days to come as promised by the Old and New Testament prophets, offers hope and encouragement regarding life after death, and answers many common questions about the inevitable end of days. These 31 easy-to-read short chapters will inspire you to live boldly and expectantly in today's world.